THE GRACE OF A NIGHTINGALE

THE GRACE OF A NIGHTINGALE

A MEMOIR
OF VULNERABILITY, HOPE AND LOVE
MARY ANNE WILLOW

ArrowGate

Published by Arrow Gate Publishing Ltd
London

17 16 15 14 13 12 11 10 9 8

Arrow Gate Publishing's titles may be purchased in bulk for educational,
business, fund-raising, or sales promotional use. For information, please
email info@arrowgatepublishing.com

A CIP catalogue record for this book is available from the British Library

ISBN 978-1-913142-00-1

www.arrowgatepublishing.com

Arrow Gate Publishing Ltd Reg. No. 8376606

Editor
Helen Fazal

Arrow Gate Publishing Ltd's policy is to use papers that are natural, renew-
able and recyclable products and made from wood grown in sustainable
forests. The logging and manufacturing processes are expected to conform
to the environmental regulations of the country of origin

For my husband

For encouraging and inspiring me, for his eagerness to love me and teaching me to do the same, for not losing faith in my book and me, and for his creative artwork and beautiful title for this book

There is a vitality, a life force, a quickening which is translated through you into action, and because there is only one of you in all time, this expression is unique. And if you block it, it will never exist through any other medium and be lost. The world will not have it. It is not your business to determine how good it is, nor how valuable it is, nor how it compares with other expressions. It is your business to keep it yours clearly and directly, to keep the channel open. You do not even have to believe in yourself or your work. You have to keep yourself open and aware directly to the urges that motivate you. Keep the channel open.

Martha Graham to biographer Agnes de Mille
in Martha: The Life and Work of Martha Graham

CONTENTS

Preface

The names of all individuals have been changed and identifying features and some occupations have been modified or excluded to preserve anonymity. The purpose of this is to protect people's privacy without damaging the integrity of the storytelling. For the sake of compression, certain characters and events are composites. This enabled me to avoid encumbering the narrative with detail derived from the ingrained complexity of some situations. However, the chronology is largely precise.

When recounting these events, I tried to avoid embellishing the rhythm and detail of the stories in my favour. Moreover, I did not want to manipulate the reader by presenting my experiences in an exaggerated or sensational manner. I would hope that wisdom through the wake of suffering, blended with distance from some of the incidents I relate, has minimised any such conceitedness. Nevertheless, I can't say I've completely avoided all of these hazards successfully.

From the distant ruins of my past, there are both unwelcome and inspirational memories which have been revisited in order to write these memoirs. It was rather like dismantling a Russian doll that contains innumerable diminishing replicas of myself, each with her own story to tell. As each cocooning image was delicately uncovered, at times it induced defensive and protective thoughts, while at others it evoked anxiety and paranoia. All of this I was aware of and I have tried to resist their influence in the pursuit of authenticity. Despite profound tiredness and shattered hopes, the agony of carrying my untold story far exceeded the power of such thoughts, which enabled me to write these memoirs, a process imbued with its own pain. At times I wanted to deny or run away from my suffering and imperfections. But I was given the grace to trust and surrender to the wounds and failures of my life, knowing they have taught me more than my triumphs. While I now acclaim some of these events as successes, I only recognise such experiences in retrospect. I have attempted to be honest and truthful throughout. Because of this, I have had to grapple with fear: fear of being judged, blamed and accused when certain events and circumstances could have been faced with less selfishness, naivety or vanity.

> *I have no desire to suffer twice, in reality and then in retrospect.*
>
> **Sophocles,**
> Oedipus Rex

Hidden untold secrets have been brought out into the light and exposed. I have striven to resist the urge to sanitise, exaggerate or embellish the truth. There was always a stronger light beckoning beyond the dark tunnel of fear and failure.

You may find these stories elicit a personal response through your own unique emotions and thoughts. As they resonate with your past experiences, you may encounter an unknown inner disturbance: past hurts and forgotten memories may be reawakened. I would encourage you to reflect on such experiences to discover a deeper wondrous inner knowing and freedom. Alternatively, you may recognise hidden gifts and radical hope previously buried by fear, insecurity or self-limiting false beliefs.

> *Our treasure lies hidden in the field of our own experience and in the inner life which results from that experience.*
>
> **Gerard W. Hughes,**
> God of Surprises

Hidden beneath the imperative to remain truthful to my vulnerable, complex and complicated personality is a mottled labyrinth of contradictions, which I have tried to convey throughout these lived experiences. Despite the temptation to erase or deny these for fear of disparagement, contradiction is inherent in the human condition. There will always be a tension between personal freedom and solitude, intimacy and social community, power and powerlessness, attachment and separation, spirituality and materialism.

Through the paradoxes of my life, I recognised my own changing sub-personalities. Through crucial moments of change I have learned that I do not need to blame others or to justify myself, neither do I need to rely on the good opinions of others. I have been willing to develop, grow and heal in pursuit of my own distinctiveness. This has been painful and exhausting as my wounded ego abandoned unhelpful relationships, thoughts and behaviours in exchange for uncertainty and an aching emptiness. At times I was tempted to run away from my past to avoid confronting my suffering and imperfections. But deep down I knew no one else could undertake this task – it had to be me. Thankfully, there was always an inner sense of blessed trust, which enabled me to take risks in pursuit of my authentic self.

Throughout these memoirs, I have come to embrace a deep-seeking, non-rational inner wisdom, searching for the true, authentic nature of love. It is a love free from condition, achievement, duty, expectation, gain and exploitation. There is a constant thread, a deep longing which is found within human vulnerability. It is a soulful desire for union with the divine which manifests herself in nature and human life.

I invite you to join me as I journey across a dystopian topography in search of freedom, healing, beauty, love and my soul-friend, my *anam cara*. There are many milestones, doorways, cul-de-sacs, valleys and hilltops. At times I have had to scramble through rugged darkness, endure bleak, intense loneliness, neglect, betrayal and abuse. Paradoxically, while struggling with cruelty and harshness, this pilgrimage has been comforted by beauty, hope, mystery, tenderness and light. Simple acts of human and animal kindness and soft words have carried me to places of restoration and healing. There have been many encounters along the way. While some folk were able to respond with loving sensitivity and generosity, others fled, ignored, betrayed, took advantage of my vulnerability or simply acted as my judge and jury. I discovered how pain and suffering are accompanied by loneliness, humiliation, degradation, stigma and powerlessness. Words become a futile distant expression of the anguish, shame and despair in the sufferer's heart and soul.

Come with me, and we will travel through the landscape of my life. You will encounter different textured rhythms from the fast and ragged, mellow and calm, short and exacting, to the smooth silence of stillness. You may find this daunting and bewildering or perhaps alluring. I will carefully guide you through the rubble into places where there is hope, love, beauty, joy and a deep soulful equanimity.

The future is not some place we are going to but one we are creating
The paths to it are not found but made,
And the making of those pathways
Changes both the maker and the destination.
John H. Schaar,
Legitimacy in the Modern State

So why did I feel compelled to write these stories? Partly for me and partly for you, the reader, and to honour God. I needed to recover my voice and find freedom from silence, oppression, shame, blame and marginalisation by disclosing the truth. I have described these events according to how I perceived them, and through the telling, I have reached a place of healing. This has enabled me to be restored to my true self – the person I was intended to become. I have discovered what I believe to be my own distinct identity while shedding false illusions shaped by abuse and oppression. There was a strong and powerful sense of determination to recover from tragedy, failure and suffering. Avoiding the distractions of bitterness, envy and resentment were essential, as was avoiding the adoption of a fatalistic tone. The nature of the storytelling has been deliberately styled so as not to moan or indulge in self-pity. These fruitless characteristics would only seek to collude with misery and undermine any conveyance of inspiration. Moreover, I do not wish to preach nor be disrespectful.

I have come to relate to other people with a deeper understanding and compassion. Past hurts and unresolved pain have been transformed into loving, peaceful acceptance. I have experienced a deeper connection and comfort within as, beyond all expectation, I have become reconciled with some of those who have harmed me. This was not an instant response but one graced with the passage of time and will no doubt continue throughout my life.

Only by my relentless faith and love of God can I share these stories. The courage to do so is a gift and one which I hope will inspire others to recover from disappointment, harm, tragedy and failure. Your willingness to read my memoirs means you have the talent of curiosity mixed with a spirit of enquiry. I hope, by virtue of these simple acts, you will recognise our common humanity, enabling you to connect with others in the experiences of life.

May God bless you and protect you; may She smile on you and be gracious to you; may She show you Her favour and give you Her peace.

Numbers 6:24–26

Mary Anne Willow
March 2019

Chapter 1

The Unmothered Child
1962 – 1969

*They are the sons and daughters of Life's
longing for itself.
They come through you but not
from you,
And though they are with you yet
they belong not to you.*

Kahlil Gibran, 'On Children'

What is your earliest childhood memory? When you are asked this
question, what images come alive from a hidden place deep within
your mind? I was asked this during a counselling course I embarked
on at the age of 27 in a small college based in Northampton. It was
autumn 1989, and my inner world was about to unravel like a ball of
barbed wire as I was transported back twenty-four years to a violent
scene in our family home in South Yorkshire.

I was three years old and watching my father, like a deranged
baboon, beating my mother with one of her pink fluffy wedge slippers.
Terrified, I clung to my 18-month-old brother Lee, as Mum crawled
away from this animal. My last glimpse of her was on the staircase
dragging herself to a place of safety. It seemed like many sullen days
went by until I saw her again, sitting up in bed, battered, bruised and
desolate.

Images of pain and fear echoed from the rubble of my childhood. I
was reliving an experience which had shaped my identity, shackling
me with emotional responsibility for my baby brother and casting me
as a mediator between my warring parents.

Mum was a small lady, only 5 feet tall, with blazing red hair. She
adopted the role of the tormentor, Dad's tormentor. Dad was distant

and emotionally remote, and the only attention my mother received from him was brutal. She would provoke him through nagging, uncooperative selfishness. Food would be deliberately burnt, and mealtimes were frequently the scene of arguments and fighting. Dad was huge, 6 feet 2 inches tall, with black hair and massive spade-like hands. He would respond by lashing out, followed by the inevitable guilt, a slow, steady trickle of remorse, making Mum feel powerful and victorious. This toxic pattern of abuse would continue until my father's death in 1997.

Far from a loving, nurturing atmosphere full of fun and playful creativity, our home was tense, hostile and threatening. I was always on the alert during the quiet times, when the calm felt brittle and delicate. War could break out at any moment, creating chaos and turbulence, smashing our fragile family wide open into raw pieces of misery.

Trenches of hate seem to have buried many of my memories. There are very few to recall. Did I ever play? Did I have Christmas and birthday celebrations? Did I have friends? Was I ever happy and carefree? Did I skip or sing or laugh? Who did I turn to for safety, consolation and affirmation? Who loved me? I struggle to find images to answer these questions.

Night-time comfort came in the form of a pink woollen blanket with a pink satin border. Safe in the refuge of my bedroom, my faithful blanket embraced me as I lay in bed. I would pick off tiny balls of wool, rolling them between my fingers. Then, before drifting off to sleep, I would swallow them to avoid any reproach from my parents.

I have a faint memory of playing in yellow cornfields at the end of our back garden. I would make dens there, peaceful, quiet retreats where the secret invisible beauty of birdsong brought an atmosphere of hope and calm. As I nestled in the safe shelter of high, sweet-smelling golden stalks, I daydreamed about living in a faraway place surrounded by green hills, forests, silver flowing streams and colourful wildlife. This innocent vision was to be realised many years later.

But these moments of serenity were fleeting and overshadowed by memories of neglect and abuse. I was often faced with my mother's anger in my absence when I returned to the house. Unpredictable, irrational and unprovoked beatings continued for years. Even brushing my hair was used as an opportunity to vent her anger, pulling and tugging, using the hairbrush as a weapon to hurt me. I have no recollection of her ever harming Lee. Instead, she chose to adore him. Years later I asked her why she resorted to such brutal behaviour towards me. She responded that transferring my father's violence and aggression onto me gave her a feeling of power and control; rather than containing her negative feelings, she'd used me as an emotional dustbin. Throughout her life, I longed for an apology, some remorse, some sense of regret, but I never once heard her say sorry.

While my mother took pleasure in hitting me, my father often beat my brother. This young boy would be taken to another room and brutally attacked by a large, powerful man. His screams still haunt me today.

At Christmas, my nanna and grandad would visit from the north west of England, where both my parents had grown up. They were gentle, unassuming folk, and they were to become my first mat carriers, a source of spiritual power, hope and love. Mat carriers is a term I have created based on the New Testament story of the paralysed man whose friends lowered him through the roof to hear Jesus speak. It tells how others can carry us to Jesus when we are too sick and weak to help ourselves. Through Jesus, we find healing and hope when life seems desolate. When I reflect on how I survived a childhood of severe neglect and abuse, this story explains how the love of others has carried me, helping me to find the courage and hope to keep going and the belief that life can get better. I am moved by the perseverance, ingenuity and faith of the man's friends.

And I saw the river
over which every soul must pass
to reach the kingdom of heaven
and the name of that river was suffering:
and I saw a boat that carries souls across the river
and the name of that boat was
love.

St John of the Cross,
Spiritual Canticle

My grandparents were calm and caring people with a natural inner serenity, and I knew I was unconditionally loved and cherished by them. They didn't shower me with material goods; they gave me their devotion and selfless love. They demonstrated human qualities unfamiliar to me, which brought a shimmering light into a dark, ugly world of fear and trepidation.

I was discovering an alternative way of being. I made a decision, albeit childlike and unconscious, that I was not going to mirror the destructive pattern of behaviour of my mother and father. A pearl of inner wisdom was whispering to me, and a light shone on a different path through life.

Wisdom is bright, and does not dim.
By those who love her she is readily seen,
And found by those who look for her.
Quick to anticipate those who desire her, she makes
herself known to them.
Watch for her early and you will have no trouble;
You will find her sitting at your gates.
Book of Wisdom 6:12 –17

My grandparents' loving-kindness opened a door for me, a door of trust and faith in others, a secret seeing, which helped me to develop the emotional resilience I would need to survive torture and despair in years to come.

I have often wondered whether my teachers had any inkling about what was happening at home. Did I give out any signs and hints? What did I draw? Were there any telling images? What about the stories I wrote? Perhaps I wanted to protect my parents, to shield myself from the abandonment and rejection so often threatened by my father. He would frequently produce the family suitcase telling Mum that either he would leave or that she had to. Who would take care of Lee and me?

The newborn baby or small child is completely
dependent on her parents, and since their caring is
essential for her existence, she does all she can to avoid
losing them. From the very first day onward, she will
muster all her resources to this end, like a small plant
that turns to the sun in order to survive.
Alice Miller,
The Drama of the Gifted Child

I learned to normalise the abnormal. This was my coping pattern, as I came to understand during my psychodynamic therapy. Even at a very young age, I was adopting the role of carer and protector towards both Lee and Mum. This gave me a sense of being needed, providing the security I craved. This ability to care for others later manifested itself in a career choice which would serve me well. I was becoming the enabler within the family. This was my role. I would protect and harmonise dangerous situations regardless of the consequences for me. I realised I could reduce anxiety and minimise conflict. I was also the cleaner, the emotional cleaner clearing up the mess. I fixed things and kept them emotionally tidy, often by taking blame on myself. The fault was with me, which made everyone else feel comfortable and calmer.

At the age of four, I had to go into hospital for the removal of my tonsils and adenoids. I can vividly recall the dismal Nightingale ward in a wooden single-storey building. Each side of the room had a row of beds for both adults and children and in the middle was a large paraffin heater, where the night staff would sit chatting.

On the day of my surgery, alone with no parents, I was approached by two men wheeling a trolley. I screamed and struggled, and they were unable to lift me from my bed until further help arrived. It took four members of staff to move me. I was wheeled to a cold, bleak room with my arms and legs pinned down. A black mask was placed over my face, and a foul-smelling vapour transported me to unconsciousness. My next memory was one of severe throat pain and feeling lonely and frightened. I stared out of the window behind my iron-framed bed crying out for my parents. Outside it was dark and raining. A nurse threatened that if I didn't stop crying, I would never see my parents again. There was no tenderness, reassurance or cuddles to recall from that hospital stay.

Two years later I experienced the most humiliating, degrading and cruel event, which began with an innocent adventure.

I had returned to school after the summer holidays, and autumn was unfolding with its promise of warm, rich colours and harvest. One late afternoon, Greta, the girl next door, invited me to explore the school grounds with her. The school gate was not far from home and could be seen from our front door. Greta was older than me, and I had been told not to play with her as she was considered a bad influence.

We wandered around aimlessly for a while, but I began to feel uneasy and told her I wanted to go home. Dusk was setting in, and I knew that not only was I forbidden from playing with her, but also that we shouldn't be in the school grounds after hours. Enjoying the thrill of our youthful trespassing, she took no notice of my increasing agitation.

At last, we headed towards the school gates to find Dad waiting with the school caretaker. I couldn't have been more afraid. There was an eerie silence as he grabbed my hand and led me home. I tried to explain what had happened, but he didn't listen. Nothing was going to ease the situation into one which felt less intimidating.

My pleas for understanding were ignored. Dad was deafened by his uncontrollable fury, and a blanket of blame and shame descended on me as we approached the house. My heart was racing as terror numbed my body. I knew my father was capable of acts of violence and abuse. Now it would be my turn to face his punishment.

There was no delighted response from those who were pleased I was safe. I was taken into the kitchen and stripped naked in front of Lee and Mum in preparation for a beating. Spread across my father's lap, face down, my body went limp as I submitted to the thrashing. My last image of this ugly domestic scene was of Lee and Mum smirking. Were they an amused audience delighting in my terror, or was this a nervous and anxious expression from those who were powerless to help? As Dad hit my bare flesh with his large, strong hand, I faded into oblivion. My only thought was a realisation that I did not belong here with this family. I could not and would not.

I came to recognise this deeply buried memory during my psychotherapy in later years. It was evoked by watching a scene on the television where a group of Jewish women and children had been placed naked in a pit awaiting their execution. They were grubby, cold, and emaciated, their faces full of abject fear and humiliation. Looking down on them was a group of Nazi soldiers, laughing and taunting them before they were shot. Viewing this atrocity enabled me to name my own shame and indignity, which had been deliberately caused by the evil acts of others. I felt a kindred spirit with these women and children. Although I can never know what passed through the hearts and minds of those terrified victims of war, this shared pain and anguish connected me to others, enabling me to discover a deeper sense of empathy, an invisible intimacy and grief that reconciled me with my own shame.

Only a couple of other memories followed me into adulthood from my first home. I remember the lascivious behaviour of my father as he bathed me in the kitchen sink and then applied castor oil cream to my genitals. This felt awkward and uncomfortable as I was laid on my back naked looking up into his lustful eyes. I wanted to scream and run away but resigned myself to inaction, fearful that any form of objection would invite physical harm and rejection.

The other image I have is of my father sitting in an armchair in the lounge, a room I was not allowed to enter on my own. It was reserved for special occasions. We were alone together, and he told me to dance for him wearing only my petticoat and no other underwear. I was anxious and nervous as I clumsily danced in front of him barefoot, cold and timid. My body was only partially covered, my brushed cotton petticoat scarcely reaching my bottom. It lifted and flapped upwards exposing my nakedness as I clumsily hopped and jumped to his tune, a vulnerable creature used for circus entertainment. I performed with deep humiliation and distress.

I became totally disengaged and emotionally shut down. I was only seven years old but was already detached from my family and acting as a spectator to their drama. I was determined I would not need the emotional support of my parents. I wasn't sure what kind of person I would become, but to be a mirror of these people was not an option. Somehow I knew there had to be a better way of being. It would be an act of self-betrayal to accept I belonged here. Instead, I was destined to wander, lost in my mind, uncertain and sad, endlessly seeking kinship of mind and soul.

This level of self-awareness for such a young child was a gift which would make me stronger in the years to come. Pain can be transformed instead of transmitted so that your very essence is kinder and more loving.

Chapter 2

The Vulnerable Child
1969 – 1973

The best minds will tell you that when a man has begotten a child he is morally bound to tenderly care for it, protect it from hurt, shield it from disease, clothe it, feed it, bear with its waywardness ... and never in any case inflict upon it a wanton cruelty.

Mark Twain, *Letters from the Earth*

Then came my saving journey. It was May 1969, and our family was returning to live in my parents' hometown in the north west of England. My father had lost his job and was given the opportunity to go back to the factory where he had trained as a glasscutter.

I remember the night I was told we were moving house. Outside, a thunderstorm was raging. I was captivated and watched it fearlessly from my bedroom window. Black skies were passionately lit and coloured by sharp magnificent branches of lightening. The power and majesty of this event has remained with me ever since.

Initially, I was angry about leaving; I can't remember ever feeling excited about the move. We left a small rural village to live in a new-build on a large housing development. I found our new home strange: an ugly, run-down industrial town with no fields to escape to. Much of it was owned by the local glass factory and little regeneration had taken place. The estate was unfinished when we arrived, and we found ourselves living on a construction site littered with cement mixers, mechanical diggers and scaffolding, the roads as yet unsurfaced. This became our playground. Piles of bricks and mounds of sand were used for building dens and creating fantasy worlds of escape. One evening the police came to our house having received reports of vandalism. They suggested to my parents that home was a safer and more appropriate place to spend time playing. Little did they realise that the building site felt far safer to me.

At school the children were unruly and I struggled to understand the dialect. There was one girl in particular who took pleasure in bullying me in the cloakrooms as we collected our coats at home time. Her name was Sharon Morgan. Much shorter than me with stubbly red hair, she was a child version of my mother, aggressive and volatile. Each afternoon she would seek me out as I collected my coat and without any warning would inflict several blows to my stomach. I just stood and accepted the violent attacks. Why didn't I challenge her and fight back? What was I afraid of? More physical violence? Why didn't I tell my teacher, Mrs Gladstone? It was probably because Mrs Gladstone also belonged to my world of scary people with her dirty blonde beehive, long pointy thickly painted fingernails, persistent cough and reek of cigarettes. And perhaps I believed I deserved this beating.

I devised a way of combating the pain. I collected a hard-backed book from home and stuffed it down the front of my knickers to act as a piece of protective armour. *That'll show her. I won't feel anything and she'll have sore knuckles. Ha ha!* It worked, and soon afterwards she stopped. We became friends – on her terms, of course. She was from a large family living on a council estate in a deprived area, and her home life was also one of abuse and neglect. I felt a sense of sorrow and sadness for her. I couldn't hate or dislike her for what she'd done, even though she never expressed any remorse.

The move was to be overshadowed by sudden financial hardship. In May 1970, a year after buying our new house, we were about to experience more gloom: one of the most significant industrial disputes ever seen in Britain. Dad worked for the Pilkington Glass empire, where the rank-and-file workers decided to strike, all because someone made an absurd clerical error in the wages department. The strike lasted for six weeks. Dad's angry and mercurial disposition was now exacerbated by financial worry and avoidable strife. With a mortgage, bills to pay and a family to feed, he made attempts to reduce spending. He started to bake, making cheap, filling food. Large quantities of bread, and meat and potato pies with thick crusty pastry were our daily sustenance. It was a time of great anxiety as we faced the real threat of becoming homeless, all due to the actions of a few obstinate, reckless men. I wonder if they ever realised how they contributed to such widespread misery.

Moving to this strange new place was to provide me with an unexpected safe haven: my grandparents from my mother's side. From the age of seven to my nanna's death when I was eleven, I spent every weekend and school holiday with them in their two-up two-down terraced house. The only heating was a coal fire in the living room, and the toilet was outside in the small yard where the coal was stored. My grandparents had a large wood-framed bed in the front bedroom. The back bedroom became mine, and they took delight in decorating it for me. I can still remember Nanna choosing a pale lilac paint with curtains to match. It was an unfamiliar experience to see them enjoying time with me and eager to ensure I wanted to stay with them. My happiness and comfort seemed to matter.

Across the narrow street lived old Mrs Winks. She wore a full-length wraparound pinafore, and thick stockings gathered round her swollen oedematous ankles. She had long silver-grey plaits, which she circled on either side of her head with numerous pins, like Princess Leia from Star Wars. Her little house was dark and oppressive and smelled of stale tobacco smoke. She spent most of her time sitting in front of her coal fire smoking Woodbine cigarettes, her only company two ceramic dogs sitting on either side of her fireplace. I would run errands for her to Browns, the corner shop, to be rewarded with a threepenny bit, a kind word and a grateful smile. My grandparents bought all their groceries from the Browns. An order was placed each week and then picked up after Nanna had collected her pension from the local post office. Helping others made me feel alive. I was energised, and I began to feel a sense of connection to others.

My grandad often slept downstairs, keeping the fire alight and the house warm and cosy. I would tiptoe into my nanna's room and climb into the big old bed with her. We cuddled up with a stone hot water bottle as I listened to her recounting stories of her childhood. She had been a scullery maid for local gentry and my grandad had been a coal miner. Sometimes she would get out of bed and stand by the window to ease the discomfort in her arthritic legs. I can still see her silhouetted against the small leaded window as she gazed out into the moonlight.

Grandad's family were Irish Catholics who had come to England during the potato famine. As a young boy he was involved in a mining accident which crushed his head, and his arms and hands had blue-black markings where coal dust had become marbled under the surface of his skin. He was left almost deaf with a severe speech impediment. My friends would often mock him, believing his slurred, garbled speech was due to some mental disorder. *Your grandad is a gommy*, they would giggle and sneer. I felt angry and frustrated with their childish meanness towards him. To me he was Grandad, and I could understand every word he said. His words were few and infrequent, as he chose to live his life with quiet peacefulness and calm composure. He was my Gandalf, warm and loving.

Grandad was deeply devoted to both his Catholic faith and to my nanna. He loved her from the moment he saw her forty years before, walking home across the fields after what she termed 'a day's service'. Grandad spotted her, a vulnerable young woman alone in the dark, so he started to follow her each evening, making sure she arrived home safely. My nanna recognised him. He was known as a quiet man and was often alone. She came to know later that he was isolated, stigmatised and misunderstood due to his speech difficulties. I doubt he was ever offered any form of speech therapy, either before or after the creation of the NHS. Eventually, they met, and Nanna's friendship helped improve Grandad's speech. They fell in love, married and had only one child – my mum.

It was during these storytelling nights that Nanna told me about a lump she had developed while straining to lift furniture. It was about the size of a small tomato, was quite hard and situated in the top left-hand side of her left breast. She begged me not to tell my mother about it; I believe that she too was afraid of her daughter. But she was also frightened of a diagnosis of cancer and the treatment it would entail. It was our secret and became an unintentional burden, which I would carry for many years to come.

What was my mum's earliest childhood memory? What was her childhood like? I asked her these questions many years later when searching to understand her deliberate cruelty towards me. I needed to convert my bewilderment into comprehension. Nothing made sense. Her parents were loving, devoted and humble, but they had a daughter who probably had an undiagnosed personality disorder. How did this happen? Mum described her childhood as one of happiness and security. There was little money, but she felt cherished and had all that she could have wanted and needed. Maybe Grandad was an overly strict disciplinarian, indoctrinating her with his Catholicism? Not so. Mum valued and respected his devotion and her own experiences of attending church as a child. He would encourage her without forcing his religion on her.

I am sure that Grandad had a relationship with a loving God, not a God who induces fear, shame and guilt. Grandad did not bear prejudice through his faith but only love. How else could he marry a non-Catholic and raise his only daughter with non-judgemental parenting, free from religious dogma?

You can show love to others by not wishing that they should be better Christians.

Francis of Assisi,
cited by Richard Rohr in Eager to Love

Indelible memories of lost contentment often revisit me. I see these as an expression of a divine love once known and impossible to forget. I remember Nanna teaching me how to bake cakes and biscuits. Sometimes we played a shopping game with a toy cash till which we would use to exchange pennies for sweets. Nanna was patient and quiet, the antithesis of the volatile nature of my mother. She was kind and generous, materially poor but rich in gentleness and acts of love. I remember once visiting a neighbour whose daughter had recently given birth. Nanna gave her fifty pence as a gift for the baby. I remember thinking: This is a lot of money, Nanna, money which you struggle to find week to week to buy groceries. Now I understand that Nanna was free of slavery to money. The joy of giving was far stronger than the worry of poverty. There was always enough when we needed it.

Grandad and I went for walks in the local park, with its natural woodland area. There was an abundance of springtime flowers, an endless carpet of bluebells, their beauty bursting into life with a fresh, youthful scent. I felt glad to be alive and carefree, not wary and troubled by threatening, violent family dynamics. These walks created more priceless treasured memories within my developing inner landscape. This first knowing encounter with such beauty was a gentle awakening to a divine passion.

Fridays were always exciting. This was when my mother would take me to stay with my grandparents. I couldn't wait. Each week there would be the same drama as Mum sat shaking and sobbing, recounting stories of domestic abuse to my nanna. She would smoke one cigarette after another, frequently popping pills to alleviate her anxiety. Despite how young I was, I knew she depended on both an anti-anxiolytic, Valium, and Mogadon, a potent sedative.

Nanna paced anxiously up and down as she was sucked into my mother's pit of gloomy domestic violence and abuse. It seemed so simple to me: 'Let's come and live with Nanna and Grandad, Mummy,' I would plead. I was afraid she would be killed. As I look back, I can see how this pattern of behaviour became the breeding ground for the abuse I would later suffer in my own adult life.

Lee seemed unaware of all this. He was happy to live at home and somehow blended in with the family dramas. Now aged 7, his relationship with my father strengthened with time, as they were able to share laddish hobbies and interests. Mum continued to favour Lee. His boyish unruliness was rewarded and even revered. His antics amused my parents, and they proudly recounted stories of his anti-social behaviour. He boosted their impoverished self-esteem, which was devoid of any moral etiquette. I was always the odd one out, puzzled and mystified by their immoral attitudes.

Lee joined the local cub scouts. Every Wednesday they hired the local swimming pool to play water polo, and from time to time I was invited along. One evening I took a school pal, Lisa, with me. I stayed at the other end of the pool avoiding the game, as it was too aggressive for me, but Lisa found it fun and exciting. She enjoyed competitive sports. As I watched, I noticed a silver-haired scout leader making lots of effort to be close to Lisa in the water. Later, when we were drying off in the changing rooms, Lisa was puzzled and upset. She explained that while playing polo the man with silver hair had put his hand inside her swimming costume and penetrated her vaginally with his fingers. She had been sexually violated and was now bleeding. We were shocked and frightened. What should we do? Who could we tell? Perhaps it was our fault for having a happy time. No one would believe us. They'd think Lisa had encouraged him.

I was too afraid to tell Dad, and Lisa was too frightened to tell her mum, for fear of retribution. We never told anyone in authority, but accepted it as normal behaviour. We did not know how to speak out and ask for help; we thought it was our fault and carried blame and shame home with us. Today we would call this man a paedophile, but we had never heard of such a word. For many many years, I carried through my life journey the burden of not being believed and the willingness to blame myself for events.

There were often strange happenings whereby men and boys deliberately committed sexual indecencies. Lisa and I once independently encountered a teenager who was frequently seen riding around the local streets on his motorbike. He would stop and immediately start to masturbate in front of us. I chose to laugh nervously and flee. Lisa opted for a less passive response and actually attacked him, knocking him off his bike.

Kerb-crawlers were frequent: men stopping and asking if I wanted a lift. There was one occasion I was being pestered while on my way home from Lisa's. I was wearing a pair of wooden sandals. This chap was insistent and a nuisance, and I was frightened. I told him to go away and leave me alone. He wouldn't. I turned and booted the side of his car, yelling, 'Go away! Go away! Leave me alone!' He panicked and fled, probably with a dint in his car door.

I was often watched and followed by a neighbour. He lived next door but one to me and was married with two young children. If I was in the back garden, I would see him from his bedroom window watching and smiling. Was this someone revelling in seeing a young child lost in the moment, or was it something more sinister? He would suddenly appear on my journey home from school. Jovial and chatty he would ask about my day, but even as a child, I sensed this was inappropriate. What was he doing here? Was it a coincidence or deliberate? Should I be rude and ignore this menace, or should I dutifully answer his questions? I would give some awkward response and speed away.

Then there was the strange young man I noticed while making my way home from school. My journey involved walking along the canal bank, a well-worn path connecting our estate to the local town. While it was used as a shortcut into town, it was nevertheless isolated, and I rarely saw anyone there. The opposite side was overgrown, and people never walked along it. However, I started to notice a tall, thin man over there most evenings, struggling through the undergrowth. He wore an ex-army green jacket and jeans and had shoulder-length hair in need of a wash.

One afternoon in the school holidays, I was sitting at the top of the bank of scrub above the canal watching the traffic below. I noticed the creepy man walking along the roadside at a time I would ordinarily be walking home from school. He was behaving oddly. Instead of using the wooden steps to climb the hill, he decided to scramble up the bank adjacent to the steps like some agitated primate. I kept glancing at him to check on his movements. He was now a few yards behind me, sitting down to stroke a stray dog. Phew! He's not going to bother me, I thought. Then, with no warning, I turned to see him charging towards me wearing only turquoise underpants, which he was in the process of removing. He was the predator, I his prey. I giggled nervously and, an invisible sledge beneath me flew down the hillside faster than fast. The nervous speed mixed with terror was exhilarating and exciting. He didn't catch me. I won.

Later that evening on my way to bed, I said triumphantly, 'Guess what happened to me today, Daddy?' I thought I was recounting a funny adventure, but my father reacted with rage. I was severely reprimanded for delaying my story. The police were called and I was asked to give a statement. The police officer seemed to think I was inventing stories for attention. They would keep a lookout and I was to report any further incidents. My father was dissatisfied with this and took the law into his own hands.

The next evening Dad planted me in the same spot at the same time armed with a pot of pepper. I was instructed to re-enact what had happened the previous day. I was being used to lure this man back again. I felt like a sweetie jar sitting on the top shelf in a corner shop being used to entice this odd man to climb up and help himself. Dad was hiding in some bushes. Would he manage to get hold of me before Dad could capture him? What would he do to me? The pepper was my only protection and was to be thrown into this man's eyes should he get anywhere near.

We waited. I sat watching in silence. Then there he was at the same time, scrambling up the hill in the same peculiar manner. He was closing in on me with fervent speed and excitement. There was no pausing to stroke stray dogs – this time I was not going to escape. He was getting faster and faster. What do I do, what do I do? Why am I here? This is crazy! Then, out of nowhere, Dad lunged at him, grabbed him by the collar and, like a large human crane, lifted him off the ground, scooping him up with his huge shovel hands and effortlessly suspending him in mid-air. He was marched off to a telephone box where my father called the police. They promptly arrested him and I gave a statement. He made a full confession to this and other indecencies, and also admitted to attempted rape. The victim lived just up the road and was the same age as me.

Against this background of fear and threats, I found solace in reading and listening to music. I discovered a secret friend called Jill. In the Ruby Ferguson stories, Jill had exciting adventures with her two ponies, Danny Boy and Rapide. She was active and independent and treated boys as equals. Jill's forthright character and love of ponies prefigured the shape my future life would take. Favourite songs were David Cassidy's 'I think I love you' and 'Close to you' by The Carpenters. These twin pleasures, music and books, became the food of an invisible love, giving me a magic mat on which I could float off to a faraway place of light and hope. As I let myself be carried away by the rhythm of sound, I felt alive and vibrant, my imagination excited by words and stories as I escaped the reality of a hostile domestic prison.

My brother was having adventures camping, cycling and exploring. Aged only ten he was bought a second-hand motorbike to ride on local wasteland. He began to lie and steal, which were traits he retained into his adult life. He would steal from Grandad, shops, his school and me. Money and possessions would disappear. Clothing was acquired through shoplifting. I was given a Collins English Dictionary for my eleventh birthday as I started secondary school. This was stolen and sold, along with a much-treasured cassette player and melodica. My purse was often emptied of cash, leaving me no bus fare or dinner money. I would have to walk to school and make sure I had plenty to eat for breakfast. Sometimes I would make an extra toast to snack on later in the day. I tried to complain to my parents, but they seemed to find my brother's behaviour amusing. They relished his disruptive antics. They were proud of him.

But, despite the tempestuous nature of our relationship, I always loved and cared for Lee. A deep sense of responsibility had taken root, and his well-being mattered to me.

One Friday evening my life would change forever. I was about to experience a defining weekend that would bring chaos and confusion into my world. It began with my Friday excitement. I was going for my weekend at Nanna's. Mum and I arrived only to find Nanna sitting in a chair nursing her right arm, in terrible pain. She had tripped on a cracked paving stone, fallen and badly hurt her arm. She had not informed anyone. There was no phone and she was frightened. Mum angrily took her off to the local hospital to be checked out.

I sat with Grandad in front of the crackling coal fire with its red flames and waited anxiously for their return. We sat up all night waiting. There was no phone to tell us what was happening, only dark, still, empty silence, as if we were underground waiting for a light to emerge.

Nanna never came back to her own house. While at the hospital with what turned out to be a fractured radius she was examined and the lump in her left breast was discovered. She had cancer, and it was inoperable. It was a large fungating mass which was about to invade her body causing unbearable pain, suffering and ultimately death. Those few happy years I had been blessed with at Nanna's were over, and they were never coming back.

Should I have told my mum sooner about Nanna's lump? Loyalty to my nanna meant everything to me. I loved her with all my heart and I wanted her to trust me. I could not betray her to Mum. I had no understanding of cancer, disease, pain and death. If I had known, would I have said anything? I don't know the answer, but I do know that Nanna was petrified of hospitals and that any form of intervention would have terrified and overwhelmed her. So maybe this is how she wanted it to be, despite the horrid pain and suffering which were about to ravage her timid body and soft sweet soul.

Nanna and Grandad moved in with us and I had to share my bedroom with Lee. Nanna commenced a course of radiotherapy and my grandad sat by her bedside quietly praying for a miracle. Not only was I forced to spend more time in this house of violence and abuse but I also had no privacy or escape from my brother. We began to fight. He seemed to take pleasure in tormenting me while I was driven to exasperation and fury. The calm and security of my grandparents' home was gone forever. Moreover, I was having to watch the most precious person in my life suffer a slow, agonising death, and I was helpless. It was as though all the lights on the Christmas tree had gone out. No light, hope or joy.

My life is a perfect graveyard of buried hopes.

L.M. Montgomery,
Anne of Green Gables

Chapter 3

Cigarettes, Whisky and Firearms

1973 – 1976

The best revenge is to be unlike him who performed the injury.

Marcus Aurelius, *Meditations*

I started my first senior school, which occupied two sites in the town centre. I soon came to realise this too could be a place of harm and abuse. I'm sure there were kind-hearted and caring teachers, but sadly my memories involve images of humiliation and violence. When I talk to friends about this, they have very different recollections.

One of the school buildings seemed ghostly and eerie, and its playground was on the roof. It felt to me as if we were being contained in a compound, almost like being in a prisoner-of-war camp. On the other hand, my friend Beverly thought it was unique and special having a playground so high up off the ground. She was proud and excited about this. I thought it was oppressive.

I have a vivid memory of an incident I witnessed while I was on my way to a domestic science class one day. I was strolling down one of the chilly corridors when I glanced into a classroom where a geography lesson was underway with a teacher called Mr Naylor. What I saw filled me with horror. There was a room full of children silenced and threatened by this man who was standing on a chair at the front of the class. In his hands above his head, he was clutching a cane which was about to be used to inflict gross suffering. Beneath him, draped over another chair, was a small boy, crying, shaking and terrified. Mr Naylor launched himself off the chair and whipped the boy, the velocity of his acrobatics strengthening the pain he was deliberately inflicting. It was shocking and cruel.

What was Mr Naylor saying to himself? Was he projecting his own self-loathing and hatred onto the child, declaring: *If I can hurt inside then so can you.*

> *The suffering that was not consciously felt as a child*
> *can be avoided by delegating it to one's own children.*
> *The suffering is accentuated by the parents [in this case*
> *teacher] demonstrating their 'grown-upness' to avenge*
> *themselves unconsciously on their child to avenge their*
> *own earlier humiliations. They encounter their own*
> *humiliating past in the eyes of a child, and they ward it*
> *off with the power they now have.*
>
> **Alice Miller,**
> The Drama of the Gifted Child

Despite this climate of fear and menace, my results were impressive. I frequently came top of the class with A grades. I enjoyed studying and learning. I wanted to understand and explore life and the world beyond where I was living.

When I was about eleven years old, Mum began to drink. First, it was cider, then beer, and then spirits. Whisky and Pernod were her favourites. Dad was often out in the evenings, and Mum was playing around with other men. I could hear her on the phone complaining about my dad and the anguish of being married to him. He was sexually boring, was one of her many complaints. Did she ever stop to wonder what it was like being married to her? Was Dad happy? What was it like living with someone who was a drunk, emotionally unstable and unwilling to parent her children with any sense of care and concern, while his mother-in-law lay dying upstairs? Why couldn't she take any responsibility for her own actions?

Dad didn't seem to care, or perhaps he was in denial. He loved to spend time on outdoor pursuits with my brother: shooting, camping and fishing. He was motivated too by a lust for strip clubs, while also being an exhibitionist indoors. I can picture him parading around the house with no clothes on, or sitting on the loo naked and smoking, refusing to close the door.

I was angry, angry that I had to share my nanna with those who didn't seem to care for her as I did. My parents paid little attention to either of my grandparents. Both were self-obsessed and more concerned to pursue their own narcissistic interests.

Then came an opportunity. Dad asked me to babysit for a colleague called Trevor Eccles who lived on the other side of our estate. He was about ten years younger than my parents with a three-year-old daughter. His wife was pregnant with their second child. I had never done any babysitting before, so I had no idea what was involved, except that it got me out of the house for a few hours. A friend of mine babysat for her neighbour, so I asked her what to expect. She explained you got the house to yourself while the children were asleep, and while she was there she took delight in rummaging through drawers. The chap she was babysitting for kept magazines under the seat of the settee, pornographic magazines, which she found amusing.

The moment I met Trevor's wife, Carol, I felt as though I had been given a big sister. I loved her. Carol was gentle and caring. Was she providing the tender love and friendship which up to now I had received from my nanna? My need for attachment was so deep, I was starved of affection.

After my first evening of babysitting, Trevor walked me home. He wore a flamboyant shirt with a wide, open-neck collar, flared trousers and brown leather ankle boots with platform soles. It was late, and I felt timid and apprehensive as we walked through the dark, empty streets. He was drunk and giddy. As we approached the front door, he started to kiss me. He smelled of stale tobacco and alcohol. I felt sick and stunned. Paralysed by this sudden encroachment, I stared at him. He began to say how excited he was that I could become his special babysitter, so special he was going to give me a lot of money. He pushed a five-pound note and some change into my hand. It was a fortune to me. Frozen in the darkness of this unlawful moment I held out my hand, not knowing if this were a gift or a tainted curse. He left saying he would make plans to invite me round again.

The babysitting increased, and so did Trevor's ugly sexual advances towards me. It was a classic child grooming. He had gained the trust of my parents, and I was vulnerable. Life at home was horrid. My parents were abusive and violent. Mum was now addicted to alcohol and drugs (Valium, Mogadon and painkillers), my brother was a thief and hooligan, and my nanna was in the next bedroom dying agonisingly from cancer. There was a constant stench in the house. It was the smell of fungating cance... the smell of death.

Trevor would often complain about his wife and how unhappy he was. Yet in her presence, he was loving and caring. I was confused and torn. I loved Carol and had started to spend a lot of time with her. It was as though there were an angel and a demon living in the same house. I would often go round after school and have tea with her when I knew Trevor wouldn't be there. Who could I tell about his behaviour? Who would believe me? Often Trevor and Carol would spend the evening across the road with their neighbours. I would fall asleep on the settee only to be woken by Trevor kissing me, his hand up my skirt stroking my genitals trying to arouse me – and himself. He tasted of beer and tobacco. His sour, acrid breath, nastier than any medicine taken for childhood ailments, made me retch. He had made an excuse to call in to check everything was okay.

Despite her irrational behaviour, I made one attempt to tell my mum. She accused me of having a crush on Trevor and slapped me hard across the face. It was my fault! My soul was screaming to be believed. *Mummy, Mummy, please, believe me, it's not my fault. Please help me!* My heart was wounded and weeping. I later realised why she dismissed my allegations. She was having an affair with Trevor. He always knew when Dad wasn't around because they worked together, but on different shifts. He would take Mum into town and get her so drunk she was incapable of getting home. He would then come to the house to pursue me. The level of fear at home was increasing. I was not safe either from my parents or this sexual predator.

Nanna began to deteriorate. As she cried out in agony one night, the doctor was called. I begged Dad to let me see her, but this was refused. I became hysterical and was given half a Valium to send me to sleep. The next day I was packed off to stay at my other grandparents' until things had settled. A few days passed with no news until one morning a school friend who lived nearby nonchalantly said in the cloakrooms, 'Your nanna has died. I saw a long black car outside your house with men carrying a coffin indoors.' At lunchtime, I ran to the nearest phone box and tried to call home. No one answered so I called my other grandparents. Nanna had died, and so had part of me.

Anne always remembered the silvery, peaceful beauty and fragrant calm of that night. It was the last night before sorrow touched her life; and no life is ever quite the same again when once that cold, sanctifying touch has been laid upon it.

L.M. Montgomery,
Anne of Green Gables

The following Saturday I was taken back to my house for a visit. At Grandad's request, Nanna was lying in an open coffin. I was terrified and wanted to escape and run away forever. I was asked to touch and kiss her but I couldn't. Mum took my hand and firmly pressed it on Nanna's cold, waxy face. I was eleven years of age, and it was my first dead body. Why didn't anyone stop to think of me, a child whose primary human attachment was dead? Why was this touching of her dead body more important for them than the impact this would have on me? It was a reflection of the family dynamics of control and dominance.

I ran out of the house crying and distraught, overcome with fear and grief. My world felt cold, empty and devoid of any tender loving care. The most kind-hearted person I knew was dead. That night, alone on the settee at my grandparents' flat, I was tormented by ghostly images of Nanna in her coffin. I was terrified and deeply alone. I didn't want to disturb my grandparents. I was wary of them. I had witnessed Grandpa beating my brother so hard with a placemat it broke. Grandma too could be aggressive and bad-tempered, although never with me. So I phoned my mum in tears. I needed her to console and comfort me. She came to the flat and I quietly let her in, only for her to use Grandma's phone to contact Trevor and arrange a secret rendezvous with him. She then left me. The anguish and horror deepened. Abandoned and alone, my heart had again been betrayed by someone who should have cared for me and protected me.

Nanna's funeral took place on a cold, wet November morning. Mum stole all the attention while I silently wept for the sweetest and kindest lady, whose love had carried me through some of my bleakest childhood days. I sat with Grandad. He was broken but carried himself with quiet dignity, able to let Nanna go back to God in the knowledge that she was in a place where there is no more darkness, loneliness, pain or sorrow. His life was now empty, stripped of the woman who had shown him the highest form of love and devotion. Her absence would leave him lonely and isolated. He was like a wandering, lost ghost, not quite dead and hauntingly sad.

Trevor helped to carry Nanna's coffin, camouflaging himself by exploiting our family's vulnerability and tricking others into believing he was trustworthy and supportive. I resented him being there. *You don't belong here. Go away!* Why didn't I share my resentment? But who would I tell? I was silenced by fear – fear of blame and unjust punishment. I wanted to scream and flee from the pain of loss and the falsity of others. I was full of rage. As the funeral car started to drive away from the graveyard, I flung the car door open and raced back to Nanna. Kneeling in the wet mud, I sobbed, screaming for her return. Something had died within me. She was here, and now she'd gone. There was an empty place in my heart, longing and aching for her.

Love knows not its own depth until the hour of separation.

Kahlil Gibran,
The Prophet

Trevor's pursuit of me continued unabated. He would corner me in the kitchen, as this was not overlooked and he could hear footsteps if anyone was returning. *Get off me, get off me*, I silently pleaded. I don't like this. It's wrong. He stank of alcohol and cigarettes as he pawed at my body.

I'd talked about it with a friend at school, desperate for someone to believe me. She suggested I went to see my GP. It never occurred to me to tell a teacher. Fear and mistrust blocked my senses and ability to ask for help. I must tell someone and stop him. But who? He started to talk about wanting sexual intercourse. He was plotting and building up to luring me into his sordid and vulgar fantasy where he could commit the ultimate crime and steal my virginity. What do I do? No, no, no! Someone help me. Rescue me!

So I went to my GP, Doctor Clover. I was twelve years old. I had seen her previously about warts on my hand. Her advice then was to go to the local park, find a ring of toadstools (made by fairies), stand in the middle and wish the warts away. I'd thought how ridiculous she was to suggest such nonsense, and even more so for thinking I would believe her. I'd inflicted one of my hard, silent stares on her, mimicking Paddington Bear who I was currently modelling myself on. But this time I hoped she would demonstrate intelligence and compassion and take me seriously.

She didn't believe me. This came as no surprise given my experience with adults to date. She told me I was a naughty, silly girl making up such ludicrous stories. It was my fault again. This constant theme of not being believed was becoming a familiar darkness, which was obstructing the light of truth and which would continue to haunt me throughout my adult life. Dismissing my account of events has repeatedly caused me unnecessary suffering and harm. The responsibility for these damaging and destructive consequences not only lies with the perpetrator but those who choose not to intervene. It is not only the act of abuse but the omission of protective care that should be held to account. I find it agonisingly difficult to trust those with power and authority. In some ways, this has served me well, as I learned to resist being indoctrinated and to challenge the status quo within institutions such as school, corporate employers and then more recently the church. But it has been a lonely place, often finding myself on the fringe, isolated from my peers and social groups.

Classic stories such as *Paddington Bear* and *Anne of Green Gables* had a powerful influence on me. How was it I managed to seek out characters who had been orphaned and who had an endless capacity for innocently getting into trouble? Was this how I saw myself? Perhaps, like them, I was hoping someone would adopt me and love me. After Nanna died, I needed an escape from home at the weekends. I needed to get out of the house. I would spend my Saturdays in the public library, which was situated in a beautiful Victorian building in the centre of town. Its exuberant structure exuded elegance and style with its dark wooden spiral staircase, patterned tiled floors and decorative ironwork. Each Saturday morning, relaxed in this magnificent building, I would obsessively read about my beguiling literary friends, Paddington and Anne, both of whom vanquished for a short while my feelings of loneliness and grief. They offered me a knowledge I so desperately yearned for. I needed guidance embraced in the loving-kindness my nanna had bestowed upon me. Anne's good-hearted soul and love of nature offered me an alluring tenacity for coping with adversity.

Why must people kneel down to pray? If I really wanted to pray I'll tell you what I'd do. I'd go out into a great big field all alone or in the deep, deep woods and I'd look up into the sky—up—up—up—into that lovely blue sky that looks as if there was no end to its blueness. And then I'd just feel a prayer.
L.M. Montgomery,
Anne of Green Gables

While Paddington, with his capacity for getting into trouble, often caused by his strong sense of right and wrong, taught me street wisdom.

Two things then happened, one of which was a miracle, and the other which took me into a place of less pandemonium. After two years of secondary school, I was moved to an all-girls' grammar school where we wore a dark green uniform, either a skirt or trousers, no tie (hooray) and a pale blue checked blouse with a Peter Pan collar. Immediately I sensed a softer and more serene environment, structured and ordered with everyone striving for the best education and development. There were no boys to contend with, and no one was caned. I felt as if I had landed on safe ground having been at sea in a constant storm surrounded by mutinous rebels. There was a quiet space where I could listen and observe rather than being on high alert, in imminent danger both from the adults and my fellow pupils. My new school was in a middle-class residential area surrounded by green fields, away from the industrialised town centre.

The other miracle was that my periods arrived early, and my

periods were to save me. At the age of twelve, I started to menstruate heavily and with severe pain. Each time Trevor appeared so did my period.

Thank God, thank God! I didn't mind the pain and mess because it kept this horrible man out of my knickers. Painful periods had other benefits too. They provided the perfect excuse for not taking part in hockey and netball lessons. There is nothing scarier than a crowd of screeching, inept twelve-year-old girls battling with sticks to launch a solid ball into mid-air. No thanks. I would prefer to be indoors warm and safe from any potential injury. I'd not long had my adult front teeth, and I was going to keep them intact. So I frequently made my case: 'Sorry, Miss, I'm having a bad period. I can't do hockey.' Case closed. Indoors it is. I was becoming a rebel.

I often found myself in the eerie Victorian stone toilets unable to leave the loo due to the severity of my period pain and heaviness of bleeding. Sweating and vomiting with violent diarrhoea, I would use the paper-towel bin for a vomit bowl as my insides were evacuating down the toilet. I remember one occasion when I should have been attending a Latin lesson – which I actually seemed to enjoy – I was instead clutching the bin, slumped on the loo and howling in pain with what was becoming a familiar monthly ordeal. The door was flung open and Miss Dingle, my Latin teacher, with her flaming frizzy short auburn hair, thick bottle-bottom specs and tweed suit, shrieked and flailed her arms at me as she tried to summon me back to her regimented classroom.

'No chance, Miss, can't get off the loo. I really am having a bad period – please believe me!'

The combination of the stench and her own disgust sent her scurrying off, huffing and puffing. There was no care and concern, no attempt to ensure I had pain relief. No one asked whether my mother was aware. Didn't Miss Dingle wonder how I would get home and if there would be someone to look after me once I got there? Abandoned and isolated by my own body I wept for comfort, support and understanding. This was yet another missed opportunity to reach out and help a vulnerable young girl.

It was a sunny day when I glanced out of my bedroom window to see Lee playing on his skateboard. I had a strange, uncomfortable feeling. Something horrid was going to happen to him. My sense of knowing had come to warn me. I tried to tell him without scaring him. I became clingy, wanting to know his every move in an attempt to protect him. Lee was untroubled by my premonition. His big sister lived in a world of silly fairy stories, but his world was full of thrilling, risky adventures, which were far more real and exciting.

Nothing happened immediately. Then one morning at school before classes began, I overheard some girls recounting a dramatic story about a road accident they'd witnessed. A car had been hurtling around a bend as a young schoolboy crossed the road towards the bus stop. The boy and car collided and he was tossed into the air like a rag doll, along with his distinctive royal blue sports bag. The boy was last seen lying in the road as passers-by summoned an ambulance.

The blue bag and location were the clues I needed. My brother walked to that bus stop every morning, and he carried a blue sports bag. It had to be Lee. I was seized by cold fear. My imagination froze, protecting me from images of my little brother lying alone in the road bleeding, injured or worse still dead.

Lee escaped serious harm with only a broken leg. He spent the next six weeks in the hospital with his leg in traction. He seemed proud of his close encounter with death. So it was frequent visits to the hospital to supply him with games, toys and sweets.

Mum's dependency and abuse of alcohol increased to the point she was completely indifferent to its harmful physical and mental effects. She was consuming large quantities of whisky and couldn't dress in the morning until she had her first fix of alcohol, as her hands would shake uncontrollably. Cupboards, drawers, even the toilet cistern, were used as hiding places for bottles of Teacher's whisky. She would cunningly empty small amounts into a range of little bottles and then plant them in obvious places. These served as a decoy to fool the rummager into thinking they had succeeded when the more precious and much needed larger supplies were hidden further away in the depths of her secret hiding places. She would lie, steal and fight as though her life depended on this foul-smelling brown liquid. Even today, forty years later, I cannot abide the smell of whisky.

She was slowly killing herself through alcohol, cigarettes, drugs and self-neglect. She was a deeply unhappy and lonely woman whose life was slowly diminishing into an underworld of blackouts and self-harm. We became used to the police arriving at our door. Once, she was arrested in the local supermarket for stealing two large bottles of whisky. On another occasion, she hit a bus while driving and then failed to stop. It was not unusual for her to be forcibly removed to the local psychiatric hospital, not to be seen for several days. Neighbours would knock on the door to report her slumped in the street. It was heartbreaking to find her lying there sobbing, smeared with dirt and crusts of blood, incontinent, bruised and grazed. I tried to help her, taking her home to be bathed, fed and put to bed. Dad and Lee had very little compassion and would often call a taxi to evict her.

Mum often became violent and uncontrollable until she became unconscious from drink. Even when Dad wasn't around, she could be aggressive. I remember barricading myself and Lee into my bedroom one night when Dad was working. All went unusually quiet around 1 am. I tiptoed downstairs to find her slumped unconscious on the settee, her cigarette resting on her white dressing gown, which was slowly smouldering. Our angels were watching over us that night, as it was only a matter of time before the house would have caught fire.

I can't recall anyone offering to help her. Where were her Good Samaritans? Our neighbours were distant and unwilling to be associated with our chaos and Mum's misery. This only deepened my shame and dejection. I learned that there is a fear of those who suffer.

It takes immense courage to walk in solidarity with the suffering of others, and even our own.
Richard Rohr,
Eager to Love

The defence against anxiety within helping professions is well documented. Social systems often develop unconsciously so as to separate its members from the source of that anxiety, the patient.

I rarely invited friends home. It was too volatile, dangerous and embarrassing. Mealtimes were bedlam, as Mum would use them as an opportunity to create chaos. Irrational and paranoid arguments would erupt from nowhere. Cutlery, crockery and even food would be used as weapons by this frenzied drunken woman. It was not unusual to have a fork jabbed into the back of your hand or a plate of food land in your face. I experienced a bewildering range of emotions towards Mum. I could feel pity, fear, rage and love towards her all in one day. I missed my mum and yet I also bitterly resented her. She was a mother and wife who had become seriously ill due to alcohol and drug dependency. The trigger may have been the disappointment of her toxic, abusive relationship with my dad, which left her feeling unlovable and despised. Her life was filled with unbearable pain and suffering, alleviated by the hypnotic, stupefying effects of alcohol and drugs, and affairs with other men.

My friend Lisa wasn't afraid to call round to see me, even though Mum would often attack her and a fight would break out. Unlike me, Lisa was prepared to defend herself, and she had an advantage – she was ten inches taller than Mum. Despite this Mum was not perturbed as she lunged upwards in pursuit of Lisa's short silky black hair. Once caught, she would drag my friend's head in any direction possible until she could break free. Both would scream and shout as they lashed out at one another like a pair of frenzied street cats. Once Mum pinned us both against a wall with Dad's loaded pellet rifle, and only Lisa's height saved us. She was able to grab the gun before any shots were fired. Once the gun was removed, and the danger was averted, Lisa and I went back to being free-spirited juveniles. Giggly and silly we left the house and headed for the make-up counter at the local shops in search of eyeshadow and mascara.

I never fought back. I never tried to retaliate. Why was I so passive against the onslaught of violence and abuse? Why was I so tolerant? I could easily have restrained Mum and avoided being hit, but I never did. Part of me loved her, and she was my mum. Despite my rage and disgust, I never directed these emotions towards her but approached her in a spirit of mediation and genuine concern.

> *I have never known a child to portray his parents*
> *more negatively than he actually experienced them*
> *in childhood but always more positively – because*
> *idealization of his parents was essential for his survival.*
>
> **Alice Miller,**
> Thou Shalt Not Be Aware

One summer evening I'd been swimming with Lisa and missed the bus I was expected to catch home. I tried to phone Mum to explain, but she was drunk, angry and irrational. When I arrived home an hour later, as soon as I opened the front door, she attacked me, pulling my long hair and shrieking at me like a banshee as she dragged me into the house. Blow after blow, kick after kick I tolerated the violence. From upstairs my brother was shouting at her to stop.

Mum legitimised her actions and neglect by cruelly admitting: 'If your dad can do this to me, I can do the same to you.' Like Mr Naylor caning the small boy, was she using me to avenge the pain and harm she was experiencing? I never once saw her hit my brother. I started to call her Cruella De Vil secretly. It was my immature, childish method of fighting back. I never hit her, despite being at least six to eight inches taller than her by now.

Mum was in despair, crying out for help. She was battling with many serious and painful problems. Her mother had died from cancer, and her broken-hearted father was waiting to be re-homed by the council. Unsupported by a violent and emotionally distant husband and with little money, she had two young children to care for, complicated by the shock and worry of Lee's road traffic accident.

On top of this, she was addicted to alcohol and drugs and in an adulterous relationship with another alcoholic.

What is addiction, really? It is a sign, a signal, a symptom of distress. It is a language that tells us about a plight that must be understood.
Alice Miller,
Breaking Down the Wall of Silence

One Saturday night Mum crept downstairs and emptied all the kitchen drawers and cupboards as though we had been burgled. It was all a fake. Lights were put on and the back door opened before Mum took a knife and deliberately carved into her own face. Bleeding and dishevelled she lay on the kitchen floor screaming. The police were called. They arrived with fierce sniffer dogs that looked like ancient Germanic wolves; a helicopter was hovering overhead. It resembled a chaotic nocturnal scene from a sci-fi movie. But there was no extra-terrestrial intruder, and neither were there any burglars. Why did she do this? It was a senseless act of self-abuse. To act out such a violent drama was crazy.

The incident was inconclusive as far as the police were concerned. There was no external damage to our property, no locks were tampered with, and no windows were broken to suggest it was a genuine break-in. On the contrary, the only damage was to Mum's face and the contents of the kitchen cupboards.

I never did discuss this with her. I sensed she was too ashamed and too weak to bear the responsibility. She did not want to keep these painful and shameful memories alive.

Chapter 4

Wild, Wayward and Wandering

1976 – 1979

Whatever you can do, or dream you can, begin it. Boldness has genius, power and magic in it.

Goethe (*attrib.*)

I needed to get away. Away from the chaotic, harmful abuse and the abusers: Mum, Dad and Trevor. I needed to save my life. I started to roam around, spending my weekends staying with school friends. There were three of them who stood out. What was it that attracted me to these girls in particular? Their mums! Each one had a mother who was gentle, loving and caring. From Friday to Sunday I was cadging meals and a settee for a bed. They each lived in a different direction from our house, creating a triad network of escape. I could easily walk or catch a bus to whichever one I hadn't seen recently. These women carried me with their care and compassion, despite their own burdens and difficulties. I was mourning the loss of my nanna. They were a substitute for the mum I longed for; they mothered me and became my secret mat carriers. They carried me with their love, and I let them feed and nurture me.

I remember staying at my friend Julie's house. Julie lived on the same estate as me with her parents and two younger sisters. We had little in common other than attending the same school. I'm not even sure she liked me that much, as she was always mocking me. Although I felt uneasy, I didn't care since it was her home I was really interested in. Her acidic snipes could be tolerated in return for a meal and sleepover. Julie's dad taught at the local college while her mum worked at the sewing factory. She was timid and fretful and spent most of her time huddled in the corner of the kitchen sipping sherry. Although her own family took little notice of her, she was kind and sensitive to me, and we developed a bond of silent compassion for one another. Many years later, during a time of profound grief, my misgivings about Julie's affections for me would prove to be true.

One of Julie's sisters arrived home late one night and started to play music when we were all trying to sleep. She refused to turn it off when asked, and so her dad went downstairs, took a pair of scissors and cut the plug off every electrical appliance before going back to bed, without a word. There was often a tense domestic atmosphere, which for me was far less perilous than being at home. In fact, it was entertaining, especially since I was not the target. I'd cope with life at home from Monday to Friday in the knowledge that I could escape for a couple of days at the weekend.

In the summer months, I would sleep outdoors at the water's edge of a local dam. Hiding from the fishermen, I slept beside the tranquil misty waters of the reservoir. I was being invited into the peaceful beauty of Nature as she held and comforted me in her soothing bosom. I was oblivious of any danger, and this allowed me to escape the tyranny of home and all its turbulence. As I watched and waited for the dawn, all thoughts were silenced as my senses became sovereign to the moment.

Now a teenager, my brother was becoming a delinquent, joyriding and stealing. I didn't like the gang he hung around with; both the girls and boys were hostile and threatening. There was always a menacing, unpredictable atmosphere similar to the one at home. Fighting could erupt at any time, fuelled by alcohol and drugs. To be popular or at least to be included meant being involved in crime. Credibility and acceptance were earned by undertaking daring acts, such as stealing and taunting others. A simple glance at one of these feral kids could invite a vicious response.

The real trouble lay within the hearts of each of these children. Each started life as an innocent baby, but their personalities rapidly became distorted making them antagonistic to the world around them. Rather than demonstrating playful curiosity towards others, they were mean and spiteful with no sense of remorse. They were capable of harming themselves and others. How did this happen in so few years? Was it learned behaviour, a family pattern repeating itself and causing these children's souls to be numbed by poor parenting? Like me, were they aching to be loved and cherished by tender-hearted grown-ups? Perhaps the denial of their deepest longings shielded them from further pain and anguish. They were living lives burdened by the absence of love, deprived of their hidden and unspoken wishes.

There was a growing distance between Lee and me. He continued to steal and reminded me of the Artful Dodger in *Oliver Twist*. He didn't restrict his stealing to the unsuspecting shopkeeper or school pal, he also stole from his own family. We were taking different paths. No matter what is happening in life, good or bad, we have the freedom to make different choices. Lee and I were at a crossroads, having travelled the same road so far. He went one way, and I went the other. I was seeking out places and people I felt safe and comfortable with, places where I could rest and be nourished, although I would struggle with authority and boundaries. Lee was looking for excitement and popularity, even if this meant being a reprobate. Whereas he needed to be part of the gang, I needed my own unique identity. I didn't need peer approval, and I certainly didn't want to follow the latest trends. Lee was a follower of fashion – in the music he listened to, the hairstyle he adopted, the clothes he wore – and he was prepared to commit petty crimes to achieve this. I wanted to make my own mind up. I didn't need others' approval to determine whether my appearance would be seen as attractive or to be accepted and admired. Self-acceptance was sufficient for me.

I would create my own style and seek out music which was creative and individual. Songs had to have some meaning and intrigue. I needed stories of fascination, not indoctrination. Music was to capture my imagination and would offer me an alternative form of education to that offered by the uninspiring state. Lyrics, rhythms, sounds and melodies would allow me to escape from dreariness to a world of kindred spirits. Bands and artists such as Led Zeppelin, Neil Young, Patti Smith and Iggy Pop became my favourites, making me feel passionate, optimistic and vibrant.

Lee started to stay away from our home for days at a time. He had coupled up with another gang member, Karen, who was later to become his wife. They met aged thirteen and became inseparable. They too needed attachment and human bonding. So now we had another family member, as Lee and Karen lived between each other's homes. Mum was fiercely jealous. She bitterly resented Karen and pleaded with my father to stop her staying over, but her pleas were ignored. From time to time her frustration was unleashed, and she would hit out at Karen. This did not deter this tenacious moll. After all, she was a rough, tough gang member who was going out with a good-looking catch.

It was the long, hot summer of 1976 and I was fourteen years old. The family holiday was to be two weeks in a caravan in Blackpool. I refused. I would not go to Blackpool with the family from hell. No one was bothered that I wouldn't be joining them. Lee was pleased as it meant he could take one of his pals with him. I just didn't fit into, least of all belong in, this fractured, dysfunctional family. They didn't seem to like me, and I had mixed feelings about them.

So instead I was packed off to my granny's to sleep on her settee for two weeks. One of my schoolmates, Mandy, lived not far away. Every day we packed a bag with our black school swimming costumes, a towel and some cold toast, and headed for the dam. We wore wraparound flower-print cotton skirts, halter-neck T-shirts and bandana headscarves over our long blonde hair. We felt cool and sophisticated. Hidden by bushes, we changed into our swimsuits then swam out to the middle of the reservoir to sunbathe on a board platform used by water skiers. Despite vulgar protests from the fishermen and the spillages of diesel floating on the surface of the water, we would spend the day basking, chatting and swimming around our very own exotic island like two mermaids. Fooled by our childish bravery, we felt like invincible goddesses.

Unknown to my parents I had a set of keys to our house. Mandy and I planned a secret adventure. I told my granny I was sleeping over at Mandy's and Mandy told her mum she was staying at my granny's. Neither Granny nor Mandy's mum checked out our story. We then returned to my house and waited for darkness to fall before creeping our way over marsh and scrubland to the reservoir. We stripped off and swam naked in the cool dark waters. We were wild-hearted and reckless.

They said I shouldn't be wild-hearted
Because it meant I was uncontrollable.
They said I shouldn't be wild-hearted
Because it scared them,
And they didn't understand why –
Why I had to be so different, so restless, so questioning.
Just fit in.
Just be like us.
Just go through life half-heartedly
Like the rest of us do.
But I couldn't. The cage was utterly life-stifling.
And so I broke free,
I ran along the mountain trails
Dug deeply into the roots of the human soul,
And found something profound, courageous.

Teryn O'Brien,
'Wild-Hearted'

The ghosts of those who'd drowned in those perilous waters haunted this beauty spot, but we escaped tragedy. No sirens were waiting to steal us from this world to the next. Our angels with their divine favouritism safeguarded and sheltered our daring juvenile souls, knowing our lives were not yet complete.

I started to become disengaged at school. Prior to my nanna's death, I was in the top stream with a strong interest in both the arts and sciences. Subjects such as geography, history, religious education, chemistry and physics were studied with interest and ease. Cloud formations, chemical equations, the history of the Roman Empire, the birth of Christianity, and even Latin had once captured my imagination and intellect. Now I was developing into a wayward, wilful rebel. I had lost interest in the subjects I once loved and the approach to teaching was numbing my senses. I found the teachers stiff and dreary and the other girls snobbish. I was restless and longing for challenges and adventure. Increasingly I could not conform to the world around me. I could not be trapped by a system of indoctrination.

Education should aim at destroying free will so that after pupils are thus schooled they will be incapable throughout the rest of their lives of thinking or acting otherwise than as their school masters would have wished.

Johann Gottlieb Fichte,
Addresses to the German Nation (1807)

My thoughts and emotions were scrambled as I struggled with anger, shame and guilt. This toxic cocktail was secretly bubbling away, and I needed help. Home was horrid. Mum was a sick and vicious drunk. Dad was violent and emotionally distant. My brother was a delinquent, and my dad's friend was molesting me. During lessons, I struggled to concentrate, and it was inconceivable to undertake any homework due to the madness at home. I was distracted and tired. I dreaded the sarcastic and unhelpful feedback from the teachers. It was futile to try harder, and I was too angry to be a people-pleaser. I was disruptive in class and desperate for mischief. Anything which enabled me to avoid applying myself was appealing. My like-minded pal Lisa, who was also seeking alternative stimulation to Latin, physics, chemistry, biology and so on, enhanced this pursuit of trouble. Detention was a frequent blessing, providing a welcome delay from returning home.

We were generally rude, uncooperative and silly. We deluded ourselves that we were intellectually superior and that we were being entertaining. Blinded by our immaturity, we took delight in mocking the teachers and our fellow pupils. Our unkind and satirical wit marginalised us. I didn't care. I didn't want to be associated with nor likened to the twee conformists. They were lacking in any self-directed thought and creativity. I didn't need teachers to teach me anything, as I was quite capable of teaching myself, thank you. How, where and when was another matter, which I was overlooking.

Was I wild or disturbed or both? I certainly had problems integrating into the classroom group. I had difficulty in establishing relationships with my classmates. Moreover, I was unwilling to communicate amicably with my teachers most of the time. It was all about my terms and conditions or no terms and conditions!

Our classroom larks included moving the teachers' equipment to make it difficult for them to deliver a lesson. Not only did we hide books, but we'd also ensure that the apparatus needed for chemistry and physics practicals would mysteriously disappear. Match heads were concealed in sticks of chalk so that once they struck the blackboard, a spark would appear. The teachers were exasperated at our antics and often expressed their frustration by throwing the board rubber at us or simply banishing us from the lesson. Even when I attempted to be obedient, my behaviour was interpreted through a lens of suspicious mistrust.

Our French teacher, Mr Murphy, was a six-foot-six-inch Irishman who wore a green suit and shiny brown brogues. His hair was bright red, and he sported a long U-shaped moustache. During one lesson he was giving out our results for a recent mock exam. I was repeatedly asked in a broad Irish accent: 'How many have you scored out?' I didn't understand what I was being asked and kept replying, 'Could you repeat the question, please. I don't understand.' We went round in circles. It was futile. In an attempt to avoid the rapidly approaching standoff I offered a solution: 'Sir, why don't you try asking me in French, then I might understand.' At this Mr Murphy frogmarched me out of the classroom and insisted I stood in the corridor for the remainder of the lesson. Disappointed and dejected I felt the familiar pangs of humiliation.

Dad's denial of Mum's dependency on alcohol was compounded by his insistence on making wine. Our small semi-detached house was often cluttered with slow-bubbling demijohns containing a strange selection of wines at varying stages of maturity. He made anything from nettle or dandelion to elderflower, enhancing the alcohol strength by adding Polish vodka. Not only was this hobby an immediate supply of highly potent alcohol for Mum, but it also gave me an opportunity to be mischievous.

It was Friday morning and a double chemistry lesson with Mr Stevens, a young teacher fresh from university. Some of the older girls had a crush on him, but to me, he was just a skinny bloke with spots and a thin goatee beard. He wrote offensive comments in my workbook in minuscule, anally retentive red ink. *This is an absolute disgrace!* was not uncommon. If you only knew, Mr Stevens, how difficult it was for me to consider doing your homework. Most of it was hurriedly scrawled in the toilets at the mercy of pine disinfectant and being snitched on by the swotty sixth form prefects.

The chemistry classroom was a classic Victorian science laboratory with rows of polished dark-wood benches. Each bench was punctuated with gas taps and frayed flexible orange hoses supplying foul-smelling gas to Bunsen burners. At the front of the room was a commanding elevated platform on which stood a huge wooden teacher's desk; it was like an altar facing out towards its audience of pubescent schoolgirls. Lisa and I were made to sit on the front row, not because we required extra help, but because we were inattentive and disruptive. We were tenaciously disobedient, which was our silver lining to a cloud of constraint.

I planned it all. I needed no encouragement or motivation other than wanting to perform a silly prank. I syphoned some of Dad's impure wine into an old glass-lined thermos flask. Today, Mr Stevens, I was going to perform my very own experiment. I would discreetly administer a unique potion to Lisa, which she would never forget, and the timing of which was crucial for its comedic effect. Very little equipment was required, and there would be no spillages. Was my reckless behaviour a sign that I found the chains of conforming to this culture too heavy to bear, and I was determined to be an untamed spirit? Or was I just stupid and careless? Either way, I pursued my plan regardless of the consequences.

Lisa was very willing to participate in my experiment and gladly drank from the flask throughout the lesson. I did not touch a drop! How did we get away with this, as we were sitting directly beneath Mr Stevens' wooden throne while he fastidiously marked our homework?

Then it started to go horribly wrong. Oh no! Lisa was summoned to join Mr Stevens on the stage to discuss her homework. By now she was a happy, playful underage drunk. 'Certainly, Mr Stevens,' she animatedly replied. She staggered onto the stage and started to undo her Peter Pan collared blouse while standing behind him. *I'm going to strangle you, Lisa – what are you doing!* I silently screamed. We will get expelled for this! I was frantic, as well as entertained by her audacious behaviour.

Mr Stevens must have known something untoward was going on but was paralysed by its unprecedented nature. Dealing with a drunken teenager who was stripping off her blouse behind him did not feature in his teacher training. Did he too find it amusing? His face descended closer and closer to the open book on his desk. He looked neither left nor right by even one degree, pretending that he hadn't noticed what was happening. Was he wise or weak? Whatever he was, his benevolent pretence rewarded all concerned: he didn't have the daunting task of confronting us culprits, and we were saved from the wrath of the headmistress.

The lesson ended. I acted quickly and dragged Lisa down to the toilets where I filled one of the large stone sinks with cold water and plunged her head into it in an attempt to sober her up. Arms flailing she reluctantly submitted to my torture, and our unconfessed misdemeanour escaped punishment. Even today Lisa claims she is no longer able to put her head underwater thanks to me.

No one in authority seemed to notice my deteriorating behaviour. If they did, why didn't they act? Did any of the teaching staff suspect anything detrimental was happening to me? Why was I failing to achieve? Were there any mitigating circumstances which would explain my academic decline, as I switched from achieving high grades to producing no work at all? Was my diminishing performance so insidious it was unnoticeable? Were the teachers so consumed by their workload that I was invisible? Perhaps they had labelled me a disaffected, disengaged teenager whose only prospect for employment would be in one of the many local factories.

I dreaded returning home after school. If I wasn't fortunate enough to land myself in detention, I would wander around the town centre putting off the inevitable journey back to the house from hell. Years later I would extend my working day beyond 5 pm, choosing to work longer than was necessary. It took me a long time to realise why. It was a form of distraction as I tried to fool my unconscious into believing these painful memories didn't exist. I still experience an eerie empty feeling between the hours of four and six in the afternoon.

Truancy became appealing. I had several legitimate reasons, all of which rationalised my absence from school. I was constantly tired. Sleep was disturbed and troublesome. My periods were heavy and painful. I was frequently battered, bruised and sore, making sitting on hard school chairs even more uncomfortable. I was unable to do my homework and too ashamed to explain why to the teachers. I avoided facing their annoyance and merrily skipped lessons.

I dreaded parents' evening. Mum arriving in her dishevelled, drunken state was not an option, and neither was Dad and his volatile outbursts of rage. So I faked letters, letters which lied about my absence from school and my parents' absence from parents' evening. I got found out. I arrived home one day to find Dad smouldering dangerously, like an incensed dragon. He was holding one of my letters in his hand. The headmistress had written to him. I wanted to giggle with panicky fear for my immediate future. I knew his silence could lead to violence, and I knew I might not be granted a chance to explain myself. But nothing was said. Nothing happened other than we attended an appointment with the headmistress in her palatial office where Dad repented for both of us and promised I would rectify my defiance. Once dismissed from her authority, Dad only spoke once about this: 'Next time, don't get caught.' It wasn't the act of truancy which deserved punishment; for Dad, it was being caught.

So, troubled and lost, I carried on defying dogmatic state instruction, replacing it with a wandering search for love and hope. Deep within the alcoves of my heart, a compelling energy blinded me to the peril of my ways.

During those long summer days of 1976, I decided to get a job. I wanted to work and earn money. A powerful survival instinct was telling me I needed to be capable of generating an income. If I could get myself a Saturday job, then it would get me out of the house, and I would have my own money, making me less dependent on my parents.

I went into the town and started asking for work. I began with the stallholders in the local indoor market, and by the end of the day, I had a job selling women's clothes with three Asian brothers from Manchester: Ahmad, Ejaz and Ismail. All three of them smelled of curry blended with stale body odour, and they all had greasy hair. They wore European clothes, which were dirty and frayed, and their shoes were shabby and scuffed. They drove a battered, rusty white van. Ismail was the eldest and Ejaz the youngest. Ahmad seemed to work most Saturdays, while Ismail and Ejaz would appear randomly. Ejaz had long fingers and strange eyes, one of which looked sideways, so it was always difficult knowing where to look when I was talking to him. It was like playing eyeball ping-pong. Resisting my urge to laugh, I tried to give each eye equal attention by switching from the left to the right. I probably seemed fidgety and unable to concentrate, which would be an accurate assessment of my inner state.

I loved my Saturday job. I enjoyed chatting with the customers as they browsed through the racks of clothes. I felt new vibrant energy freeing me from the tyranny and misery of domestic oppression and discovered a new self-respect and sense of my personal worth as my self-esteem started to grow. There was a strong sense of community as the stallholders visited one another's stalls to chitchat. The effect on me was a newfound sense of loving belonging, which I desperately longed for. My whole being ached for an authentic encounter with true love.

We share a common journey of wanting to love and be loved; that we want to feel safe, comfortable, and connected; that we want to belong – somewhere... We're afraid of exposure and vulnerability. We're afraid of the unknown. We're afraid to be wrong. We're afraid of abandonment. We're afraid of weakness, of truly trusting, and the fragility of letting go.

Jonathon Stalls,
What Really Frightens Us

There was one stall close by which sold vinyl records. They played music throughout the day, awakening and carrying my soul to places of exquisite beauty and love. What an unexpected surprise to discover how an indoor market record stall could evoke such a wondrous atmosphere: songs such as 'Mississippi' by Pussy Cat, Dr Hook's 'A Little Bit More' and 'You are My Love' by Liverpool Express. These sounds became my invisible Saturday mat carrier.

I was gaining increasing freedom and autonomy, and my dependency on my parents was fading. During my lunch break, I would treat myself to a freshly baked cheese and onion pasty followed by a warm doughnut. I used my weekly wage of £3.50 to buy clothes and pay for bus fares. I was also learning valuable social skills. I had to approach folk and offer assistance, either to make a decision and buy or to consider alternatives for the undecided. I took a genuine interest in the customers and wanted to help them. My job also gave me the courage to stop babysitting for Trevor. I had an excuse. I was too tired from my Saturday job – and I was also earning my own money. I found the inner strength to assert myself against this drunken molester and resist his predatory invitations.

But things were not all rosy in my land of retail dreams. I had exchanged a molester for three child groomers. I'm not sure how it began, but Ahmad, Ejaz and Ismail came to know I was from a vulnerable background. It could have been because Mum would often turn up at the stall drunk and dishevelled. Sobbing, battered and rambling, she would be invited behind the stall to sit and drink tea. Shut out from the world, she was seduced by the deceptions of these three men as they disingenuously tried to console her. I just felt shame and embarrassment. I was afraid her behaviour would reflect badly on me and would not be tolerated. I would be sacked for humiliating them and their business. Fear of rejection suppressed any sense of compassion for my vulnerable, suffering mother. I shunned her instead of reaching out lovingly.

The Saturday routine would consist of Ahmad sitting behind his stall, concealed by hanging acrylic cardigans and jumpers. From his hiding place, he would ogle the browsing women. Depending on the size of their breasts, he would dictate who would serve the shopper: the bigger the breasts, the more likely it was that Ahmad himself would offer assistance. All three men took delight in talking about sex, sex with their numerous wives and lovers. Ejaz purported to be an airline engineer at Manchester Airport in addition to his share in the stall. He would boast about his clandestine sexual pursuits with women from the airlines. Graphic words and phrases were used to describe the sordid details of their sexual conquests. I may not have understood the words they used, yet I was repulsed.

Ahmad would unexpectedly give me extra cash when he considered me to be especially hard-working. He was manipulating me and trying to lower my defences. Then the physical contact started: the occasional hand on my knee when I sat next to him, or the way he pressed one of his fingers into the palm of my hand when I handed over cash from a customer, a coded invitation for sex.

This was wrong. This was horrid and frightening. *Resist these lewd obsessions and grow in grace*, was being whispered to me. A mysterious caution was warning me. It was not something I could hear from the outside, neither was it something Paddington nor Anne had advised. A hidden wisdom not yet understood was speaking to me.

Ahmad started to pressurise me. He demanded I should wear skirts as he disliked the jeans I wore each week. I was now five feet eight inches tall with disproportionately long skinny legs. I felt safe in trousers, especially when I was having one of my heavy periods. The security of these clothes was important to me. Skirts and dresses were frivolous and impractical. The final threat was given: 'Either turn up wearing a skirt next week or be sacked.' Ahmad was insistent.

I fretted all week. Worried myself stupid. My mind spiralled in a vortex of anxiety. The following Saturday morning, wearing jeans, I sat on a bench in the town centre tearfully agonising with a school pal.

Suddenly I felt a valiant energy bursting inside.

I made an impulsive decision.

Without any further discussion, I marched to the stall, looked Ahmad in the eye, and told him to stuff his job: 'I'm not wearing a skirt and I'm not coming back!'

I proudly stomped away with my newfound dogged resolve.

Life at home remained chaotic and miserable. If Dad wasn't doing shift work, he was at a local strip club or away with Lee camping and fishing. Mum was her usual drunken disturbed self. She would crash around the house looking for a fight, reeking of whisky, chain-smoking, irrational and psychotic. In my bedroom, I had an old wing-backed chair that I used to barricade myself in with as a protection against her tyranny. I would wedge the top of it under the door handle, blocking any attempt to get into my room. This would shield me from any physical violence but not from the torment of her constant emotional terrorism. Eventually, she would exhaust herself in the search for a fight and collapse in a stupor. There was solace in her alcohol-induced world away from the pain of reality.

It was during one of these tempestuous evenings, weary and desolate, gazing out into a moonless night, that I had a life-changing experience. It's strange how wisdom visits when things seem utterly hopeless. Lost in an empty darkness, there was nowhere my mind could transport me for relief. My imagination was lifeless, and I was trapped. Then there was a silver glimmer, a whisper. I was being given just what I needed at the right time. A mysterious happening of divine grace was etching a fine precious script of wisdom and freedom around me. I sat on the side of my bed and entered a psychological labyrinth in pursuit of finding freedom, hope and change. I asked myself Kipling's six questions, the five Ws and the one H: What, Why, When, How, Where and Who.

I had to take some kind of action. I could no longer live like this. I realised my parents would not change, so I had to. I did not, nor ever would, belong here. So where did I belong? Again I asked myself, and again I didn't know. Sometimes it's about knowing what isn't before what is. To do nothing was not an option. I was going to crawl out of this gutter of despair and find a trail of escape. This was my first encounter with a threshold of knowing.

What would be my way forward? As I saw it, there were four options:

Option 1

What do other girls do around here? Get pregnant and move into a council flat. Being a single mum filled me with abject fear. I was no more capable of looking after a baby on my own than flying to the moon! My body was not ready to be subjected to this, and my mind wasn't mature enough. Sense was telling me not to choose this road. This was not my path.

Option 2

I could leave school and look for a job. However, the employment prospects, particularly in this misogynistic industrial town in the seventies, were grim. I would have to become a mindless conformist wearing a pencil skirt and stilettos and trot around an office carrying files (for men). Or, even worse, I could work in one of the local factories alongside groups of feral women, who terrified me.

Option 3

Prostitution. During a recent biology lesson, I was sitting next to Gillian, who told me how she went to London during a half-term holiday and lost her purse. She resorted to selling sex to raise the cash to travel home; she was planning to leave home at sixteen when she finished school and head down to London to become a full-time prostitute. I cringed with shock and revulsion. I wanted to grab her hand and tell her it was demeaning and dangerous work. She could get hurt, be taken advantage of by a pimp and catch a venereal disease. Gillian was a shy and demure girl. I would never have imagined she was capable of becoming an illegal sex worker. I could see her working with small children in a kindergarten or in a nursing home for the elderly. Was she really serious about this? Was this her escape from this miserable town?

Gillian did not match my naive and judgemental stereotypical image of a prostitute. Prostitutes were rough, tough and shameless women who loitered around train stations riddled with drugs, alcohol and disease. They wore salacious, degrading clothes. They were revolting and ugly. Gillian's story was challenging my perception of these vulnerable women. I fleetingly let my imagination gaze at a dark situation, wondering if this could be a way out for me. I asked myself, could I become a sex worker? What if I went to London with Gillian? We could rent a flat together and become best friends and look after one another. When we'd saved enough money we could buy our own place, learn to drive and go on holiday. Could I really do this?

Option 4

I could get an education and then reassess my options. What was the best I could achieve given my circumstances? I could set myself the goal of achieving five O levels. Is it possible to become socially mobile with just five O levels? If I were going to achieve this, I would need somewhere to study. It was impossible at home. I could go to social services and ask to be fostered. I could live temporarily with a family, which would encourage me to study.

I chose Option 4. I would get five O levels. I knew a social worker who had visited Mum at home. I arranged a secret meeting and asked to be fostered. At school, I chose to concentrate on the sciences. Unlike the vagueness of history and geography, which attracted my better grades, these seemed practical and useful and could lead to a vocational job.

Next, I told Dad about the foster family and how I wanted to move out in order to study. I did not anticipate his response. Conditioned to expect anger, I was prepared for a battle. Instead, he calmly asked me to stay. He couldn't cope without me. He needed my help with the day-to-day domestic chores, which I had taken responsibility for. Each week Dad would do the food shopping while I would do the washing and cleaning. I hadn't realised how much he depended on me. I agreed to stay but needed a contingency plan. It never occurred to me to ask my father for help. I would solve my own problems. Trusting either of my parents was not an option. I neither liked nor respected them. I was also deeply ashamed of them.

Why didn't I ask for help at school? Many of the teachers seemed to dislike kids. Scathing comments written in red ink were frequently used as feedback to the toils of homework. Classroom sarcasm was used to humiliate and ridicule the powerless. I had insulated myself from this menacing culture by secretly scorning and mocking the teachers. Frequently playing truant, I would wander the town centre shopping precinct bored and disillusioned. The Our Price record shop was the main attraction. It was here I would explore the artistic vinyl works of my favourite bands: Led Zeppelin, Neil Young, Iggy Pop, Cream, Yes, The Clash, Talking Heads, The Cure, Bowie, Patti Smith and Rickie Lee Jones.

My dreams of freedom relied on the teachers' ability to teach and my willingness to learn. I became anxious. There was a risk of failure. I felt desperate and vulnerable. It was easier not to dream and remain detached. Truancy had previously provided relief and escape, but now I needed to conform and tolerate the taunts and insults if I was going to achieve my five O levels. I would relinquish the tantalising beauty of my youthful freedom in exchange for a more mature pathway to adulthood.

My anxiety was compounded by my all-girls' school amalgamating with the local boys' school. The boys' school had a culture of male belligerence; it was fixated on rugby and was overtly sexist, choosing to employ all male staff, often not for their intellectual calibre but because they were capable of throwing a rugby ball. The geeks and flat-chested girls didn't stand a chance in this testosterone-dominated environment. Sporty boys, regardless of their deficient academic ability, were promoted to prefect status. Those girls who were willing to endure standing by the cold, muddy touchline of rowdy rugby matches in exchange for the glee of making the boys mugs of tea also received recognition. I was completely discounted, both because I was flat-chested and also because I refused to be a maid for the rugby team. The good opinions of this supercilious bunch were meaningless to me.

A pal of mine known for her feistiness was made head girl. To this day she believes this decision was not based on her commitment to study but her DD bra size; the male teachers were not aroused by her searing intellect and charismatic leadership but by her voluptuous young body. Fortunately, she had the strength of character to sabotage the teachers' lustfulness by championing female rights.

My plan to escape from home began with a punishing study schedule, starting at 4.30am each day when the house was safe and everyone was asleep. There was no fighting and no bullying. I snatched a few hours to study, calmly nestled in the tranquillity of dawn. I was able to apply myself to my schoolwork. I could concentrate without fear of being attacked.

I must have attempted about twenty O levels in total. I had endless grade Ds and Es, and then eventually I reached my target of five passes: four grade Cs and one grade B. The grade B was in Physical Science, a combination of physics and chemistry. The teacher, Mr Wilson, was probably the only teacher who never picked on me.

What would I do now? I started to explore job options. Nothing appealed to me. Shop, factory and secretarial work were the main choices. Thankfully I remained unconvinced I was destined for any of these. I resisted and went back to school to commence A levels.

Then fate dealt me a glimmer of hope disguised as a wet, cold trip to Wales.

Chapter 5

Welsh Seagulls
1979 – 1980

Knowledge of the self is the mother of all knowledge. So it is incumbent on me to know my self, to know it completely, to know its minutiae, its characteristics, its subtleties, and its very atoms.

Kahlil Gibran, *The Prophet*

It was the May bank holiday and my life was about to be transformed. A school pal invited me to spend the weekend with her family. They were heading to a quaint coastal town in north Wales with their small caravan. Of course, I would grab any opportunity to be away from home.

It was while we were in Wales that I developed the idea of working in a hotel. It would give me a safe place to live, and I could earn some money. This unspoilt traditional resort was far more alluring than the industrialised slums of my hometown. It seemed to stand still in time, its long sandy beach and picturesque harbour bordered by a dramatically beautiful estuary. Immediately behind the town were spectacular mountains. There were walks and trails into places of wild beauty; ancient follies kept secret stories and scandals of mystery and intrigue.

I was able to convince Dad it was a good idea as it would only be for the summer period, but in truth, I had a powerful urge to get right away. I knew this wasn't possible nor practical while I was at school working for my A levels, but it would only be a short time until the day came when I could leave forever. I trekked round every hotel asking for a job. My lack of waitressing and heavy-duty work experience deterred any potential employer from considering me. I was also very skinny, so folk assumed I lacked the stamina for hard physical work.

At last, I reached the furthest hotel in town at the far end of the promenade. It was owned and managed by a young couple, Alan and Brenda, who had three small children. Alan took the initiative and interviewed me there and then. During our discussion, Brenda entered the room and without any introduction asked to see my hands. She inspected both saying, 'These are working hands – yes, she can have a job.'

I was offered employment from June to September 1979. This would be one of the defining periods of my life, rich with beauty, wisdom and love. I persuaded Dad my absence was in his best interests as it would cost him less if I were away from home for the summer holidays: his food bill would diminish. He agreed, and I was free to go.

I went by train and never regretted it for a second.

Something within was guiding me. I had an inner ache, a longing to live my life to the full. This ache would lead to other opportunities. A faint whisper was calling me. I had the courage to trust this path. Courage is not the absence of fear, but is when something else is more compelling. Resisting fear was a necessary act in pursuit of my destiny. I had the strength to ignore the fear.

Alan was a tall, thin, nervous man with a bald patch on the crown of his head, making him look like a monk. He had a twitch, which made his head shake, and a nervous stutter. He wore wooden clogs, accentuating his long skinny legs. Brenda was plump and short with a pageboy haircut. She often got upset about her weight, which had escalated following the recent birth of their third son. While Alan was a quiet and thoughtful man, Brenda was moody and cantankerous. They had met at university where she was studying home economics, and he was studying accountancy. They combined their skills, got married and bought a hotel business. They were ambitious, hard-working risk-takers.

They shared one of the large family bedrooms with their three sons for the entire holiday season, which ran from Easter to the end of October. There was a resident au pair who took care of the boys while Alan and Brenda organised and managed the hotel, often from 6 am to midnight seven days a week. During the winter months, they would spend time modernising and refurbishing the hotel.

I was given a room on the top floor shared by two other girls, Susan and Jane. Susan was a student from Norfolk and Jane was from South Wales. Susan was gentle, elegant and witty; she had silky long black hair and was tall and pretty. Jane had shoulder-length wavy blonde hair, and behind her piercing blue eyes was a world of pain and neglect. She was untamed and uncouth, abandoned by her teenage mum and for most of her childhood parented by her grandmother who bitterly resented her. She was like a wild stray cat prowling for food in the form of love and tenderness. I was always wary of Jane as I was sure she would relish a good scrap. There was an angry aura about her as if she was harbouring unresolved grief and sorrow, which she was desperate to project onto someone else.

Our room was sparsely furnished but bright and airy. There was one double and one single bed and a small, flimsy wardrobe to share between three of us. We inserted nails into one of the walls so we could hang our washed knickers to dry. I got the single bed, which was next to a large sash window overlooking the beach and the sea beyond. It was quiet and safe, with expansive sea views. The sound of silvery moonlit waves lulled me into a deep womb-like sleep every night. My senses were enthralled with magical sounds, scenery and smell from this coastal refuge. My soul was free to dance and celebrate. At last, I was experiencing a sense of equanimity. This encounter with the life and rhythms of the coast stirred my soul and imagination.

How sweet the moonlight sleeps upon this bank!
Here we will sit, and let the sounds of music
Creep in our ears: soft stillness and the night
Become the touches of sweet harmony.

William Shakespeare,
The Merchant of Venice

At last, I could luxuriate in a place of timeless peace and calm. I had found a shelter where I could belong.

I worked six days a week on a range of duties throughout the hotel: taking round early morning teas, cleaning the bar from the night before, serving breakfasts and then cleaning the guests' bedrooms. I wore a black dress with a white collar and a small black and white check apron; for my chambermaid duties, it was a plain navy dress. We were allowed the afternoon off unless there was a coach party of day-trippers wanting lunch, and then it was back on duty at 4 pm to prepare and serve the evening meal.

Our meals were the same as the hotel menu. We began the day with a full English cooked breakfast followed by endless tea, marmalade and toast. Evening meals were typical English dishes, such as roast turkey, gammon and egg, or scampi and chips, starting with cherry-topped melon boats or vegetable or tomato soup. We were allowed a mid-morning break in the kitchen, and then it was back to work.

The job I detested the most was cleaning the men's loo adjacent to the bar first thing in the morning. The whole room stank of stale tobacco, and I would retch and sweat as I cleaned the splattered urine and smeared faeces in the lavatory stalls. Saturday was changeover day when all the rooms were made ready for the next cohort of guests. After the mammoth task of changing the beds and cleaning the hotel from top to bottom, we would line up with our backs against the wall as if we were awaiting a firing squad. Before she handed us our weekly wage, Brenda inspected each room, bathroom, toilet, corridor and landing. Only when she was satisfied would we be paid.

It was hard work, and I was strangely grateful. I had a purpose, and I could visibly prove myself. I found an inner strength and resolve, liberated from the restraints of home and school.

In the evenings we would wander down to the harbour for a mug of hot chocolate. I had a favourite café, which had outdoor wooden booths overlooking the sea and was lit with fairy lights. Before being allowed out, we had to tell Brenda where we were going and who we were going with. We were expected to be back no later than 10.30pm. Alan and Brenda wanted to ensure we had enough sleep for the next day's work, but they also felt responsible for our welfare. Many of the girls from other hotels were known for their late-night sexual encounters with boys from the funfair. Not only was this risky and potentially harmful for the girls, but it also damaged their employers' reputation. Alan and Brenda blended good business acumen with genuine care and concern for their staff.

For the first time since my nanna died, I mattered to someone. I had boundaries and strict discipline, which I respected and valued. I felt safe and wanted. I was motivated to work hard. It wasn't because we were praised, promoted or rewarded financially, but because I discovered I had a natural desire to do my best. I had a work ethic. My self-esteem had found food and light through work and achievement in an atmosphere of structure and routine. Clarity of purpose and meaning had replaced chaos and confusion. My dedication to my job was bringing me growth and a sense of self-worth. My soul was thriving in this seaside sanctuary. I could breathe and dream of a future which was not going to be subjected to the torments and tyranny of my parents, brother and teachers. I was unshackled from their toxic cruelty. No longer would I be their shock absorber, their emotional dustbin.

There was a man called Gareth who worked as a domestic in the hotel kitchen. Brenda's family had known him for many years. He was orphaned and had severe learning difficulties. Alan and Brenda took care of him, providing lodgings and paid work in the kitchen: loading and unloading the dishwasher and mopping the floor. He always had a fag hanging out of his mouth or in his hand, and his fingers were heavily stained from his chain smoking. He had few teeth, and those that remained were black, rotten and shark-like. He rarely shaved nor made any attempt to wash or bathe, so he stank of body odour. Gareth spent his weekly earnings on cigarettes and beer.

Only once did I visit his room, when he had overslept one morning. Over thirty years later, I have an indelible memory of the reek of foul, acidic urine, a stained mattress and a few items of clothing strewn across the floor; there was neither furniture nor bed linen. Gareth was known for having violent outbursts, and more than once had smashed up the hotel dining room. Alan and Brenda must have denied him any furniture for his own safety. Without them, he would have been an addict sleeping rough or locked away in some psychiatric hospital. Instead, he had a room, paid work and was cared for by this young family.

Once a month a retired couple named Mr and Mrs Williams came to stay at the hotel. In their late sixties, they were reserved and reticent, preferring each other's company to mixing with other guests. Early one morning Mrs Williams fled the hotel. What we found reminds me of the Kipper and the Corpse scene from Fawlty Towers. Mr Williams had died in his sleep. It transpired that Mr and Mrs Williams were married, but not to one another. Mrs Williams had scurried away in the hope of hiding her scandalous infidelity from her husband and family. She denied any knowledge of Mr Williams and refused to claim any association with him or his body. Furthermore, the real Mrs Williams, now both widowed and betrayed, was furious and she too abandoned the corpse of her deviant dead husband.

We were shocked and saddened by this sudden death, as we were all fond of this quiet couple. It was also upsetting to see how their infidelity caused such misery for two families whose lives would be affected forever by what had happened. The memories of happy times would now be exchanged for the pain of broken trust and rejection. Could they have been happily married if they were capable of such calculated acts of disloyalty? Was neither of them concerned that their deceit might cause pain for their respective partners?

This was not the first time my own values and beliefs were being challenged. For me, loyalty and dedication were absolute. This is what I had witnessed in the relationship between my grandad and nanna. Lies and deception were what I had experienced both from my abuser and my parents. Was the thrill of secrecy for this hotel couple so exciting it overcame moral scruples? Were they long-lost lovers reuniting after years of being apart, separated by the wrong choice of marriage partner? Maybe they were trying to revive memories of lost youthful love, so naive, so immature, so unsophisticated, and yet so charming. Was this a means of coping with their dread of the indignities of ageing?

This unexpected death was devastating and shattering for me, stirring my feelings of grief, reawakening the emptiness of loss from my nanna's death. I was angry, and it felt unfair. I was beginning to understand that we have a limited time on earth and that we have no way of knowing when our time is up. Life is for living to the full while we can.

Alan and Brenda were worried about how this incident would affect the reputation of the hotel. It was known for being a family-friendly haven, not a hideaway for clandestine liaisons. We had to remove the body without the other guests noticing. The hotel was served by two parallel staircases joined by a series of corridors and landings. Alan and Gareth clumsily tried to carry the corpse downstairs, Gareth mumbling obscenities while Alan twitched, stuttered and stumbled down, twisting and turning to avoid being seen. Several attempts were made to move the body without being seen by the other guests before it was handed over to the undertaker.

It struck me how we so easily transformed Mr Williams into a 'thing'. He was no longer 'he' but 'it', an object which couldn't be hurt or harmed. He couldn't talk back and complain about our uncaring manner. He didn't have any say in the matter. I was unhappy at the complete lack of respect we were showing his body, but I was also powerless to protest for fear of losing what really mattered to me: living and working at the hotel.

Another memory of that summer involves Jane. She fell in love with a local restaurant owner, well known in the area as a womaniser. He seemed much older than us but was probably in his mid-twenties. Jane decided to move in with him, much to Alan and Brenda's disapproval, but she was headstrong enough to cope with their censure. She was willing to jeopardise her livelihood for this unpleasant man, whereas I longed to be thought well of by them. I wanted to please them. My self-esteem was becoming dependent on their good opinion and my employment. This opportunity was so precious to me I would not have been prepared to risk losing it.

Jane became pregnant and was bullied to have an abortion by her boyfriend. Their relationship fell apart, and she was homeless. Alan and Brenda offered her a room and job back at the hotel. Shortly afterwards she started to see a Turkish man who visited the town once a week with his clothes stall. He lavished her with gifts and flattered her fragile ego. He offered to take her on holiday to his hometown in Turkey. Jane was elated. She had never been abroad before. Alan and Brenda were concerned about her well-being and tried to dissuade her from travelling.

Jane never returned. She was arrested at the airport on her flight home. Her suitcase contained hidden drugs – drugs she was not aware of, drugs which had been secretly concealed by her boyfriend. He denied all knowledge of them and Jane went to jail, despite Alan and Brenda's attempts to defend her.

In different ways, Jane and Gareth's stories taught me how easily other people's misfortunes could be mine; I was aware that 'there by the grace of God go I'. I too could make choices which could lead to all kinds of problems: unwanted pregnancy, drug and alcohol abuse, homelessness, destitution and social isolation. Random circumstances over which I would have no control could disadvantage me. None of us is immune to the misfortunes of life.

I didn't dwell on my dismal circumstances at home but felt blessed and fortunate. I had an increased ability to view my life with optimism and hope. I felt humbled and enlightened. My enthusiasm for the future was growing. Instead of feeling like a powerless victim, I realised how privileged and fortunate I was. I had opportunities and choices which were no longer limited by my thoughts. An inner transformation was taking place, and I started to shed some of the resentments and bitterness I harboured towards others. I felt happier and less anxious. I was learning that I was free to determine my attitude regardless of my circumstances. There was no reason why I should be demoralised and unhappy.

Alan and Brenda carried me, taught and guided me. They had become mat carriers. Their willingness to risk employing an inexperienced young girl helped to change the course of my life, helping me to thrive and find freedom. They infused my life with light, hope and beauty. They exemplified God's abounding grace and mercy. Their trust enabled me to embark upon a pathway that if denied could have led to disastrous consequences.

Their caring nature towards the less fortunate would also influence my life. Providing Gareth with employment and accommodation was not an easy task. He needed constant supervision when they were already overburdened with their responsibilities managing the hotel and parenting three boys. Yet they were willing to provide and take responsibility for him. Concern for Jane's welfare and supporting her in court were further examples of their benevolence. They could have easily blamed and shamed her for her gullibility, proving they were right and she was at fault. Their egos could have been nourished with a sanctimonious response. But they didn't. They chose kindness and generosity. They chose not to be daunted by their selfless choices.

Before I left, I took some time out to reflect on my experience over the summer. Sitting quietly on the beach in the early autumn haze, calmly gazing across the rolling waves, breathing in the fragrant sea air, I slowly began to reconstruct what had happened throughout my stay. I began to look deeply into the rubble of my life, and I soon uncovered pieces of knowledge about myself. There was a stranger living in me, a young woman with a gentle and quiet spirit. I befriended her and listened. This was my true self calling out, showing me the way. I was starting to make sense of this unique seaside experience. I was getting to know myself in more depth. I was finding freedom from the unknown. Lost in the moment, old assumptions were being washed away by the rhythm of the sea. There was a sense of inner space where grace was able to flow and tenderly touch my soul. Beautiful fresh insights were emerging from this emptiness. Like the seagulls above I was no longer stranded by limitation. I was learning to fly.

This time of withdrawal and contemplation became a glistening revelation. I felt excited and alert, despite not knowing what future treasures were awaiting me. I had no fixed images to dream about. My imagination had been crushed, banished into the murky past; my mind was fraught with the struggle of trying to cope with my nightmare family.

What had I learned about myself so far? I'd discovered that I enjoyed helping people; I had found inner contentment and harmony from serving others. My self-confidence was growing. I had a purpose. I suddenly mattered, not because I could be used for others' malevolent pleasure, but because I had something of worth to offer. I could be rewarded with gratitude and appreciation, not punished and humiliated. I felt valued and worthy of others' good opinion. I'd had a knowing encounter with mercy and benevolence.

One of the secrets of life is that all that's really worth doing is what we do for others.

Lewis Carroll,
The Letters of Lewis Carroll

Belonging to a team of like-minded folk was energising. I relished the hard work and irregular, unsocial hours. A regular pattern of living was dull and monotonous. I was motivated by principles of kindness, compassion and beauty. My spirit of enquiry relished problem-solving and learning new skills, especially when it involved caring for other people. It mattered to me that others felt comfortable, at ease and happy.

As I prepared to leave the hotel, I plucked up the courage to ask for a character reference, knowing that Alan and Brenda valued my work and efforts. At the end of the summer season, I reluctantly returned home. I felt angry about leaving my seaside retreat, but somehow I knew that all would be well. I began to trust in the mystery of my life.

We have to learn to distinguish the true self, the deep down self from the superficial.

Gerard W. Hughes,
God, Where Are You?

Chapter 6

Longing and Belonging

1980

The little reed bending to the force of the wind soon stood upright again, when the storm had passed over.

Aesop, *Fables*

How do you choose the optimal career pathway at seventeen years of age with minimal qualifications, only casual work experience, and a chaotic and abusive home life? You live in a misogynistic industrial town where unemployment is at its highest ever, unplanned teenage pregnancy is widespread, and your teachers are sadistic. You have not yet proved yourself either intellectually or emotionally. You cannot provide sufficient evidence that your character is worthy of commitment. Will others judge you according to what you seem to be now rather than what you can become? What do they know about you so far? You belong to a dysfunctional family, your mother is an alcoholic, and your father has a raging temper. Your brother is a hooligan, he steals and tells lies. You are the family carer burdened by domestic responsibilities as well as acting as the mediator. You have repeatedly failed your O Levels. Your teachers have a poor opinion of you, as you are disruptive, unreliable and distracted. You lack respect for those in authority and are capable of being rude, insulting and generally obnoxious towards anyone and everyone.

How does any potential employer with the power to change and transform your life see beyond your history and take a chance? Do they have the courage to resist fear? Fear of employing someone who could let them down. Fear of damaging their credibility, should you prove to be a disappointment. What's in it for them? Why should anyone employ and train you when they can choose someone safe and reliable? And what if, in pursuit of their own personal ambitions for power and control, they use this opportunity to take advantage of your vulnerability and subject you to further abuse, exploitation and bullying? Do you withhold information about yourself and only display attractive characteristics? Do you fake who you really are – like a shop window advertising items worthy of investment while unwanted damaged goods are hidden in the storeroom away from scrutiny?

I felt like two people: the girl who dreamed of living happily among tall trees in forests of silent surprise beside rivers of dancing salmon and innocent wildlife, and the girl who was miserable in a place with harmful people. Was it possible to distort and falsify information about myself so that I became more desirable and attractive, someone worth employing? Would I be capable of inventing a false self-esteem to disguise my true self, which felt worthless and inadequate? And would it matter if this challenged my underdeveloped integrity? I just wanted to be given a chance.

Since returning home from my seaside haven, where I had discovered an unimaginable richness of health and vitality, I was plagued by a sense of worthlessness. I was inconsequential and unlovable. The familiar struggle against feelings of self-doubt and helplessness threatened to imprison me and thwart my efforts to find light and freedom. My monstrous, poisonous history was threatening and tormenting me. My mind was torn between falling into an abyss caused by the endless suffering that was my home life and listening to a persuasive silent whisper of hope, hope that my destiny could be graced with love, generosity and human kindness, all of which I had witnessed from my nanna and grandad. I needed someone to rescue me. I needed a mat carrier to carry me to a place of peace, hope and contentment.

Disheartened by the dismal vitriolic bondage of my life, I was restless and profoundly miserable. I experienced a kaleidoscope of feelings and behaviours. At school I was rebellious, disillusioned and full of anger. At home I was the carer and the diplomat, trying to soothe and harmonise the family dynamics. I desperately wanted to believe I could invent a future free from torment, conflict and abuse.

After the initial turbulence of returning home, I started to be comfortable with the uncertainty of not knowing what the future was preparing for me. I had a sense of expectation. My silent destiny was being created. Alchemic magic was taking place. Despite my despairing vulnerability, I somehow felt blindly optimistic. Something quite mysterious was conspiring to help me create a better future. I did not feel I needed to be in control. I was neither fearful of the unknown nor afraid to ignore the familiar but was hoping that a journey would emerge, a journey away from this barren landscape into one which was scrupulously fertile. Boldness, patience and determination would accompany me, the teenage wayfarer.

Mum was still drinking heavily and was constantly in trouble with the police. She was in and out of the local psychiatric hospital. Dad was bad-tempered and violent. Lee was now expelled from school and involved with local gangs. I didn't tell my parents about his stealing. Vivid images of cruel corporal punishment fortified my resolve to protect him from my father, despite his guilt. His future might become even more desolate if he was found out. But what didn't occur to me was that by concealing his behaviour I was also interfering with the possibility of him mending his ways. I was giving him the false impression that he could escape punishment and allowing him to avoid the realisation that he was heading for a life of criminality. Remaining silent seemed heroic and exciting. I had learned the art of silence by burying and denying my own abuse and true feelings. My blighted ability to trust those in authority was sufficient justification for withholding information. Loyalty to my brother also enabled me to retaliate against my parents, giving me a sense of power over them. I never told anyone, other than to boast to a few school pals.

Of course, if I had told Mum and Dad, I could have had my revenge on Lee. He'd have been punished and taught a painful lesson for stealing from me. But my anger and resentment towards my parents was more powerful. So I kept quiet. This was my secret from them. They did not deserve my loyalty. I selfishly and arrogantly betrayed them, my silence missing an opportunity to prevent Lee from becoming a villain.

Again my inner voice was busily whispering, *I do not, I cannot belong here.* Where did I belong? These questions obsessively plagued and tormented me. It was as though a well-meaning spirit was warning me. I was frustrated. I just couldn't settle. My mood constantly fluctuated. I was lost, isolated and lonely. And yet, at the same time, I was feeling alive, more alive than ever, despite the suffering and misery I was enduring.

I felt uncluttered from any vain and petty teenage preoccupations. The girls at school – the 'in crowd' – seemed to spend endless hours worrying and fretting about their hairstyles, the colour of their tights, current trends in mascara, blusher and lip gloss, the latest fashions from Chelsea Girl. Who bloody cares? I screamed to myself. I was becoming increasingly marginalised.

I discovered my own style. I was slim and tall for my age, about 5 feet 8 inches. I had bright blue eyes and long blonde hair and was often told I resembled Lindsay Wagner who played the bionic woman in the American television series. I lived in flared Wrangler jeans, suede desert boots, cheesecloth shirts and a black velvet jacket. I wore black mascara and brown eyeshadow; around my neck was a black velvet choker, which I had made myself. My boots and clothes were all bought with my lunch money and bus fare. Chips and scraps from the nearby fish and chip shop were cheaper, tastier and more satisfying than school dinners. It also meant I could get away from the prison atmosphere of school for half an hour, despite this being against the school rules. I would covertly hide and eat with a schoolmate in a cobbled alley behind a terrace of slum houses. Despite the litter, dog poo and vulgar graffiti around me, I still found this a more restful and relaxed atmosphere than the regimented dining arrangements at school. I was happy to be outside, free from the chaotic sounds of hungry kids slurping, burping and flicking unwanted food at one another.

On the days when I had no money because Lee had taken it from my purse, I would make six to eight rounds of toast for my lunch before leaving home. This was often eaten by the morning break, so lunchtime would be spent trying to persuade one of the rich girls to buy me a Kit Kat from the tuck shop.

Despite my craving to belong, to be accepted, I could not conform to the majority. I was determined to be an individual with my own principles and ideals. The trappings of popularity, fashion and material possessions would not seduce me. I was becoming foolishly arrogant and conceited in an attempt to strengthen my fragile ego and self-esteem. I was full of contradictions. I resisted the urge to run away, to flee from the despair that frequently engulfed me. Until I had some sense of knowing which direction to travel, I had to find a way of tolerating this horrid incarceration. Staying put was my best but also my worst option. I was beginning to realise life was about mystery and paradox.

My resilience grew as I surrendered my spirit to this messy, chaotic drama. I resisted enacting my angry impulses. Somehow I still found an inner strength to remain steadfast and calm, despite feeling torn between opposing thoughts of either sudden escape or sticking it out until I had some notion of which way to go. If I left home, how would I earn enough money to be independent? Where would I live? Would I end up destitute?

Carefully listening for guidance from my inner voice like a small child gently waiting for reassurance I slowly realised I could suffer one of two things: the pain of discipline or the pain of regret or disappointment. I was experiencing both the pain of discipline and the pain of disappointment. It wasn't an either-or situation but a blend of both. As I look back now, I realise this frustrating lesson was showing me how life is not black and white but full of uncertainty and subtle nuances. Regret had not made its acquaintance with me yet, or at least regret for which I was responsible.

My original plan of getting an education – five O levels – had been accomplished, but what now? I went back to the sixth form to commence A levels in sciences and general studies. This seemed like the best option, although I was less than enthusiastic about it. I longed to be back in my seaside home. I was mourning for the peace, tranquillity and beauty I had briefly yet indelibly encountered.

It was Friday morning, and I was meant to be at school for A Level biology with Mr Milligan, a tyrant who had unmistakably been employed for his rugby skills and who was devoid of any academic ability including basic spelling. He reminded me of a silent movie villain as he sat on his elevated bench stroking his moustache and looking like some hung-over predator. He stared at us fiendishly in search of his next victim and would prowl around the classroom carrying a femur as a weapon ready to taunt us. He could strike at any time. He relished giving pupils humiliating and embarrassing names. Adding the word 'creature' to our surname was a favourite. We all dreaded becoming his next specimen to be verbally dissected and discarded.

I boiled with rage. I felt as if I was inside a crucible, helpless and trapped. I wanted to lash out and fight back. I was desperate for him to teach us something. I needed to learn and develop if I was to stand any chance of escaping my derelict life. I needed him to help me not terrorise me. He was lazy and incompetent, and I realised he neither could nor would teach us. I couldn't face him. I felt sick at the thought of sitting in his lesson, anxious that he would single me out, as he frequently did. I was different from the others, as they were the year below me. It had taken me an extra year and three resits to pass my O levels.

So I chose not to suffer under the cruel dictatorship of Menacing Milligan but caught a bus into town. As I headed off, I was feeling miserable and lonely. I had failed to get Mum up and give her breakfast. She was in bed, soiled and agitated, incapable of dressing herself due to her usual morning tremors. My pity for her was futile. I felt utterly helpless and wretched. Leaving her alone like this made me feel heartless and cruel. It was as if I had abandoned a wounded, desperate child.

Unknown to me, my life was about to change forever. My destiny was entering a threshold of profound enlightenment. My path was about to take an unprecedented turning towards freedom. Mercy was being poured out onto me, leaving very little for my mum.

I sat staring from the window of the bus, my mind full of gloomy thoughts. I planned to idle away a couple of hours before making my way to school. All mixed up, I didn't know where to go or what to do. I felt so alone and dispirited. *What will become of me? Oh, what will become of me?* I silently lamented.

I drifted into the job centre. I knew someone who worked there and I was hoping to scrounge a cup of coffee and fill the gap of loneliness with some trivial conversation. Then, as I walked through the door, there before me was a flip chart on a huge stand with big bold writing on it:

Urgent
Nurses wanted
5 O Levels
Must be hard-working
Shift work 37.5 hours per week
4 weeks annual leave
£250 per month (approx.)
With accommodation
Apply Now

I read and read this, over and over again, saying to myself, *Eureka! Eureka! That's it!* Like staring at an exquisite priceless work of art, I experienced a sudden and striking revelation. It was my first knowing epiphany.

There you will show me what my soul has been seeking.
St John of the Cross,
Spiritual Canticle

This is what I'd been searching for. This is what I'd been prepared for. This is where I'd been led. Nothing is wasted. My experience in the hotel had served a purpose, showing me the way into nursing, but most of my learning lay hidden beneath the debris at home amid the dreadful human suffering and abuse. Later, throughout my nursing career, I would come to realise how caring for Mum taught me tolerance and compassion, while others offered only prejudice and indifference.

Many years later, when my parents were decorating my old bedroom, they discovered something quite astonishing: at the age of seven, when we first arrived at the newly built house and before my room was wallpapered, I had sketched a small female outline and called her Florence Nightingale. What was I thinking when I drew this sketch? Did I imagine myself being a nurse one day, or was it that I longed for a nurse to care for my wounded soul?

I yearned to be free, like Keats' Nightingale 'singing of the summer in full-throated ease … far away from the weariness, the fever and the fret'. With light wings, I could soar freely above and away from this misery. I started to plot my escape. If I was successful with an application for nursing, I would have a roof over my head, somewhere safe to live and study, and I could earn enough money to live on. I would learn useful knowledge and skills in a practical, hands-on job caring for people. I could have a career. Nursing was offering me a future, providing me with a chance to become part of a profession – an international profession if I wanted it. There was hope for me despite the mess I was living in at home. I could have a purpose and make a meaningful contribution towards helping those who were sick and in need. I just had to scrape enough courage together to reach for it.

Then the spirit of gloom reappeared, an apparition of melancholy plagued me. Is this how Scrooge felt each time he was visited by the Ghost of Christmas Past? What if I didn't get accepted? I was afraid of failure, a familiar shadow that had haunted me after having to retake so many O level exams. Perhaps this was why I wanted to leave school, because I was weary of ridicule. I couldn't face any more humiliation and disappointment.

Would nursing put an end to this? Would it rescue me and provide me with a safe and secure place to live, thrive and prosper? I was faced with a choice – either to see myself as a perpetual failure or to try to succeed in nursing.

I agonised for days. I was frightened of telling Mum and Dad. How would they cope without me? Who would defend Mum and Lee? Mum was at risk of serious self-harm as well as injury from my father's beatings. She was so vulnerable. I was terrified. If something horrible happened to her or Lee, I would be the one to blame, it would all be my fault. I was paralysed by anxiety, torn between my loyalty to my family and my dream of becoming free.

If only I could resist thoughts of failure and betrayal and listen to my true self. I had a chance to significantly change and improve the circumstances of my life. I could live in a safe and stable place, in a calm atmosphere where I could learn and grow, somewhere I could feel valued and respected.

My inner voice encouraged me to try. *At least have a go.*

Chapter 7

An Irreversible Ending
1980

Life's but a walking shadow, a poor player,
That struts and frets his hour upon the stage,
And then is heard no more. It is a tale
Told by an idiot, full of sound and fury,
Signifying nothing.

Shakespeare, *Macbeth*

Do I leave and let my family struggle? Will they implode when I have gone? I was enslaved by emotional and domestic responsibilities, but the attractiveness of nursing was tugging me towards escape. It was 1980 and I was making my decision to the strains of Randy Crawford singing 'One day I'll fly away'.

Even before I put in my application, I made my announcement. I took a deep breath and blurted out: 'I'm going into nursing and leaving home.' There. I'd said it. I'm going – come what may! Strengthened by my brief taste of freedom over the previous summer, I was adamant. There was neither guilt nor self-reproach: *I can't rescue you nor fix your problems, so I need to take care of me. It's not my responsibility to look after you. You should be looking after me.*

I chose to tell Mum and Dad when we were all sitting round the kitchen table one suppertime. We only sat together occasionally, when Dad was at home. It was the usual scene of senseless drunken brawling, squabbling, shrieking and threats. Mum would brandish her cutlery, stabbing with her fork and waving her knife in our faces.

The atmosphere was tense, but I still went ahead with telling them what my intentions were.

What happened next was like a volcano erupting. A crusty scab had broken away from a bulging abscess so that the putrid foul-smelling pus beneath the surface was forcefully discharged. Mum's immediate intoxicated reaction was to pick up her plate of food and fling it into my face. It was as though there was a poltergeist in the room throwing crockery all around us. She was never eager to eat, as her appetite was suppressed by her addiction to alcohol. Instead, she was hungry for combat like some dangerous wild feline creature who could strike at any moment. She lunged across the table, hissing, clawing and grabbing at my long blonde hair. I was dripping with the remains of a burnt roast pork, soggy veg and lumpy gravy. I winced as Mum scratched, spat and pulled out clumps of hair. Screaming and hissing hysterically she dragged my head frantically in all directions until Dad managed to stop her. The fight continued between the two of them, surrounded by broken crockery, inedible cold food and cutlery scattered on the floor. Again it hadn't occurred to me to defend myself or fight back. I felt powerless against this sick, demented woman who was inconsolable in her rage, controlled by her addiction to alcohol.

Or perhaps the reason I didn't fight back was that I sensed her inner state. Maybe she was the one who felt worthless and unloved – unloved by her husband and her moody teenage daughter. Consumed by grief and misery, she didn't have the strength to overcome alcohol's hold over her life. I was confused by my turbulent, erratic thoughts and feelings. My mood bounced between deep pity and sadness, rage, fear and fatigue to the dark gallows of teenage humour. Self-loathing and bewilderment were my companions through my teenage angst and desolation.

To this day I avoid eating gravy or sauces, especially dark-coloured sauces. They are painful reminders of that unforgettable scene, which resembled a pack of wild animals misplaced in an unfamiliar human world. I still associate carved red meat, vegetables, potatoes and gravy with the pain of my mum's alcoholism and Dad's brutality.

It was done. I had made my decision. It was an irreversible ending. I'd told them I was leaving and that I wouldn't change my mind. I was going to apply to become a student nurse and leave school. My gritty wilfulness fuelled my unwavering determination to go ahead with this plan. And so I did.

I put all my efforts into ensuring I had a persuasive application. Failure was not an option. I was desperate, and I was leaving home whatever happened. I tried my best to ensure there were no mistakes; there were no crossings out and I'd summoned my best handwriting.

Enclosing a copy of the reference I had been given by Alan and Brenda, I sent the form off in a neat brown envelope.

A few weeks later I was invited for an interview.

The week before a school pal called Tracy also had an interview at the same hospital. Although I didn't mix much with Tracy, I liked her; she was quiet and kind, not moody and attention-seeking like so many of the others. She was one of the 'good girls', a diligent pupil and liked by all the teachers. I couldn't see any reason why she should not be accepted for student nurse training. I hoped we would both get a place so we could pair up and help one another. I offered to go with her for support. This would also serve as a reconnaissance mission for me to glean information to help me prepare for my interview the following week.

When I met Tracy at the bus stop, I was immediately struck by her appearance. She wasn't very tall, probably less than five feet, with waist-length wavy brown hair which accentuated her lack of height. I'd expected her to look formal and smart with her hair pinned up like nurses do, but she was wearing a full skirt, which billowed down to her ankles, and a baggy jumper in shades of cream and chocolate brown. Her hair was free and flowing. Tracy looked as if she were heading off to the Glastonbury music festival, not a career-defining interview.

I felt nervous and worried for her but tried not to show it. I was struggling to make conversation and felt anxious, twiddling my hands as I used to do when I pulled the wool off my comfort blanket as a small child. I tried to be reassuring and relaxed, for her sake. I asked myself why she hadn't made more effort with her appearance. Why hadn't she bothered to tidy her hair and wear a smart, formal outfit? To me it was common sense. Perhaps she had been given poor advice. Was I over-reacting? Whatever it was, I promised myself I would try to look more professional. I wasn't sure how, as I didn't own the clothes I had in mind and I didn't have the money to buy them. What was I going to do? I couldn't attend an interview wearing my jeans and velvet jacket. I began to think about who I could borrow from.

We arrived at the School of Nursing and were shown into the common room by a tall, serious woman who wore black tights and white stilettos. She asked us to wait. Posters on display boards depicted wounds, limb fractures, injection sites and various strange anatomical procedures. There was a drinks machine in the corner, quietly hissing away. From it oozed a faint smell of hot chocolate.

We tried to look serious and mature when we really wanted to giggle nervously. So we sat and whispered to each other like two small fidgety children sitting in assembly. A short man in a grey suit appeared from a nearby office. He wore round glasses and had close-cropped grey hair. His name was Mr Watts, and he was head of nurse training at the hospital. He didn't smile but looked at us sternly as he called Tracy into his office. She stood up shakily and followed him.

Tracy was refused a place for nurse training. No explanation was offered other than she had been unsuccessful. Could her rejection be my good fortune? It might mean there would still be a spare place for me. I would make sure I presented myself differently. I would wear a smart, formal outfit and tie my hair up in a tight bun.

I was shocked at Tracy's failure to be accepted on the course and felt anxious. Everyone knew that the hospital was desperate for nurses, but they were turning potential students away. If someone as pleasant as Tracy was rejected, then there was no hope for me. It unnerved me. My self-confidence was non-existent, despite the positive experience of working at the hotel. My inner running commentary kept insisting I was useless and stupid. It was hard for me to believe I was capable of achieving something good and rewarding. I tried to resist these self-generated accusations. My fragile soul was tormented, but I was going to try. I needed to defy my negative emotions and unhelpful thoughts. My spirit of determination was emerging like a phoenix rising out of the ashes.

I wouldn't allow my negative self-abasement to manifest itself in destructive behaviours, which could sabotage my chances. I was transforming my inner essence into a positive and life-enhancing energy. I was beginning to fly, finding the strength to live the life that I would love. Not for one moment would I waste my heart on fear anymore.

My mind was racing as I quizzed Tracy about the questions she was asked, worried that my lack of interview experience would disadvantage me. I knew they would want me to explain why I was applying to be a Registered General Nurse (RGN) rather than an Enrolled Nurse (EN). RGN training took three years and required five O levels, including maths and English, whereas EN training only took two years and required only three O levels. Since it had taken me at least twenty attempts to achieve my five O levels, I felt they might want to minimise any academic risk by suggesting a shorter course that required fewer qualifications.

I toyed with the idea of saying the obvious: 'I've always wanted to be a nurse. Ever since I was a little girl, it has been a dream of mine. It's a calling, a vocation.' But this wasn't the truth. In fact, I wanted a challenging career. I needed to strive and reach my full potential and not be held back by academic hierarchies. Until only a few weeks before, I'd had no conscious inclination to train to be a nurse. I tried to piece together a different story based on my experience in the hotel: I enjoy caring for people, I like working unsocial hours and I have a strong work ethic.

Should I tell them the truth? I was so desperate for approval. I wanted to beg them: *Please believe in me. Please don't judge me by my school history. I want a second chance to prove myself.* Then maybe they would be persuaded I was trustworthy and bright enough to succeed. I wasn't going to waste their time and I would respect this opportunity. I'm good enough. I'm not bad and I'm not mad, despite my family background. I began to panic and felt sick. I was frightened that they would see me as disingenuous ... that they would not believe me ... that I might be a serial failure. Heaven knows, I thought this about myself often enough.

So why bother to invite me to an interview? Surely I must have a chance. They must be curious about me. The shame of my family background plagued me. Painful feelings of ineligibility and incapability reverberated through my body. I was almost paralysed by my spiralling anxiety.

> *We pay a price for everything we get or take in this world; and although ambitions are well worth having, they are not to be cheaply won, but exact their dues of work and self-denial, anxiety and discouragement.*
>
> **L.M. Montgomery,**
> Anne of Green Gables

My mind was like a monkey swinging from tree to tree in a dark, dank forest, each branch representing some negative image of myself, all the reasons why I was not worthy to become a student nurse. My dysfunctional family had ruined my chances of being accepted on a career pathway, a path which could give me self-respect and hope. This unselfconscious extraordinary power of negative thinking was sending me deeper and deeper into despair. My dream of a life of love, beauty and purpose was becoming increasingly remote.

I felt doomed. What if I let go of these self-destructive, harmful branches? Would I crash to the ground, or would I be carried by some invisible hand to a place of safety? Was I immune from being damaged and destroyed beyond recovery? Perhaps there were invisible mysterious guardian angels, the most wonderful rays of God's protective light, which would save me from myself. I agonised and agonised about what to do. I battled with my self-limiting beliefs. The siege of fear was threatening my future, moment by moment.

Then, like some valiant Joan of Arc, I refused to retreat. I confronted my inner enemy of fear and used it to my advantage. It became an energy that propelled me towards solutions rather than being fixated on problems. I began to look for friends who could lend me the clothes I needed for the interview. The influence of fear began to fade.

I borrowed a high-neck pink floaty blouse from one pal and a knee-length maroon pencil skirt from another. The blouse had a sweet ribbon, which you could tie at the top. I wore my flat black school shoes and American tan tights. This outfit was in complete contrast to my usual hippie image. It felt incongruous and uncomfortable. I scraped my long blonde hair up into a severe mound at the back of my head and avoided any make-up. I looked scarily serious, choked by the Mary Poppins blouse, the prudish skirt restricting my movement to a hobble. This combined with the weight of my hair on my head irritated and frustrated me.

I went on my own to the interview, sweaty with nerves. Once again I was asked to wait in the common room. It wasn't long before Mr Watts called me in to his office where three chairs were arranged in a triangle. I was asked to sit at the tip. Beside Mr Watts sat a tall, slim woman with flaming red hair. She was wearing the dark green uniform of one of the highest ranks of nursing officer. Even while seated she must have been a foot taller than Mr Watts. If I looked severe in my outfit, then this woman was terrifying. She was sitting bolt upright, her arms crossed, piercing me with a witch-like glare. Her pale, lined face seemed incapable of smiling. She exuded menace and looked ready to reduce me to some kind of pickled specimen to store in a jar in a dark cupboard. What compounded our introduction was her strong Glaswegian accent. I couldn't understand a word she said. It was all riddles and nonsense. Absolute gobbledegook!

Her red hair reminded me of my mum. This immediately transported me to a place of alarm and dread. Should I walk out now and flee from their torture and intimidation. What excuse could I give? I've changed my mind. I'm too scared to go through with this. I feel sick. I have made a mistake, and I'm sorry to waste your time. Anyway, I'm not good enough, I'm useless and wayward.

Mr Watts began by saying he recognised me. He asked if I was with another girl who'd been there for an interview the previous week.

'Yes,' I replied. 'I came along with my friend Tracy for support.'

I started to twiddle my fingers with nervousness, and my right leg wouldn't stop twitching. Reminding me of Tracy also reminded me she had been rejected. What chance did I have? If they could turn down Tracy, then they could certainly reject me.

They took it in turns to fire questions at me. I had to keep asking the red-haired nursing officer to repeat herself. I sometimes took a guess at what she wanted to know. There were questions such as how would I cope with shift work, working weekends, bank holidays and Christmas. How would I feel about not being able to stay out late and go to parties? Would caring for sick children upset me? How would I cope with death and dying? I made connections to my own life experience as I answered these questions: many years of babysitting, looking after Nanna when she had breast cancer, and then the unsocial working hours at the hotel. I was piecing the puzzle together elegantly.

Then Mr Watts' manner changed. He seemed softer and less stern as he asked me why I had taken so many attempts to pass five O Levels. My mouth was already dry and sticky. My top lip was persistently sticking to my teeth as I frantically tried to think of a reason other than the truth. Was he the villainous pied piper luring me with his magic, trying to trap me? Was I being manipulated by his secret charm so that he could find reasons to reject me? Like my teachers, did he think I was a failure and unworthy of the privilege of a place in nursing? Or was he a virtuous leader and character builder? Could he help me rid myself of this legacy of abuse and hardship by offering me a future in nursing? He was so powerful. He had the power to transform or ruin my prospects.

I surrendered to telling the truth. Taken aback by his astuteness, bluffing my way out was impossible. So, beneath the familiar dark cloud of shame and embarrassment, I explained my mother was an alcoholic and I was the family carer. Studying at home was difficult as I'd had to shoulder additional responsibilities.

With Mr Watts' next questions I was given a dilemma. I found myself on the edge of an emotional and psychological cliff. If I jumped, would I fly? Or should I retreat and return home to a life of drudgery and abuse?

'If you are offered a place what will happen to your mother and family? Who will care for them? How will they cope?'

I didn't have any answers because I hadn't thought about it. I hadn't got this far with my planning. I didn't know what would happen to them. How could I know? I had been concentrating on the easy things: what to wear for my interview and why I wanted to be a nurse. My mind went blank. My motivation and concentration were faltering. I was stunned. My body went limp and weak as I stared at both of them, utterly overwhelmed with despondency. I wanted to cry like a child desperate for loving comfort and reassurance. I felt cold as I sat alone in this strange room at the local hospital facing two people who had it in their gift to change my life forever.

There was no denying I was the family carer. Mr Watts had a valuable point. What if I were to abandon them? What would become of them? I couldn't see myself as their long-term carer. I couldn't look after them indefinitely. Something was driving me. Something was calling me away.

My response was one which shocked me. I was not proud of what I said; it was one of the toughest things I have ever had to say. I felt cruel and selfish. But it came from a place of wisdom and valiant hope within me, a place which had been quietly waiting to reveal itself.

'This is my life, and I am going to make something better of it. I want a career and to be a professional person. I want to be educated without undertaking full-time studies. My family will have to learn to take care of themselves.'

I have no further memory of the interview. All I can recall was later wandering around the town centre dazed and despondent. I felt so alone and miserable with no one to talk to, no one to listen to my story, no one to help me deconstruct what had happened, to convert my apprehension into comprehension. Had I sabotaged my prospects by disclosing the truth about my family? I felt confused and full of self-doubt. Had I betrayed them? Would my willingness to abandon them be seen as a character defect?

A small brown envelope arrived a week later: reality was about to impose new expectations. My heart was racing as I snatched the letter off the floor and hurriedly ran upstairs to my bedroom, hoping no one had noticed. I felt like a thief fleeing from a crime scene.

I told no one I had been offered a place to commence nurse training in July 1980. I hid the letter underneath my pillow, hoping this would vanquish my nausea and panic. I slept on it for a week. I felt lost within an inner numbness and frightened by my imagination. I couldn't do this. It wasn't because I couldn't leave my home and family. For the past week, my head had been visited by horrible visions of the sick and dying, brutal images of my nanna's tender body mutilated by breast cancer, her cries for help echoing in the night as the pain overwhelmed her.

My imaginings began to lead me down a dark path of misery. I constantly doubted my ability to cope with the prospect of caring for the sick. My fear of suffering seemed worse than suffering itself. My legacy of failure continued to torment me. Just like my schoolteachers, I told myself: 'You are stupid, you are worthless, you are pathetic and a disgrace.' What small, undeveloped fragments of self-esteem I had were being rapidly eroded.

I had fantasies of people bleeding to death, people covered in poo or soaked in stinking urine.

Body parts missing or children screaming.

Dead waxy bodies being transported to the freezing cold mortuary.

People wailing and screaming from pain, loss and grief.

I can't cope with this. I'm not ready for this.

I was craving loving tenderness, someone to hold me and caringly stroke my face, someone to whisper words of reassurance and love.

I was lost in a place of inertia. I was petrified.

Mr Watts became my next mat carrier. He helped to carry me away from hatred and oppression and to lead me to a place of opportunity where I would thrive and be healed. He rescued me from the wreckage of violent abuse. He led me from a derelict place into hope for tomorrow.

He was offering me a chance.

All that I was longing for, compassion, trust and hope, was being given to me abundantly. I could choose this path and try to make my life meaningful; I could learn and develop, study and grow. I could help others and become part of a profession. My journey so far had not been wasted. I could add value and make a contribution by serving others. If I accepted this offer, it wouldn't be easy. I realised this path would ask me to continue to walk alongside human suffering.

I made my decision. I stopped groping for direction and asking for purpose and meaning. I accepted the offer and my life changed in ways far beyond my limited imaginings. An undiscovered world was about to open up in front of me.

But before I embarked on this new journey, there was one more trip I had to make. If I didn't do it then, I may never have the chance again. I knew this would be my only opportunity. I went back to my seaside retreat for another season. I plucked up the courage to write and ask if my place for nurse training could be deferred from July to the autumn intake to enable me to return to the hotel. I felt I had to do this to equip myself with further skills in preparation for nursing. I was nervous about asking for something I needed. I was worried I would be giving the wrong impression. Would I be seen as delaying my commitment so that I could frivolously fritter away the summer in some sleazy seaside town with its bright neon lights, funfair rides, candyfloss and slot machines?

My longing to return to my sacred place by the sea was more compelling. I resisted submitting to the fear of others' imagined false impressions. I had to go back one more time. My fear was blended with courage – they seemed to be made of the same ingredients. I had the strength of mind to face my demons, to confront my unreal imaginings. I had to respond to this beckoning. If I didn't, I would feel less alive. I had to fulfil this passion, a yearning to be intimate once again with the wild and unpredictable landscape of the coast.

I imagined myself as an old lady reflecting on the decisions I had made throughout my life. I was afraid of dying full of regret for a path not taken. Was I risking it all for the memory? Was I trying to relive my nostalgic images and feelings of contentment? Or was this visit about creating something new and lasting? The truth was it was a mixture of the two, a combination of reflecting on what had gone before and opening my mind to new experiences.

My request was granted. I was offered a place in the autumn. I quit school, packed my bags and scurried off to the hotel.

This final visit was somehow richer than before. I was able to refine my people skills when serving the guests. I felt less self-conscious and socially awkward. No longer did I feel lost and unsure about my future; I was happier and more relaxed. The dread of returning home had faded, knowing I would soon have my own accommodation at the hospital. Throughout the summer I was able to save my wages. My ambition was to learn to drive once I had started my nurse training. I was learning to be self-sufficient and financially independent.

During my quieter moments, I had a deeper sense of who I was becoming: a young woman who was growing away from a shattered family towards a future of hope and optimism. I was beginning to feel the wondrous spirit of emancipation as I spent warm sunny afternoons on the beach in deep conversation with myself. I began to imagine how good my life could be.

Chapter 8

The Call of the Nightingale
1980 – 1983

Coping with the intimate demands of caring for the sick would require love, grace and a self-giving humility. The humility of a self-knowledge grounded in truth, patience with others, simplicity of life, attentive listening to others, courage to overcome difficulties and a compassionate heart.

St Bonaventure, cited by Ilia Delio in *The Humility of God*

Can you remember the first day of one of your most significant life-changing choices, such as the day you started paid work? Did you have any inclination your life was about to be defined by this? Did you even realise you were making such a profound and significant change to the course of your life? Were you aware of the threshold you were crossing?

It was 26 October 1980 and I was about to fall in love. In love with nursing.

I arrived at the nurses' residence on a cold and foggy autumn Sunday evening. Crisp golden-brown leaves danced around the entrance to this antiquated Victorian building which was to become my home and sanctuary. The next day I would commence three years of Registered General Nurse training.

Inside was a labyrinth of long dismal corridors, each one punctuated by a series of single rooms. There was a pervasive smell of disinfectant. I was shown to my room on the first floor by the warden, a short lady with grey hair. She wasn't overly friendly, but pleasantly civil with a dutiful smile. I was given a key to my room and some instructions for the following day.

I had a single bed with starched hospital sheets, a coarse blanket and a coverlet bearing the hospital name in large bold red letters. There was a corner basin and a set of chunky dark-wood drawers. Tucked below a small window was a wooden desk and chair. The simplicity of these austere surroundings evoked a deep sense of homecoming and peace. This was the place I needed to be.

The room was comfortably quiet. The only sound was hot water cascading through a large cast-iron radiator as it generously heated the room. I expected to hear nervous chatter echoing from other students who were arriving, or perhaps existing students who were living there, but there was nothing, just a placid silence, like a dormitory in a cloistered convent.

The contrast to what I had left behind gave me a feeling of warmth and calm. I felt safe and secure, free to relinquish my constant fear of being attacked and ridiculed. I have often thanked my angels for withholding information about what lay ahead. Had I known then what life had in store for me, I would have panicked and denied this opportunity. Instead, I would have allowed myself to drift. Florence Nightingale's words 'How very little can be done under the spirit of fear' perfectly describe my life in nursing.

The career I had embarked on would demand strength and resilience. The witnessing of human pain, sorrow and loss would often leave me feeling agonisingly helpless. When dealing with the many forms of human suffering I would be utterly wretched and bereft at the absence of meaning.

You have power over your mind – not outside events. Realise this and you will find strength.

Marcus Aurelius,
Meditations

As I set off on my expedition towards the Promised Land of transformation, the other members of my fragmented family were each starting on their own journey. We scattered far and wide.

Now aged 17, Lee had gone to Portsmouth to join the Royal Navy. Dad seemed more relaxed and had accepted a new, less demanding role at work. It was casual work in the factory warehouse driving a forklift truck. The shift pattern was simpler and less taxing. He wasn't so tired and there were fewer violent outbursts. His change in mood was partly a consequence of both his children leaving home and so relieving him of his responsibilities for providing for two teenagers. But, more importantly, Mum was finally admitted to a pioneering residential centre for the treatment of alcohol addiction. She didn't have to suffer the degrading incarceration of the psychiatric ward, but was looked after in a sixteen-bed inpatient clinic purpose-built to provide medically assisted detoxification and psychosocial interventions. It was newly built with light and spacious rooms and a warm and welcoming atmosphere. Above all, it had a compassionate culture.

Broken and disturbed, Mum voluntarily went into this unit where she spent the next few months. I only remember visiting her once. I didn't want to see her. I was ashamed and deeply sceptical she would ever relinquish her lust for alcohol. I silently ranted and raged as my soul cried out for the love she had not been able to give me. She'd neglected me, humiliated me and failed to protect me when I was vulnerable. I couldn't and wouldn't trust her. She had told too many lies. She was a possessed psychotic vixen, cunning, cruel and selfish. I was so angry, and I hated her. Mum's emotional poverty had wounded both of us, and we both needed healing. I continued to lament my aberrant childhood. The whole family had suffered the damaging indignities of this debilitating disease. Dad would mix his visits to Mum with his craving for strip clubs. I was disgusted by him and cringed when he came near me. I felt devoid of any affection for him.

Some years later I asked Mum what it was that had enabled her to find the motivation to defeat her addiction to alcohol when her life was so chaotic. Everything around her was still the same, apart from Lee and me leaving home. Dad was still Dad, emotionally unavailable and self-absorbed. Both her parents were now dead, and she had no siblings to turn to. Our home was still a squalid mess: shabby, soiled carpets, torn and damaged furnishings, broken and cracked crockery – all symbolic of the state of our family.

Mum had willingly surrendered her shrewish character for a journey of tender healing. What gave her courage to withstand the agony of withdrawal from her crutch whisky? It was love. Loving care crept into her life from the kindness of strangers. It came from the nurses and doctors in the addiction unit. Mum explained how she felt genuinely cared for, loved and respected by these people. Her healing came from the willingness of others to help her, as in the parable of the Good Samaritan. She sensed they believed in her worthiness, her integrity and her authenticity. Her past lies and failings didn't matter. The staff did not judge her. They acknowledged she had a genuine illness, which needed healing not condemnation. There was no shame and no blame, only love.

There are palaces whose gates only open to tears. In the desert of the heart let the healing fountain start.

The Zohar,
cited by Daniel O'Leary in *Already Within*

Holding her hand, the staff would patiently listen as her soul trembled with tearful grief for the life her hopes and dreams never had. They became her mat carriers. They would not let her suffering and adversity crush her, but carried her to a place of grace, peace and lifelong healing. They soothed her and allowed her to grieve and mourn. Mum knew she could trust their compassion and genuine desire to help her. She could let go of the pain and misery while others carried her in the name of love.

Following her discharge she never drank alcohol again. She took up full-time employment with the Inland Revenue and rebuilt her life. She remained married to my dad until his death in 1997.

I clung to my resentment of my mother; I found it hard to believe she had changed, and full of bitterness I vowed never to forgive her. My doubt was an insidious virus infecting my new beginnings. I became doubtful and gloomy about my ability to succeed at my nurse training. Had I been taking refuge in my own fantasies, fooling myself I was clever enough? Tormented by the memory of the acidic comments so often claimed as truths by my teachers, I began to believe I was an imposter. Perhaps I was only offered a place out of pity because I had shared information about my family. I began to sabotage my own success. I wasn't intelligent enough, and neither was I worthy of something good happening to me. Only bad things happened in my life; it was all my fault. I was the one to blame. I was about to commence my nurse training convinced I was a fraud.

Then a flicker of light broke through. My true self asserted itself, not the damaged and wounded self, but somehow deep down in my soul I started to believe nursing was my own unique journey. I deserved this opportunity and it was a gift to me. I turned my back on my morbid predictions. I discovered an inner resilience, which I could use to my benefit. I had the choice of shunning my dismal circumstances and opting for a future of hope and prosperity.

I arrived at the School of Nurse Training at 8.45am on Monday, 27 October 1980. There were thirty of us altogether, all female. Most of us were aged between eighteen and twenty-five, with a few mature students, mainly women who had spent their twenties raising a family. Each of us was assigned our own personal tutor, one of whom was a nun, a quiet, shy woman. The other three included a tall, skinny man who was meticulous and pedantic and a gentle and easy-going woman who was approaching retirement. My tutor, Miss Jenkins, was young and ambitious with an imperious manner and had only recently taken up teaching. She insisted on high standards both academically and clinically. A strict code of conduct was to be adhered to and included topics such as confidentiality, time-keeping and image. She governed us by command and control. It was her way or the highway.

We began our three years of training with eight weeks of theory entitled Introductory Block. This consisted of lectures in anatomy and physiology, nursing care, documentation, and basic life support. They took place in a single-storey wooden building adjacent to the old Victorian hospital, which had once been a workhouse.

Elderly patients were often terrified, believing they really were in the workhouse. They would scream out in the night to be rescued by their loved ones or saved by some holy angel. They lived in fear of not returning home to their families. The ghostly atmosphere of this stark building with its prison-like high walls and windows was hardly conducive to healing and recovery. Long, dark corridors echoed to footsteps, trolleys, beds and machinery and were haunted by the cries of the sick and bereaved. Henry Marsh had a similar experience when he worked as a houseman in a dilapidated old hospital in London.

The building had housed a workhouse in the nineteenth century and it was said it had not yet escaped its dismal previous reputation with the local population. It was the sort of hospital which made the British public's devotion to the NHS quite incomprehensible, with the patients housed like cattle in the old workhouse rooms – large and ugly rooms with dozens of beds lined up on either side. The casualty department was on the ground floor and the intensive care unit on the first floor immediately above it. But there was only one lift in the hospital, which was a quarter of a mile down the hospital corridor.

Henry Marsh,
Do No Harm

This would not be my first hospital with such an archaic layout. I was to later experience a similar setting which would hinder efficient patient care.

We sat in rows of single desks as we were indoctrinated with the rules, procedures and practices of caring for the sick. Each session was delivered with military precision.

Shortly after lunch one day, Miss Jenkins seemed flustered and distracted. She announced the timetable had been changed, as Mr Watts had requested to see us. In he came and slowly patrolled around the room as if he were searching for his next culprit. His voice was authoritarian and grim as he recounted a tragedy involving two second-year student nurses. They had been suspended, suspected of stealing controlled drugs. With no warning one of them had flung herself off the top of a multi-storey car park and died instantly. Sharp gasps for air could be heard around the room. We were all stunned, frozen with shock.

Mr Watts' message was clear: *Thou shalt not lie and thou shalt not steal.* Trust and confidentiality were paramount. This shocking story threatened my fragile poise. I was shunted into an unexpected psychological voyage. I became afraid. Before now I'd had nothing of value to lose, but suddenly I was beginning to fear loss. This was unfamiliar and strange to me. Fresh hopes and dreams had evolved since embarking on this professional journey; failing to fulfil these was not an option.

I might be asked to leave due to insufficient intellectual capability or incompetence. Furthermore, poor standards of professional conduct such as drunkenness, stealing, lying and breaches of confidentiality could also lead to dismissal. I was terrified of deviating from the code of conduct. But why? Didn't I trust myself to conform? Until now my only record of institutional behaviour was at school, where for five years I revelled in being disruptive and antagonistic. But now I was spellbound by my aspirations. The allure of learning and growing was drawing me to a place where I could thrive. I refused to allow myself to be confined by fearful imaginings. My soul was inviting me to discover the gift of freedom from oppression and the inner richness of self-expression, each of which would help to refine and heal my wounded heart.

I was taking no risks. My days of youthful mischief were over. It was time to grow up and conform. But there was one more message coming my way. This would be my first cultural lesson in becoming a respectable professional, but it would sting. My self-made defensive walls were under attack.

In front of my peers, I was abruptly summoned by Miss Jenkins. Embarrassed and shocked I followed her without question. Electric fear shot through my thin teenage body as I walked heavily to her sombre office. My heart was pounding, my mouth was as dry as blotting paper, and I felt dizzy with trepidation as I entered the windowless room. On the shelf was a collection of large nursing textbooks, titles such as Ross and Wilson's *Anatomy and Physiology*, Harrison's *Textbook of Medicine*, Bailliere's *Nurses Dictionary*, *Caring for the Surgical and Medical Patient, Paediatrics and Geriatrics*. I struggled to breathe normally.

From a corner of the room, a skeleton was staring at me, a pale and pulseless personal assistant, like some Marcel Duchamp sculpture. Before me was Miss Jenkins' large wooden desk with a chair next to it, waiting for me. There were no elaborate introductions to soften the encounter. *What is it? What is it? What have I done wrong?* I assumed I must be at fault even before I had heard the accusation against me. I sat and waited. Miss Jenkins took aim and fired without hesitation.

'You have an attitude problem, Nurse Willow. You are standoffish towards others.'

I was startled by her remark, but I realised I had to respond in a way which was pleasing to her, despite wanting to contest the validity of her allegation. What I really wanted to say was: No, no. Please understand me. You're wrong. I'm not behaving badly. It's my way of coping in a world where I feel threatened. This is how I survive. I'm not standoffish, I'm sensitive and nervous in company, especially with large groups of girls.

Until this moment I had little awareness of how others saw me. Fond memories from my positive summer experiences in the hotel were in hiding. Miss Jenkins' mirror told a different story. It had sharp edges and it hurt. I felt scared and vulnerable in front of this woman. To protect my fragile sense of self I had learned to clad myself in the armour of fake self-confidence. I was over-compensating for my insecurity, feelings of insignificance and poor self-worth. It was my way of coping with adults who held some form of power over me. Until now this approach had served me well, but not anymore. It was incompatible with the philosophy being engendered here in this place of caring for the sick.

I was having a Road to Damascus experience. It was painful and I smarted. If this had happened at school I would have replied with smug sarcasm. I had no time to think. I felt trapped and tethered by fear. Either I conformed and attracted good feedback from then on or I risked being expelled from the course. My fear of failure was growing like Jack's beanstalk except there was no magic and no castle to flee to.

I was an easy target for this emotionally unintelligent and inexperienced teacher. Her primary motivation was not to be concerned about my well-being but her need to assert her authority. I shrank into my chair, my skin clammy as I squirmed in distress. Bewildered by this ambush, I apologised: 'I'm sorry, Miss Jenkins. I had no idea. I will try to be friendlier and less aloof.' It's all I could offer her. I hid my true feelings of fear and deflation.

This experience left a profound impression on me. I was wrong and Miss Jenkins was right. Once again I was powerless before the poor opinions of others. I couldn't fight back, knowing she had the power to either ruin or enhance my future. It was an intense clashing moment of shadows and light. How could I contest this ridiculous misunderstanding? I was confused and emotionally bruised.

If she had chosen a more compassionate and engaging approach maybe we both would have learned something and our relationship would have strengthened. Why didn't she ask me how I was enjoying the course and how I was coping. Was I settling into the nurses' home? I felt wounded and blistered by her critical assumptions. The thorns of fear and suspicion now perforated our developing relationship. From then on I would be on high alert, wary of any verbal missiles aimed at my self-esteem. An invisible thread of trust was broken by this one single incident. Without delay, I became the model compliant student. I was responsible, conscientious and reliable. I was an ambassador for nursing.

Following eight weeks of Introductory Block we were cast out onto the turbulent sea of clinical practice. The first year was a combination of medicine and surgery; the second year covered night duty in general medicine, and then it was back to day shifts for paediatrics, A&E, theatre, geriatrics, and psychiatry; our final year was a consolidation of medicine and surgery. There were assignments and exams throughout the three years until we sat our final exams.

I immersed myself in my studies and clinical placements. I discovered a new diligence and determination which enabled me to achieve high grades ranging from B+ to A+. The distance from failure increased with each assignment and clinical assessment. My appetite to learn was insatiable. I was attempting to dodge painful feelings of shame, judgement and blame. I had developed a false addictive belief system: perfectionism. I studied tirelessly. The higher my grades the less likely I was to be criticised. Anything less than B+ was unacceptable to me as I obsessively tried to overcome entrenched feelings of inadequacy. I strove to become the best I could be. But this goal was slippery and elusive. I never quite arrived there. Essays would be drafted and redrafted as I learned about the process of nursing the sick and dying; at the same time, I was trying to heal my own psychological wounds.

Halfway through my training, on 2 April 1982, an inconceivable fear and gloom arrived: the Falklands War. Three days later Lee was to exchange war at home for the HMS *Invincible* as it headed off to the South Atlantic. He was 17 years old and seduced by the glamour of war. He accepted the standard propaganda of militarism and sailed off in search of his own inner hero. How else would he be noticed and gain the accolades he craved? Perhaps if he'd seen himself first as son, brother, lover and future father, he would have shifted his loyalties from the drums of war to creating peace and love at home.

I was working in A&E at the time. I became distracted and anxious with the anticipation of grief. Despite being at loggerheads with my brother, I worried about him and was afraid he would be killed. I cared about him. Deep-rooted protective feelings re-emerged sending my emotions into turmoil.

The constant flow of patients in and out of A&E brought snippets of news throughout my shifts, news which at times was exaggerated and embellished or just plain nonsense. Factually incorrect details would be passed around like toys to play with. There were stories about bombings and about those wounded or killed by bullets, missiles and raging fires. I heard about the destruction of ships, helicopters, submarines and aircraft. There were tales about men being taken prisoner, and about torture and executions. The difficulty I experienced in uncovering the truth was not helped by newspaper propaganda. There was no internet or mobile phone to check out the veracity of the claims. While on duty I had to rely on word of mouth from the public, which was distorted and unreliable. Staff huddled in corners to discuss the drama of this senseless conflict. I wanted to scream out in fear and dread: *My baby brother is out there on a cramped ship, not realising the implications of his folly!*

I struggled as images of young men, wounded, mutilated and dying, competed with my concentration. Lee was there, barely out of boyhood, lost in his fantasy hero world fighting for his Queen and country, where in reality he was just another nameless seaman obeying orders for a political campaign.

This conflict was a perfect excuse for Mum to start drinking again. The anxiety might threaten her resolve, and once again she'd seek solace in whisky. Each time I saw her throughout the campaign I expected to smell the evaporating fumes of alcohol on her breath, or maybe her eyes would tell me, the pinpoint pupils I had become so familiar with as she'd so often tried to deny being drunk. The Falklands War was her greatest test since her stay at the clinic. I counted the days and waited, convinced she would succumb.

I wrote Lee letters telling stories about my less heroic life as a student nurse. I filled shoeboxes with gifts of chocolate and biscuits. I made music tapes and enclosed photos.

Then it was all over. The Argentinians surrendered on 14 June, and on 17 September 1982, the *Invincible* sailed into Portsmouth harbour. I was there with Mum, Dad and two of Lee's pals to celebrate his homecoming. It was a luminously bright sunny day as a vast crowd of friends, lovers and relatives jubilantly waved their Union Jack flags, sang and cheered to welcome their heroes home.

Inch by inch this monumental metal structure slipped into the dock. Hardly a ripple formed on the water as it glided silently and effortlessly back to its home. It stroked the clouds and touched the sunshine with its colossal size. It was a floating city before us. The crowd cheered, the band played, and as I looked at Mum tears started to roll down my cheeks. I felt deep forgiveness towards her. She had not touched a drop of alcohol throughout the war. She'd had every opportunity and a clear excuse but she had resisted. I knew from this moment on she would not drink again and she never did. My intense anger towards her was replaced with loving pity. My heart was moving towards her as I stepped away from bitter suspicion and doubt. I felt reunited with her as she returned from the exile of her addiction. I spent many moments watching her in the glistening Solent sunshine profoundly grateful for the rarity of her healing. Resentful images of the suffering she had caused herself and all of us were transformed into beauty and light as I gazed lovingly at her. I admired her courage as she had patiently waited throughout those few months for Lee to return. Her addiction to alcohol had been banished for good.

Not only had Lee returned from the abyss of war but Mum too. I tiptoed into a new era, one where I had a mum for the first time in twenty years. It would take many more years to grieve for the poverty of my unmothered childhood. A profound sense of loving forgiveness stirred and carried me from a bleak desert of angst to a verdant plain of healing and wonder. The sordid debris of years of intense conflict and pain was being jettisoned. My soul was being cleansed and freed of dark inner shadows. An invisible benevolence was emerging from within me, carrying me towards a loving light full of radiant hope and new beginnings. This was one of my mat carriers, faithfully loving me and guiding me through a valley of suffering to an opening of reconciliation.

I continued to study relentlessly, and I passed each assignment and test the first time. But would this be enough to pass my final exams? What if I failed them? I would only be allowed three attempts. I trusted nothing and no one. My endeavours continued throughout my course with unfaltering commitment. I never went close to the threatening border of failure, but I was still emotionally hungry and discontented. My self-esteem remained fragile. Not only was I experiencing a lack of trust in my relationship with Miss Jenkins, but I struggled to believe in my own abilities.

I was still restless. All I had to do was to pass my final exams, and I would be ready to cross the threshold from student to qualified Registered General Nurse.

Chapter 9

Carpe Diem

1983 – 1984

*A courageous heart will go forth and
engage with life despite confusion
and fear
A fearful heart will be hesitant and will
tend to hold back
A heavy heart will make for a gloomy
unlived life.*

John O'Donohue, *Benedictus*

It was 1 November 1983. I woke early in my small room in the nurses' home after a night of agitated uncertainty. Vivid jumbled images had invaded my sleep, their hyperactive nonsense robbing me of rest and comfort. It was the day of my Registered General Nurse final exam results. Paralysed by fear, I asked a nursing pal to collect them from the hospital post room. Off she raced with childlike enthusiasm, running across the crisp, chilly hospital grounds in her slippers and dressing gown. I buried myself under the duvet hoping it would console my nerves with its luxurious cosiness as I waited for news.

Through my third floor window, I could hear a shrill yelling. I leapt out of my duvet bunker and peered out of the small window. My friend was waving an open envelope shrieking, 'You've passed! You've passed!' All the striving to attain this professional licence had been successful. I was now a fully qualified Registered General Nurse. I had achieved the goal I had worked so hard for and which I had been so desperate to reach.

But after the initial joy and relief, I felt unsettled, trapped and restless. It wasn't enough. I immediately started to search for a gateway to a better place, a new path, a new venture cloaked with hope and prosperity.

I was offered a short-term contract as a staff nurse on a 30-bed female surgical ward. During my training, this had been one of three areas I had found lacking in acceptable standards of care. Needless to say, my observations had made me unpopular. Power struggles prevailed in an atmosphere of stale custom and ritualistic practice. The ward sister was lazy, forgetful and incapable of leading her ship of fools. Rather than challenging her, the ward staff colluded with her to protect themselves and the status quo. None of them had worked in any other hospital since qualifying, and their knowledge and experience were limited to that one ward. No one was willing to mutiny. Everyday conversations revolved around trivia which had no relevance to nursing practice. Trust and respect were faint as they drifted from one shift to another.

Frustrated and disillusioned, I could not escape the thought that there had to be a better way of doing things. Perhaps it was time to leave behind that which I had outgrown, in pursuit of my true life's desires. Feeling melancholy, one dark foggy winter's evening I caught a bus into town to meet some friends. As I sat on the damp smoky bus, I entered a trance-like state. It was as if I were on a balcony looking down onto a stage, with the other passengers the actors and the play a tragedy of those worn and wearied by struggle and deprivation. Coughing, mumbling and spluttering, we were all chugging along through the cold and dark. Sitting a few rows in front of me was a group of youths. They taunted and jeered the other passengers. Vulgar, threatening language combined with spitting and flicking nose pickings entertained their troubled souls. *I can't do this, I can't live with this*, I silently screamed. *I need peaceful beauty and fragrant tranquillity, not this vile intimidation.* I knew I had to make a decision about the course my life would take.

A life that continues to remain on the safe side of its own habits and repetitions, that never engages with risk of its own possibility, remains the unlived life. There is within each heart a hidden voice that calls out for freedom and creativity.

John O'Donohue,
Benedictus

I had to get away. Not by fleeing in terror and confusion like some tortured migrant, but with thoughtful planning and exploration. I became the lonely seeker in search of a place where I could belong and flourish. How would I recognise the place that would be my destiny? I had an awareness within me which was my guide. I listened and trusted that I would be shown where it was that I was intended to be. The process had begun with acknowledging where I didn't want to be. Once I had admitted that I didn't belong in this place, I sensed an emerging path was revealing itself. An inner wisdom once again was whispering. There was an invisible beckoning.

I wasn't afraid. I was willing to take the next steps. It was no longer an option to stay where I was. It was too emotionally uncomfortable to deny my true sense of calling. Like St Peter, I stepped out of my boat onto the sea of uncertainty, trusting I would not drown.

Cambridge, I asked myself. Where is that? An internationally-renowned newly built teaching hospital was recruiting recently qualified staff nurses. It would be such a contrast to my decaying Victorian general hospital. I asked if anyone knew about Cambridge. I was told strange stories about this faraway land: privileged people punting down the River Cam, May balls, debutantes in silk taffeta gowns, aristocrats, pink champagne, swarms of bicycles, and dons in swirling academic robes. I jumped to the conclusion that the others had invented these stories to tease and upset me; it was all so far removed from what I knew, it never occurred to me that these tales could actually be true.

The week before I was due to leave for Cambridge, Mum arrived at the nurses' home with her arm in a sling, her face scratched and bruised. Dad had beaten her again. Weepy and tired she recounted another story of senseless domestic conflict. I was torn. Should I go to Cambridge and leave my parents to battle with one another? Would others judge me to have abandoned my poor mother? Who would mediate if I went? Would it make any difference if I stayed? I was frustrated and angry. Here I was on the threshold of a life-changing adventure, and once again my parents were presenting me with a dilemma. It was as though they were trying to sabotage my decision to leave. But when I tuned out what was happening to me and concentrated on them, I was overwhelmed with pity. Their situation radiated sadness. I could no longer be part of that. I was being called away. Despite my worries and concerns, I had to leave.

It was Sunday, 4 March 1984 and Mum and Dad were driving me to Cambridge. Two tatty old suitcases were tied to the roof of the white Hillman Avenger, and I was hidden underneath bags and boxes on the back seat, clouded in Mum's Players No. 6 cigarette smoke.

We arrived outside Old Addenbrooke's hospital and looked for the nurses' accommodation. Dad and I went inside to collect my key and room details. We wandered through the cold, echoing corridors. The bleakness of the atmosphere made me feel as if we were inside some vast abandoned tomb, soulless and incapable of sustaining life. There was little evidence of structural improvements since the building first opened over two hundred years before and, as it awaited closure, it was on the brink of being uninhabitable. The 'new site' Addenbrooke's was slowly replacing this archaic institution.

My dingy room had a single wartime iron-framed bed covered with a hospital blanket; next to it was a small, shabby wooden wardrobe. The mattress was torn and stained, its fabric threadbare through many years of cushioning weary bodies. There was one electrical point, a round-pinned 3-amp socket. Dad became anxious, knowing none of my appliances would fit, including my essential alarm clock. He knocked on other residents' doors to plead for a plug and screwdriver.

My window overlooked an operating theatre and I could hear a whirring sound as a huge glaring theatre light illuminated the heads and shoulders of the doctors and nurses whose job it was to relieve disease, pain and suffering, perhaps saving someone's life. The bottom half of the glass was opaque, concealing the patient from view. In the kitchen were a wobbly gas stove and a fridge. Inside the fridge was decaying food, the smell causing me to retch.

Once we were back outside, Dad became upset about the poor conditions I was expected to live in and refused to unpack the car. I was surprised by his reaction. Dad was familiar with poverty. He had grown up with the legacy of the Second World War when basic commodities such as butter, meat, tea and coal were rationed, and children played on bombsites. Undernourished, he had been dragged up rather than brought up. He and his four brothers shared a double bed in a two-bedroom terraced house in a slum area of town. His parents slept in the adjacent room. Their only heating came from a coal fire in the front room. The toilet was outside in the backyard along with chickens who provided eggs and meat. Dad knew what it was like to rough it.

I calmly insisted that I had to give it a try. Dad had hardly ever tried to protect me, and these few unforgettable moments on this quiet spring Sunday were a rare encounter with his gentler side. I gained a fleeting glimpse of his capacity for compassion. I could see that he felt helpless at having to let go of his tenacious only daughter.

The decision to stay triggered a surge of fortitude and determination in me. I was going to make this work. There was no going back. I bought a toaster, kettle, two mugs and a large green plastic bucket for washing clothes. I lived off tea, toast and takeaways or simple bread and cheese. At night it was essential to wear slippers to visit the bathroom as the corridor was littered with cockroaches. Before I got into bed, I would inspect the bedclothes in case any of them had found their way under the pillow or sheets.

I lost weight and began to improve my fitness, every day cycling around this charming and spectacular historic city. My time in Cambridge was extraordinary. It is a truly special place. The city's cultural heritage is its soul, its majestic architecture blending with fields of green. The contrast to my hometown was striking. I felt as though I had landed a role in a romantic fairy-tale ballet. I'd forsaken cultural decay for a picturesque metropolitan kingdom. Betting shops, off-licences and derelict buildings defaced with vulgar graffiti had been exchanged for museums, art galleries and botanical gardens. Drifts of spring flowers adorned the banks of the River Cam as it flowed through the city, crossed by the famous Mathematical Bridge and the Bridge of Sighs. I would wander through this divine place transfixed by its exquisite buildings and people. Its eclectic citizens fascinated me; the cultural diversity was mesmerising.

But there were ricochets of adjustment, and at times I seriously doubted I had the resilience to cope. I felt inept and self-conscious. When I spoke with my northern English accent, I felt instantly stigmatised. How easy it had been to chat with strangers back at home – on the bus, in shops and cafés. Not here! No, there was a different kind of social etiquette, which I had to learn fast if I was going to settle. Folk were reticent, reluctant to engage spontaneously without due thought and consideration. I was unsettled and kept pondering whether I would ever feel sufficiently accepted to stay. I needed a sense of permanency and connection, which seemed so remote.

A moment of enlightenment occurred one sunny April morning. I was climbing the steps to the Fitzwilliam Museum to see its collection of Egyptian, Greek and Roman artefacts. A sense of calm came over me, and I stood still and silent, listening to my inner voice of wisdom. Again I was being guided. *Stay and let this place help you to grow. Let go of the past. Do not cling to that which will stifle you.*

The nurse next door to me was also from the north of England. I was grateful for this coincidence, although we didn't seem to have much else in common. Her name was Debbie, and she had been working permanent night duty at the hospital for just over a year. Debbie was shy and quiet and reluctant to mix with others.

It was May 1984, and we were both on night duty. On the morning after we had finished our last shift, Debbie was excited as she was going to London to stay with her boyfriend for a week. I planned to spend my days off exploring and learning more about the city.

The following day, about 11 am, Debbie, appeared at my door unexpectedly. She was tense and agitated. 'What's wrong?' I nervously asked. 'I thought you were away for a week? What's brought you back so quickly?'

'If you were in trouble who would you go to?' she replied. 'Who would you trust? Like me, you're living in a strange place a long way from home and your family.'

'I'd go to see my nursing officer as I would have to hope that I could trust her confidentiality based on our professional code of conduct.' There was a particular officer I had in mind, and I had developed a good rapport with her. 'I can't think of anyone else I would trust.'

'I can't do that. It's too complicated.' She didn't explain why and I sensed she didn't want to talk about it, so I didn't ask her. She changed the subject. 'Do you fancy coming out for lunch?'

I'd made plans with another neighbour, Louise.

'Why not join us instead?' I suggested.

She agreed, and the three of us ambled down to a riverside pub. Louise and Debbie drank heavily: bottles of lager and pints of beer. I stuck to orange juice. I was nervous about drinking alcohol at lunchtime, especially when recovering from the fatigue associated with night duty. I was also conscious of its ill effects; I had painful memories of watching my mother.

After about six rounds of drinks, I left them to go shopping. I was excited about buying the latest Smiths album. I bought some biscuits and Earl Grey tea and hurried back to play my new record.

The kettle was on and the music playing when Debbie appeared at my door again.

'How are you?' I asked.

'I'm okay. I've sorted things out.'

She came into my room and sat on my bed for the first time.

'What have you done? Have you arranged to see a solicitor?'

'No,' she said, and that was all. I made her a cup of tea and she fell asleep on my bed. I couldn't ask Louise to help me move her since she too was sleeping before her night duty.

I turned down the music and wrote some chatty letters to friends.

Debbie continued to sleep heavily. When Louise woke, I asked her to help me get her back to her room to sleep off the booze. We got her back on her feet, and each took an arm to support her as we coaxed her back to her bed. I turned her on her side and covered her with a blanket, leaving the door unlocked so I could pop in to check on her later.

Louise told me she'd had a long intimate chat with Debbie about her problems after I had left the pub to go shopping, but she didn't go into details as Debbie had asked her not to. I suggested we tell the home warden and ask her to check on Debbie later, but Louise didn't want to involve anyone else. She was uncompromising, firmly stating that it was no one else's business. This didn't make sense to me. Why couldn't we ask for support? Louise was older than me with a more senior nursing position. I felt that she was asserting her professional authority, and I passively submitted. I didn't listen to my own inner voice. I gave away my own personal power.

I went out for a takeaway supper and an evening stroll. I wanted to enjoy the awakening of spring in this pretty city. Louise was going to check on Debbie before she went on night duty at 9 pm. I arrived back soon after, took my shoes off and started to get ready to read a book in bed with a cup of tea, again listening to my new Smiths album. On my way down the corridor to fill the kettle, I decided to see how Debbie was and ask if she wanted a cuppa. I could hear laughter coming from the street outside – giddy students enjoying an evening away from their intense academic pursuits. I knocked on her door. There was no answer. I tried the door, which I expected to be locked, thinking she had woken while I was out and decided to go to bed for the night. It slowly opened. The floor creaked as I crept in towards a thick silence.

'Debbie, are you alright? It's me, Mary Anne,' I whispered. The room was dim and eerily still. I could see Debbie was in the same position I had left her in, on her side on the bed, facing the door. As I approached her everything froze in time. The macabre scene in front of me couldn't be real. This was a nightmare unfolding, and I was about to wake up and find myself tucked up in bed listening to Marr and Morrissey plaintively singing a doleful tune.

It was no dream. Debbie was dead. Her face was mottled and blue, and her mouth was covered in froth. She was lifeless. I panicked and ran to my room to grab an artificial plastic airway. Nurses carry these in their uniform pocket in case of an emergency. I had automatically reverted to my nursing role and acted as I would in a ward situation: ABC – Airway, Breathing, Circulation. Frantic and shaking I ran back to her and attempted to insert the airway into her mouth. My heart was racing and my chest felt tight as I tried to breathe against a desperate crushing terror.

I ran to get help. I fled down three flights of stairs into the main corridor of the hospital screaming, 'Get me some help, please help my friend!' I felt responsible. I was besieged by frenzied irrational thoughts. I had done something to cause this. I had killed her. This was all my fault and I would be blamed. I shouldn't have left her alone. I should have stayed with her. Why did I leave her? I could have prevented this.

Only a sleepy porter could be seen through the haze of my hysteria. Then the night-duty nursing sister appeared. She looked startled and confused about what to do. She ran to get a doctor. A young junior doctor arrived. He too reacted with shock and bewilderment. I grabbed his arm and told him to run. We raced through the marble corridors and into the nurses' home, back to Debbie. He looked at her and shakily searched her cool, limp body for a pulse. Nothing. There was no sign of life. We stared at one another. 'We have to try,' I said.

We heaved Debbie's body onto the bare wooden floor and attempted to resuscitate her. Air from her lungs escaped and made us both jump. We looked at one another in shock. For a second I thought that perhaps she was alive after all and I had made a big mistake. But I hadn't. I grabbed a towel and wiped away the froth from her blue lips so I could breathe air into her motionless lungs. The terrified doctor repeatedly pushed against her chest. I was so horribly frightened I felt as though I was about to be sick as I desperately tried to bring Debbie back to life.

The nursing sister and porter carried the resuscitation equipment up the endless flights of stairs, as the lift was turned off at night. Their mountainous ascent seemed to take forever. But it was a waste of time. The electrical sockets in our rooms were incompatible with the modern equipment. They were obsolete and outmoded. More and more medical staff arrived, but to no avail. The room quickly became crowded and noisy as folk tried hard to revive Debbie, but she had died some time ago and was soon declared officially dead.

That afternoon when I had gone shopping Debbie told Louise she was a lesbian and was being blackmailed by a former lover. Louise was bisexual, so I imagine Debbie felt safe sharing this with her. Perhaps they were kindred spirits.

The police were summoned. Debbie's room was searched for clues into the cause of her death as I was interviewed in my room next door. I sat in an old worn armchair feeling stony cold and dazed. I was stunned into a state of numb emptiness, frozen in the moment. I could hear movement coming from Debbie's room. The police were crawling and scratching around, looking for something to explain her sudden death. Like an unwanted rash, they encroached on her personal belongings and treasured keepsakes. They were inspecting each and every drawer, cupboard, box, tin and envelope. Like an army of insects, they invaded every nook and cranny. I silently appealed to them: *Please cover her body over. Please be sensitive and respect her privacy and dignity. Don't treat her like some worthless, unlovable corpse.* I felt so protective towards the safety of her deceased body, which only a few hours ago was alive. I wanted them to go away so I could mourn for her.

The police officer who interviewed me had silver-grey hair and a thick moustache. His name was Kevin. He was kind and easy to talk to, and even disclosed that his girlfriend had once been a lesbian before falling in love with him. He was totally accepting of his girlfriend's sexuality past and present. There was no hint of shame or disgust.

There was no evidence of suicide. No note. No drugs. No self-harm.

I didn't go to Debbie's funeral. I don't know why. I seem to recall her family wanted her death to be kept private and hidden. Perhaps they felt ashamed of her and were unable to face the truth about her sexuality, or perhaps the circumstances of her death were too traumatic and shocking to share with strangers. Stigma and discrimination, blended with anguish, shrouded the emptiness of Debbie's life.

While I can still recount the conversations which took place on the day of Debbie's death, my memory after that is blurred. I felt desperately lonely and diminished. A wall of darkness disconnected me from friends. I would wander aimlessly by the river and around the city streets feeling exiled and isolated. By contrast, I noticed I had a heightened sensitivity to the beauty around me. My surroundings displayed more presence and sharpness of shape and vividness of colour. The world was lit with iridescent light, in contrast to the dullness I had previously known. The enchanting beauty of this city embraced me. I thought I would fall apart in the shadow of the tragedy of Debbie's unlived life, but somehow an invisible loving spirit helped me to cope. Despite my anguish, fine threads of light peeped through my bleakness. My soul was delicately soothed as invisible angels of mercy watched over me.

Alone in this sleepy corner which is forever England, tormented by regret and blame, I turned to my faithful companion: music. I was gripped by self-contempt in the wake of Debbie's death, but somehow melodies and lyrics permeated my inner turmoil. Comforting, soothing rhythms and soulful songs carried me to a place of calm and hope. Slowly I distanced myself from the enslavement of blame.

Once again in my life, I was saved by beauty – the beauty of nature as well as of music. My senses were the threshold to the preservation of my soul; they allowed invisible miracles to take place. Nature and music were my mat carriers, restoring my spirit so that I could carry on despite what had happened.

The coroner concluded it was a sudden unexplained adult death, an adult cot death. The story was turned into a cheap scandal, splashed across the front page of the local press: *Gay nurse dies after heavy drinking session.* Debbie's vulnerable short life was shamelessly paraded to sell more newspapers.

Chapter 10

Pride and Prestige
1984 – 1989

If you neglect your own immensity
your life path becomes repressive and
unnatural – you cannot drift endlessly.

John O'Donohue, *Eternal Echoes*

Riddled with fear and insecurity, I was determined to ensure I would always be employable. I told myself I must keep learning and growing to remain up-to-date and skilled. The more qualifications I had, the less likely I was to be overlooked and seen as someone who was lazy and complacent. I needed to prove that I was intelligent and competent – fit for purpose. I was willing to forfeit holidays and an active social life, consigning myself to study and hard work. I was deeply conscientious, and my free time was often spent reading and studying. My self-confidence strengthened as I saw job opportunities beginning to open up in front of me. I needed to earn enough money to provide a place to live and be independent now that I was free from the tyranny of my parents. This was what drove me; it was never about status, nor was it about money for its own sake. I looked for posts in increasingly complex and sophisticated areas of nursing.

I aimed to be the best I could be, but however much I achieved, I didn't trust my accomplishments and success. My motivation was based on a sense of worthlessness and inadequacy. I wasn't good enough, so I had to keep improving myself. It was too risky to settle for the status quo; just living my life was not enough. I would later discover I was struggling with imposter syndrome: an inability to believe in one's own achievements and a fear of being exposed as a fraud. These anxieties were compounded by my longing for love and security. I wanted to matter to someone, to be their significant other. The more I ached for this, the harder I worked and studied.

These self-imposed demands did bring good luck. I had the good fortune to work in another world-renowned prestigious hospital, Papworth, which was also in Cambridgeshire. Its culture dynamic and transformational, it was a magnet for an international workforce, and people would travel from the other side of the world to work there. I was excited and thrived on an atmosphere of exemplary clinical practice, working beside some of the world's best surgeons, nurses, physiotherapists and pharmacists. I met princesses and politicians, dukes and prime ministers. But at the heart of it was always the patient and family; improving and saving lives was our raison d'etre. I loved being part of this amazing hospital, which achieved the highest standards of patient care and staff satisfaction. I truly felt I belonged to a community. We all worked with shared values, striving for excellence as we served the patients and their families. In return, we felt valued and proud of our endeavours. We all mattered.

I was involved in nursing patients who had undergone pioneering surgery, and my clinical skills developed in new and unimaginable ways. I far exceeded my wildest expectations, pushing myself into fresh areas of study and expertise. I qualified as a teacher, counsellor and a senior nurse leader. Yet I was still dissatisfied with my accomplishments. There was always more to learn, more to achieve.

I rarely went home to see my parents. Their lives had become almost settled since I'd left. They had modernised their house and started to travel abroad on holidays, often trips to exotic destinations to meet up with Lee, who would be on some naval expedition. But the old tenacious ghost of domestic abuse lingered. I still received the familiar phone calls from Mum, who would be sobbing after a fight with Dad. These episodes always followed a pattern. They'd have a disagreement, and neither of them would give in. Mum would then goad Dad into a fight, and he would lash out, after which they led separate lives for weeks on end, sleeping and eating apart. Mum became the victim and Dad the perpetrator of violence. She would manipulate his guilt to get her own way; it made her feel powerful. She was the winner, and my father gave in to her to atone for his bad behaviour. And so life went on. I never heard either of them say sorry to one another. There was no remorse and no regret. A holiday would then be booked, and round and round the merry-go-round they tirelessly spun. There was no rapturous magic nor bright, coloured lights and music, just an undying bittersweet tangled web which trapped them both. Feeling powerless to help, I tried to comfort and support Mum in our frequent phone calls. I always reminded her she could leave Dad. She never did.

I began to sense I was being called to teach. Not satisfied with my clinical accomplishments, I was restless. I was also struggling with my boss who was micro-managing me. She had an excessive almost neurotic need to control and check my work. She obsessively inspected and monitored every detail in search of fault and imperfection. The atmosphere was one of suspicion and mistrust. We just clashed. She was constantly irritated when I didn't consult her, and I felt undermined and suffocated. I was captive to her good opinion, never daring to disagree for fear of retribution. Once again I was aware that she could use the power of her position to reprimand me, or even to discipline me.

There was a sinister dread behind my misery at working for this hypercritical, bullying woman: the familiar fear of blame which could jeopardise my career. She had a beguiling charisma and was popular with the ward consultants. Her whimsical charm lured them into a sense of confidence and security. On the other hand, I was lacking in humour and social chitchat and probably made them feel awkward as I legalistically recounted daily updates on each patient. My boss accepted all accolades for patient success with no acknowledgement of the contribution of the rest of the team, but if things were to go wrong, I dreaded the blame which could be passed on to me. Any failure would be mine. I was plagued by past feelings of shame. I was hypersensitive to these corrosive dynamics. The weapon of blame was always pointing towards me.

Driven by increasing unhappiness, I spent time pondering my long-term future. Should I move to another hospital, or go abroad – to Australia or New Zealand? Should I move closer to home to be near some of the pals I trained with, and of course my parents? Perhaps I should apply for another speciality, such as training to be a midwife or a health visitor. All of these options left me feeling despondent. None of them appealed. I would be deluding myself if I chose any of them. They were an invitation for regret.

I was lonely and miserable. I spent many evenings in tears, afraid and emotionally diminished by this woman. The problem was compounded by my status. Who could I turn to? I was a ward leader, and it was not professional etiquette to divulge my innermost worries to anyone in my team. It would be seen as weakness and inadequacy, risking my reputation and credibility. More importantly, I felt it would be disloyal to talk to the team about my frustrations behind her back. It would be seen as troublemaking, sowing seeds of discord. They could become unsettled and disruptive, ultimately affecting team performance and patient care. I had to be true to my own sense of credibility and integrity. I could not betray her, neither could I unsettle the team by confiding my unhappiness. I felt trapped. Perhaps my loyalty was misplaced, but I had to live with myself, and my conscience would not allow me to act in any other way. I had to model the behaviour I expected from others; I could not project my misery onto them. I had to turn my distress into inspirational optimism and positive encouragement.

I decided to leave. I applied for a post in teaching and moved on. It was a life-changing and life-enhancing decision.

Then, in the summer of 1988, as I was about to start my exciting new job, my life took an unexpected twist. My best friend introduced me to a pal of her brother who was working in the same town I was about to move to. His name was Andrew, and he was a close family friend, even boarding at the same private school as her brother. I naively assumed by virtue of this family history that he was a decent, trustworthy chap. Initially, everything went well, as he offered to acquaint me with local sights, cinemas, restaurants and bars. I was introduced to his family who seemed enthusiastic about Andrew's new friend.

By now most of my friends were married or in a long-term relationship. Some were expecting their first baby. I had not sailed close to this shore as I'd been too busy with my career; there were no other entanglements in my life. I cherished the freedom of being single. I was the author of my own happiness and the captain of my own ship.

> *It matters not how strait the gate,*
> *How charged with punishments the scroll,*
> *I am the master of my fate:*
> *I am the captain of my soul.*
>
> **W.E. Henley,**
> 'Invictus'

I felt strong and resilient with a deep sense of who I was and what I wanted. Now happy in my new career choice and full of optimism for the future, I no longer felt the need to find a man to share my life with. I was financially independent. I could make all my own decisions, both big and small.

My soul would weep for the lives of those who were shattered by illness and suffering; the bodies ravaged by ugly disease; the families devastated by the premature arrival of death, shredding hopes and dreams. Periods of solitude were essential to me. Long walks alone in places of divine beauty brought emotional recovery and refreshment from the demands of nursing the sick and dying. A calm found only in the company of nature would slow my racing thoughts and hectic heart, uncluttering my mind and allowing me to find acceptance of the harshness of suffering.

Being single brought experiences far beyond those I could have imagined had I stayed in my hometown or become part of a couple. My zeal to explore new places and nurture close female friendships was rewarded by my endeavours.

In the sweetness of friendship let there be laughter, and sharing of pleasures. For in the dew of little things, the heart finds its morning and is refreshed.

Kahlil Gibran,
The Prophet

I was proud of my vibrant life and its landmarks. I valued my freedom; it was a precious jewel full of glistening light and radiant colour. I could live as I wanted to. I confidently resisted relationships, as they seemed too complicated and oppressive. I was fearful of intimacy and attachment; I couldn't bear the thought of becoming emotionally dependent. It would invite vulnerability and the risk of rejection. I wasn't ready for the compromises and negotiations required when being in a couple. It never occurred to me that I could find happiness in the warmth and calm of a loving relationship.

Then my myopic single young woman existence collided with Andrew. He made it clear he liked me and wanted us to become a couple. He was serious from our first encounter. I responded with nonchalance. I felt uneasy and was puzzled by his persistence. We did have things in common. We had similar tastes in music, and between us, we had a vast, eclectic record collection. We also both enjoyed hill walking. Eventually, although I was not entirely comfortable, I ignored my instincts and started going out with him. We went on holiday together and spent Christmas with his family.

His elderly father was a gentle and quiet man who looked far older than his years. He was short, bald and had poor eyesight. He bumbled about the house taking an interest in local news and watching daytime TV. He reminded me of the home-loving hobbit Bilbo Baggins. By contrast, his mother was much younger and had a volatile nature, firing disparaging comments at her husband and at Andrew too. She seemed troubled, constantly expressing a bitter contempt towards Andrew's father. Her twisted, contorted behaviour reflected the toxicity of her soul. Like gnarled excrescences on the ancient branches of a diseased tree, her nastiness could not be concealed, constantly leaking out like a foul-smelling vapour in the unkind words she hissed and in her dark moods. She was deliberately cruel and emotionally impoverished. Her smallest act would be that of kindness.

One evening while we were visiting Andrew's parents his father became ill. He had chest pain and was sweating profusely. An ambulance was called and he was whisked away with a blue light for investigation and treatment. We all followed and spent an anxious few hours waiting in A&E until he was stable. It was a heart attack.

We arrived back at the family home in the early hours and as we stood in the kitchen waiting for the kettle to boil Andrew became upset and started pacing up and down. Without warning his mother spun round with the speed of an Olympic athlete and whipped him across the face with the tea towel, she was holding, telling him not to be so soft. It was brutal and nasty. I gasped and almost slapped her back, a reflex reaction which was difficult to control. But Andrew seemed unperturbed and stared blankly at her. He remained motionless, desensitised to her violence and empty of retaliation. Was he, like me, used to passive acceptance of abuse? It was as if I were watching a play being acted out in front of me. They were on the stage, and I was their audience. I wanted to shake him and say, 'Don't let her treat you like this. You don't deserve it!' But I didn't. I stood limply with dismay.

This incident triggered the carer and protector in me. I became emotionally embroiled and insidiously involved. With no inner blueprint to guide me towards loving relationships, other than that of my nanna and grandad, attachment had crept up and hooked me in. I now had a part to play in this dysfunctional family. I became Andrew's rescuer. I wondered why he'd been sent to boarding school while his sister remained at home. Was she the all-good golden girl and he the lost and forgotten child? The next morning we went away, leaving behind Andrew's angry mother, a woman who harboured many years of regret and unfulfilled hopes and expectations. Any nurturing maternal instincts she may once have had were long eclipsed by dark shadows of resentment.

I began to subjugate my own needs to Andrew's. Such self-sacrifice assuaged the guilt I sometimes felt about the life I had been living as a single woman, a life with my personal freedom at the heart of it. We planned a holiday to Cyprus soon after this. It was while we were away that Andrew asked me to marry him. I was dumbfounded. I did not feel worthy of marriage to this man. My mind was scrambled with conflicting thoughts. Why would he want to marry me? Was I ready for marriage? Why did we need to get married? We could just live together. His commitment seemed stronger than mine. I was scared and flattered at the same time. I was afraid of permanency and long-term commitment to a man I was unsure about. Marriage was not yet part of my life script. What if he were to desert me? Could I trust him? My poor self-image and feelings of unworthiness drowned out my inner wisdom.

We arrived home and announced our engagement. I knew it was a mistake, but I wasn't strong or wise enough to reject Andrew's proposal. An invisible force was sweeping me along. My feet were no longer on solid ground. I had slipped off the shore and like a piece of driftwood was floating in the sea. Carried along by the current, I lacked the self-awareness and self-esteem I needed to get back onto dry land. I ignored my inner wisdom. I was powerless to resist.

My feelings for Andrew were muddled. I was torn. I was comfortable with being his understanding friend but not his future wife. Something within me wanted to hold back, rewind and start again. Could hindsight protect me from making this mistake? I was unsure and uncertain. My inner world was not aligned with what I was consenting to. I was full of contradictions. Should I or shouldn't I marry him? We hadn't discussed our future together; practicalities such as how we would run our finances and changing names were overlooked. We hadn't talked about whether or not we wanted a family and, most important of all, we hadn't considered whether we shared the same values. How would we deal with our differences, important decision-making and conflict? How would we deal with hurt? I was trading my inner wisdom and courage for a shallow socially acceptable relationship. I deluded myself that it would give me immunity from further sorrow and hardship. I told myself that if I remained single, I risked being marginalised and lonely. But lurking beneath this fragile relationship were emotional monsters, which had yet to creep out and disturb the murky surface.

Both our families were instantly engulfed in wedding plans, creating an illusion of happiness and security, enabling us to avoid uncovering any emotional secrets which lay beneath the surface. Dress codes, flowers, hymns, rings, confetti, invitations, speeches and menus distracted all of us from asking if we were truly compatible. The vicar agreed to marry us after one brief administrative meeting. There was not a single probing word and no curiosity about our motives and values.

Everyone else's enthusiasm far surpassed mine. I carried on denying my true feelings and let the plans evolve. I pretended to myself and others that our marriage would work. I passively accepted my fate, afraid of disappointing everyone. And there was the embarrassment which would emerge if I did delay or cancel the wedding. All my friends had married and were planning a family so why couldn't I? It never occurred to me that I might gain respect if I introduced uncertainty about the marriage. I was shackled by the inherent childhood shame I carried. Naively, I believed getting married would give me an elevated social status. Until now I had not wanted to be like others. I had no desire to be one of the majority. So why now? My inner resolve to be true to myself weakened as the plans gained momentum.

Andrew and I argued more and more. He seemed deliberately antagonistic towards me. He enjoyed provoking me into arguments and then would disappear on his bicycle for hours on end. He started to drink more, often until he was impossible to rouse. He had an obsessive exercise and diet regime, which dictated our daily routine as well as what food we ate. There were signs he was a man of addiction and control. He needed to exert control over himself and me. Initially, I tried to please him by taking up exercise classes, and I appreciated the health benefits of aerobics or swimming, but Andrew's approach to exercise was gruelling and verged on self-abuse. Each day he would analyse and monitor his weight, his calorie intake and how many miles he had run or cycled. His obsession with fitness was incongruous with his binge drinking.

I protested to him about his controlling, critical behaviour. I wasn't thin enough, blonde enough or fit enough to live up to his expectations. As he tightened control, so I became controllable. At first, I tried harder, but then I began to feel as though I had no personal merit; I was there to impress his family and friends. My feelings were ignored, and increasingly I felt like an adornment whose sole purpose was to enhance his image. I was like a sparkling crystal Christmas decoration.

Three months before we were due to be married I snapped. Our relationship was turning sour. It felt easier to die inside and avoid conflict. There was an ever-increasing space between us. I felt lonely and unlovable. I was becoming emotionally drained as my self-confidence slipped away day by day. I felt empty and caged in by this mean and domineering man who was constantly trying to control me. In the mirror of his eyes, I knew I would always be incomplete. I was squandering my long-term happiness for ungentle woundedness.

I reached a breaking point. Crushed emotionally and overwhelmed with misery I told Andrew the wedding was off. I couldn't marry him. Marriage was not for me: I wasn't ready, and I couldn't cope.

I heaped the responsibility onto myself. It was my fault we couldn't get married. I disarmed him with self-imposed failure. I wasn't good enough for him. I wasn't wife material. It was safer to take the blame if it freed me from a lifetime of pain and unhappiness. In my desolation, it never occurred to me that I had the right to an apology. I deliberately made myself the scapegoat to alleviate my guilt for inducing disappointment and anger. I used victimhood to my advantage. It was self-preservation.

Chapter 11

The Prelude to Illumination
1989 – 1991

If I get married, I want to be very married.

Audrey Hepburn

How do you know you can spend the rest of your life married to the same person? Isn't this the promise we make when we decide to get married? Can you ever know or is it blind faith? Are we equipped with sufficient knowledge and experience to make such profound promises? Will your union be a lifetime of loving friendship with your soulmate or are you entering an underworld of fire and brimstone?

There was a ceasefire. After I announced I was too unhappy to get married, all the futile clashing arguments and quarrelling evaporated like an early morning mist in summer. Andrew took me by complete surprise. He relieved me of the responsibility for the difficulties in our relationship; he took them all from me and made them his own. He was very clear that he could put it all right. He could mend things, and it would be easy. He fully admitted he was behaving badly and asked for a second chance.

Three months later we were married. The ceremony was held in a small, quaint village church and the reception was in a hotel across the road. I don't remember much about the wedding other than hoping Andrew would not get too drunk.

Within a few months Andrew's behaviour had deteriorated again, far beyond the premarital episodes, and this time there were no acts of contrition. I vividly remember him stating that I was now his wife and he could behave as he liked. He was not going to be a doormat. It was a great victory for him. When we married, his pursuit of me came to an end. He had conquered me, and his supremacy over me would reign. I had become legally his. It was cruel and frightening to think how easily I had been manipulated by his display of penitence for his controlling behaviour. I no longer trusted him and I no longer trusted my judgement. The friable bond between us had crumbled.

During his frenzied drunken nights, he would crash into my room. I often slept alone so as to escape his tormented moods. I was worried that the effects of disturbed sleep would interfere with my ability to perform well at work. With slurred speech, he belittled me with verbal abuse and intimidation. He insisted I had given up my right to consent to sex now we were married. Images of Trevor flooded into my mind as Andrew forcibly demanded his marital entitlement. I was frozen with intense fear, powerless and unnerved. I couldn't retaliate. Alcohol-infused saliva would be smeared across my face as I was pinned down stone-like beneath his reptilian belly. Some nights, my face turned to the wall with my eyes tightly shut, he would just straddle my body to masturbate. Heedless of the anguish he was inflicting, he would curse me with venomous accusations from the dark spaces of his troubled psyche.

My soul was screaming with rage, but my childhood abuse meant I lacked the courage I needed to speak out. Feelings of shame and worthlessness robbed my voice. Somehow I deserved this. I'd been foolish enough to trust him – to marry him. I suffered silently, certain that no one would believe me if I told them what was going on. I couldn't even tell my closest friends. New scars joined the old scars that were raked across my soul. No one would ever see them, no one would ever know.

This is my dark secret of shame. I have had no voice for telling it until now.

Would this have happened had my childhood been different? Perhaps if I had known loving, protective parenting, I would have made different choices. I might have been more wary, cautious and wise. It was a cold and comfortless existence as winter visited my soul. I was imprisoned by harshness and violation. Any desire to be with this man was relinquished. Trapped in a small cell-like bedroom, my thoughts darkened as solitary sadness became my only sanctuary. I wanted to make myself invisible as I longed for refuge. Intoxicated and agitated, Andrew would barge in and order me to return to the marital bed. Vitriolic obscenities would be hissed at me in an attempt to force me out of my bunker. Like a boa constrictor, he squeezed and squeezed until I surrendered in fear. His unrelenting psychological torture eroded my strength to resist. I felt despised and loathed; I was haunted by macabre childhood memories, scenes resembling Hieronymus Bosch paintings of the extremity of human suffering: Dad beating Mum and Mum screaming out in pain. Despite the distance in time, the pity of those images remained undiminished.

Andrew's drinking got worse. Attending any social event such as a family wedding became impossible. His drunkenness resulted in him taking offence for no reason, heaping humiliation on us. His mind was riddled with psychotic conspiracies, convinced that others, including me, were plotting against him. His ability to work diminished and we became socially isolated. He told lies and became increasingly paranoid. He would interrogate and taunt me about my past, often accusing me of lying about past relationships. I would return home from work tired and drained and find him in a foul, irrational mood, his mind tormented by jealous schizoid fantasies. No amount of reassurance would placate him. I was always left feeling this unhappiness was my fault. He never expressed any remorse for his behaviour.

He made no effort to help with domestic chores and financial responsibilities as he sat drinking and smoking until the early hours. I would find him surrounded by scattered and broken objects he had smashed before falling into an alcoholic stupor, evidence of another night of mental torment and self-destruction. He even destroyed his beloved acoustic guitar. Obsessed with body image, weight and fitness, he often had bulimic episodes. He would starve himself for many hours, during which he would undertake long periods of intense exercise. Then he would binge-eat followed by self-induced purged vomiting. It was not unusual for him to pop out to the late-opening garage and return home loaded with biscuits and chocolate, all of which would then be consumed while becoming incoherently drunk.

He was a compulsive shopper. He had to buy three of everything: bicycles, cameras, CDs, vinyl, clothes. He frequently complained he was deprived of holidays and disposable income. We were financially crippled. I constantly worried about money as I watched him deliberately invite debt in order to indulge his lust for consumerism.

One day while we were in his sports car, I experienced a frightening premonition. Andrew was driving like a Mad Max warrior; he had been drinking and was taking no notice of how fast he was going. Clinging to my seat, petrified, I suddenly had a vision of the car crossing the central white line and colliding with a vehicle on the other side of the road killing us both. I never allowed myself to be a passenger with him again. I couldn't trust his temperament and his ability to avoid drink driving. I may not have had the sense to resist marrying him, but I did have the sense to stay alive.

When Andrew wasn't around, I would ring the Samaritans. I needed someone to talk to. I needed a soothing voice for fear I was falling apart and going mad. I needed to stay calm and clear-headed if I was going to survive. I vowed Andrew would not be the author of my decline, emotionally or physically. My life experiences of striving against adversity were sustaining and protecting me from becoming encumbered by further permanent affliction.

I begged him to get help, to go and see his doctor or have some form of counselling. I offered to go with him, but he scorned and rebuffed my pleas as ridiculous. I told him he was destroying our marriage, but he refused to acknowledge we were having difficulties. I went to my GP. I had seen him before about my perpetual heavy menstrual bleeding and horrid pain; this time I went to seek marital help. My tolerance was exhausted, and I wasn't coping with Andrew. I felt vulnerable and anxious about disclosing the sensitivities of what was going on. I was too ashamed to mention the sexual violation but concentrated on the day-to-day fighting, arguing and disruptive behaviours. I didn't share the paranoia and dark moods. I was afraid I wouldn't be believed.

I was told I was suffering from severe premenstrual tension and offered hormone treatment – progesterone pessaries. At least I wasn't told to go and stand in a ring of toadstools. Rushed and distracted, the GP was unable to explore the root cause of my presenting relational problems. It was easier to attribute them to my hormones. No messy emotional issues were examined; he looked through the narrow lens of solution-based medicine and fudged the issue. I felt shunned and humiliated. Did he see me as a hysterical woman with wandering womb syndrome? Just like the child who had once asked for help, yet again the clues were missed. My hormones were unrelated to my most pressing concern: my inability to cope with Andrew's personality disorder.

Choices swirled within me. What should I do? I had reached the edge of utter despair. I could disintegrate and fall into an abyss, allowing pain and suffering to engulf me, or I could summon the strength to choose life-enhancing ways of moving away to a place of tenderness and peace. I was terrified I would be swept into a vortex of madness and despair, ravaged by my own chaotic inner commentary. But I was never allowed to topple over the edge of sanity. I was becoming aware of a mysterious invisible mat carrier, wordlessly encouraging me to listen to the abiding wisdom deep within me. I was not – nor would I ever be – forsaken, despite my sense of abandonment.

For a few indelible moments of peace, my confused thoughts and negative inner voice would be silenced. I'd be momentarily freed from the bondage of fear and liberated from self-fulfilling harmful images. Somehow, as I rummaged around the rubble of my life, I was able to cope and find the strength to carry on. Despite the darkness, there was always a horizon illuminated by hope. Something within reassured me as I hovered over the fragility of choice. I found the inner strength and will to seek out purpose and confidence.

Once again I chose growth in the form of education and training. I would gain new knowledge and skills to enable me to find a path out of confusion. I immersed myself in my career as a specialist nurse lecturer. I embarked on training to teach adults and complemented this with a part-time counselling course. I wanted to understand the human condition more deeply. I was curious and mystified about human behaviour and emotions, especially my own. I wanted to relate to people with greater authenticity and compassion. Like a still silent dawn, I began to awaken to my true self.

Then a political fuse was ignited, and once again war broke out, this time the Gulf War, which started in August 1990. I postponed all personal development as I became distracted by Lee's return to a war zone. He was posted to HMS *Herald*. Unlike the jubilation of his departure on HMS *Invincible* eight years earlier, this time Lee begrudged his latest orders. He was now married and settled in his own home. The losses were greater, the gains meaningless.

This style of warfare was different. His previous encounter with the horrors of war consisted of guns, bullets and missiles. Gulf War armed forces were exposed to a unique mix of hazards not previously experienced during wartime. There were neurotoxins, such as the nerve gas sarin, the anti-nerve gas drug pyridostigmine bromide, and pesticides that affect the nervous system. The oil and smoke that spewed from hundreds of burning oil wells presented another hazard.

My life was spiralling out of control with the dynamics of war. I couldn't contemplate asking Andrew for support, for fear that he would use it as an excuse to accuse me of emotional inadequacy. He seemed both unaware and uninterested, which only heightened my sense of isolation and separation.

Once again I was paralysed by the anticipation of Lee's death. I was filling shoeboxes full of gifts: sweets and chocolate, miniature bottles of spirits, crisps and biscuits, cassette recordings and letters. I was his protective big sister. As I worried about my brother, I was also re-evaluating my life and its tortuous path. I gradually acknowledged that my marriage was terminally ill. I couldn't fix it. I had to admit defeat. My mental health was at risk if I didn't withdraw and find a safe place to heal and recover. Shame and self-contempt were not legitimate excuses to stay. I had to take responsibility for myself.

After endless warning signs, I crawled away from the wreckage of our marriage into the local nurses' residence just before our second wedding anniversary. I could no longer tolerate the abhorrent abuse.

By now there was nothing to salvage, only my own sanity. I felt emotionally bankrupt. Why had I taken so long to recognise the truth about my marriage? Was it because I had the capacity to tolerate exceptionally high levels of abuse? Did I lack belief in my emotional and moral strength? Moral dilemmas clouded and distorted my reasoning. I had taken marital vows which were binding, but these had become a form of enslavement. I had pledged loyalty, trusting a man who was incapable of loving me. I oscillated between feeling weak and inadequate, and angry – angry with myself, and with Andrew.

Others were angry too. Andrew's mother telephoned. Seething with rage, she accused me of desertion. To her I was pathetic. She had stayed in her own marriage, enduring a lifetime of unhappiness, and she thought I should do the same. But, unlike me, she'd had no prospect of escape. She didn't have the social and financial independence of my generation. She was full of bitterness, resentment and regret. Images of her face, craggy and furrowed from years of chain smoking, swamped my mind.

I was desperate to respond, to explain why I had left Andrew. It would have been easy to tell shocking tales of her son's cruel behaviour. With only a few words I could shatter her belief that Andrew was the victim of a defiant wife. But I didn't have the energy or inclination. I was silenced by guilt, shame and failure. I couldn't share the horror of what had happened. I kept it private, locked away in my heart. I hoped that by concealing the truth, I would prevent it from turning into an open wound, limiting its power to haunt me.

Mum was ashamed. She too believed in lifelong marital suffering. My decision to oppose this brought her social humiliation. Her daughter was getting a divorce after two years of marriage. How dare she! I discovered Mum was burdened by a pernicious and inescapable Catholic guilt, which disabled her rationality. This was the only time she used her latent childhood religious indoctrination, telling me I would go to Hell. She portrayed herself as a martyr, claiming she had tolerated domestic abuse and so should I. She refused to acknowledge my marriage was over. I remained a disappointment to her until the day she died.

It was August 1991, and Lee was at home recovering from the Gulf War. I had a week's leave and was planning a trip to the Lake District with a pal who was a single parent. At the last minute, she was unable to join me as her daughter was poorly. The same evening I received a phone call from Lee insisting I visit him and his wife. This was no ordinary invitation.

I have no memory of Lee ever sending me a birthday or Christmas card. He never phoned or made any attempt to visit me. Only once did he plan to come to see me in Cambridge; he never arrived nor explained why he decided to cancel. All my letters, photos, cards and gifts were never acknowledged. The less effort he made, the more I tried. I convinced myself it was because he was a man and men don't make any effort to keep in touch. I believed it was my responsibility to ensure my baby brother and I had a relationship. If we were to become estranged, I would be blamed. I hadn't tried hard enough. Not given enough. Something within compelled me to love and care for him, despite his complete rejection.

There was a similar dynamic with my parents. Mum and Dad regularly visited Lee wherever his naval career took him, often bringing Karen with them. They were proud of their war hero son and enjoyed the elevated social status conferred on them when mixing with his naval officer friends. Uniforms and medals were glorified and admired. They exchanged the monotony of their dreary daily routine for social prestige, inebriated laughter, sunshine and tacky tourist attractions.

I never wanted to accompany them. Nor was I invited. I couldn't bear the thought of being abroad with them for days on end. Lee and Dad would drink heavily all day and every day. Mum would torment and provoke Dad into petty squabbles and sulky fights. Karen was cold towards me, which made conversation strained and stilted. Their bigoted humour was distasteful to me, and they would often mock and ridicule me for entertainment. It was safer not to go. We had very little in common.

I was cooped up in the noisy nurses' residence when Lee rang to ask me to visit him. I knew I had to respond; a quiet whisper was urging me to go to him. If I wasn't meant to go to the Lake District, was I being asked to go and see Lee? I trusted the call and set off the next morning, intrigued. Concealed behind his invitation was a mysterious story yet to be told.

That evening, after Karen had gone to bed, he suggested we should sit outside on the patio with a beer. As I relaxed, gazing at the full moon, the peaceful atmosphere was shattered. Lee broke down in tears. He described how he had become paranoid during his Gulf War deployment and was now experiencing suicidal thoughts. He described the fine detail of how he intended to kill himself while Karen was at work. He planned to lock himself in the garage and suffocate himself with car fumes.

Silenced by the gravity of his suffering I wept as I held him in the stillness beneath the milky moonlight. Lee was suffering from PTSD – post-traumatic stress disorder. The trauma caused by the Gulf War far exceeded the ordinary vicissitudes of life such as illness and financial hardship. Lee was overwhelmed, and the effects were catastrophic. He admitted he had buried the stress of the Falklands War to shield himself from anxiety, and his experiences in the Gulf War were triggering old memories with a highly damaging cumulative effect. In his head, he was fighting two wars. Powerful images were being evoked, scenes of terror, grief and despair. During the daytime, he was experiencing flashbacks to scenes from both wars. At night he was having bad nightmares and was sleepwalking.

Night, in which everything was lost, went reaching out, beyond stars and sun. Stars and sun, a few bright grains, went spiralling round for terror, and holding each other in embrace, there in a darkness that outpassed them all, and left them tiny and daunted. So much, and himself, infinitesimal, at the core of nothingness, and yet not nothing.

D.H. Lawrence,
Sons and Lovers

Karen seemed unaware and lacked empathy. Lee had not disclosed the gravity of his mental state to anyone, not even his wife. Their ritualistic daily routine muted any conversation which dared to move beyond the superficial. There was a clear absence of any form of intimacy between them. When Lee's behaviour deviated from the normal pattern, Karen accepted it without question. He would spend days on end locked away in their bedroom with the curtains closed, lacking the motivation and energy to venture out of his dark cave. Nothing seemed to tempt him out, not even glorious sunshine and coastal rides on his motorbike.

I instantly felt his fear and terror. My mind raced as I desperately tried to think of how we could find the best help for him. Part of me was terrified, but the other part of me switched into a caring and rescuing role. I was being pulled in two opposing directions, one concentrated on Lee's needs and the other on my own. Both were demanding and exhausting. I had to thrust aside my own marital troubles and recent separation.

Lee was too paranoid to consider sharing his story with his GP, nor did he trust the navy, who had yet to acknowledge the legitimacy of PTSD fully. He was angry at how he had been treated throughout the war. He had worked a relentless schedule of shifts: six hours on and six hours off seven days a week. As he rolled out of his bunk, another seaman got in. Anti-nerve gas tablets and injections were administered every four to six hours, interrupting sleep periods. Many doubted the efficacy of these medicines. The legacy of the Falklands War deepened Lee's anger. He was angry with his juvenile naivety at believing he had to fight for his Queen and country. His perception had changed dramatically as he felt exploited and denigrated by the navy.

A familiar pattern of projected responsibility was starting to overwhelm me. It was as if I was the only person who could help Lee through this trauma; it was a childhood drama being acted out again as I adopted the role of enabler and caretaker. But I was utterly lost and devoid of solutions. Inside I was panicking and was riddled with guilt. Where could we get help for this? Who could we turn to? I couldn't think rationally under the burden of his care. I wasn't equipped to deal with this emotionally. It was too painful.

We began by telling Karen, but she was distant and difficult to engage with. Perhaps she was paralysed by fear and lost in her own anxiety. Her way of coping was through her daily routine, which rarely altered. Each day was carefully timed, from waking in the morning to going to work, to returning home and then following her usual evening pattern. Each day was unchanged and totally predictable regardless of the turmoil around her.

I spent my week with Lee, encouraging him to venture outdoors during the day. Like a mother with a small, vulnerable child we took leisurely walks in the warmth of the summer sunshine. We talked about simple things he could do to help himself, such as avoiding alcohol and eating a healthy diet. His faith and trust in me was a heavy burden, especially since I had no grand ideas and solutions. We were facing unprecedented circumstances which neither the navy nor the NHS were acknowledging. Conflicting emotional demands and feelings of powerlessness tormented me. I was so afraid of blame and failure, but worse still, any attempt by Lee to kill himself.

I dreaded my visit coming to an end with no progress in Lee's mental state. I promised to explore different options once I was back at work. I told him and Karen I could talk to colleagues who may be aware of who to contact. But in reality, I hadn't a clue where to go for help. I felt as though I had been sucked into a quagmire with no certainty of recovery. As I was leaving, I told them I loved them both dearly and that I was confident we would find someone to help Lee. It was all an act. It was a disingenuous stage performance to engender optimism and hope while feeling helpless inside. It was all I could offer.

Forlorn and desperate I arrived back at the nurses' residence. Adjacent to my room lived a nurse whose boyfriend was hanging around waiting for her to finish her shift. He was in the RAF. I asked him what he would do if he were in my situation. His response was definite: 'There's only one option: the ship's chaplain.'

I made a single phone call, and my life was transformed forever. I contacted the Navy asking for the chaplain to my brother's ship. Without delay, I heard a voice say 'Paddy the Padre'. With only one encounter, never seen, only heard, Paddy the Padre was to become one of the most profound and significant mat carriers of my life.

Chapter 12

Priests, Ships and Hounds
1991 – 1994

I am not what happened to me, I am what I choose to become.

Carl Jung, *The Zofingia Lectures*

Why should I trust this padre? How could I discern whether he was a religious eccentric wanting to lead me down a merry path of evangelical nonsense? How would I manage to look beyond my scepticism and prejudices and have confidence in his advice when I would prefer the familiarity of a doctor or professional counsellor? I had never met him, so I had no visual evidence to judge his genuineness or capability. Nor was I religious. We had little in common which might predispose me to trust and respect him. So why was I willing to listen to him? Was I so desperate, vulnerable and in need of guidance? Yes, I was. My brother was mentally ill and at risk of suicide. There seemed to be no expertise available for his post-traumatic stress disorder. Who could I turn to? My heart was crying out for someone to help Lee. My inner chaos terrified me.

I had a brief and yet powerful conversation with Paddy the Padre, which would change the course of my life. I explained Lee's circumstances and symptoms. Paddy advised me to persuade Lee to go and see him. He would be able to support him to make contact with the help available within the navy. New forms of treatment were being established, including group therapy. I immediately responded to his concern and compassion. His voice was calm, and he listened carefully to my story. There were no interruptions as he let me talk. He did not need to satisfy his own curiosity nor dominate our conversation with his ego. He listened so that I had a quiet space to think, compose and tell my story. He seemed comfortable with silence. It was as though I was sitting next to him in the same room. I could feel his non-judgemental, celestial presence. This was my first knowing encounter with the grace of God; I was walking on holy ground and my soul knew it.

Then Paddy took me by complete surprise as he asked, 'And what about you?' What about me? I thought. With full-throttle denial I backed off, dismissing my feelings.

'I'm okay, I'm coping.'

'Given how much you care for your brother and the intensity of his emotions, surely this is difficult for you to bear? Do *you* need some support?'

I continued to deny my own feelings. I was too ashamed of my vulnerability and failings. I thanked him and politely ended our conversation. I was moved by this man's empathy and concern for me, a stranger.

I managed to persuade Lee to go and see Paddy the Padre. Despite his paranoia, he too was able to trust him. He joined group therapy and was prescribed anti-depressants. Lee and I never discussed this episode again.

I felt I could now let go and concentrate on my own troubles – how to deal with my separation from Andrew. I decided to apply for a divorce on the grounds of unreasonable behaviour. In my divorce statement, I deliberately omitted any reference to Andrew's sexual abuse. Once again I was silenced by shame. I wanted to bury the harmful images forever. I couldn't bear to externalise them by putting them into words as this seemed to bring them back to life. The pain was too complicated and terrifying, and I was afraid of being traumatised once more. But it wasn't only the humiliation that prevented me from sharing those ugly, abusive scenes, I was also struggling with feelings of failure and guilt. I didn't want to cause Andrew pain by disclosing details of his sexual abuse. I wished him neither harm nor revenge, and part of me still believed it was my fault. I hoped there was sufficient evidence of unreasonable behaviour without needing to refer to the bedroom traumas.

Andrew didn't contest the application, nor did he ask me to delay the process, so we were divorced a few months after our second wedding anniversary. We both recognised it was inevitable. We were permanently broken.

I only ever returned to our home once. I dreaded the visit, and it took months to pluck up the courage to go. Andrew had agreed not to be there. As I entered the gloomy, lifeless house, I was shocked by what I saw. The living room resembled a shrine; it was littered with enlarged holiday photos of me. Huge glossy images were displayed everywhere. It was like walking into a photography studio, but there were no landscapes and images of nature; there was only one subject, and that was me. It was sinister and chilling. I fled in fear.

I took nothing other than my own clothes and sentimental possessions. It made the divorce tidier – a clean break – and it eased my guilt about failure. I couldn't cope with any negotiations, nor did I want any material reminders of the house of horrors. My self-confidence and self-esteem were low. As one of my pals said, I had changed from a vivacious and animated young woman to one who resembled a deer caught in headlights. I was emotionally frozen and fragile. Like thin ice on a pond, any vibration soft or harsh would shatter me.

Until recently I'd had no conscious awareness of God's presence in my life, but increasingly I was sensing something stirring within me. A mysterious beckoning led me to sacred spaces, and I would find myself sitting in empty churches and cathedrals. At first, I tried to resist but guided by a new longing I began to realise I could pursue God or deny Her. From the start, I chose to think of God as 'she' rather than 'he', a creative nurturer breathing life into all things. I was a prodigal daughter of a feminine God waking up to the divine in me. This God of mine was gentle and tender. She would bring healing and restoration.

With an unhurried and unperturbed pace, God followed my fleeing soul by Her divine grace. I had been running through the dark labyrinth of my life ever since I could remember, breathlessly searching for peace and love, but looking in all the wrong places. I was unaware of divine grace following me until my soul felt its pressure forcing me to turn to Her in that never-ending pursuit. I gave up resisting and surrendered to God's untiring labour of love. My spirit became enlightened as I stepped into a new way of being.

I fled Him, down the nights and down the days;
*   I fled Him, down the arches of the years;*
I fled Him, down the labyrinthine ways
*   Of my own mind; and in the midst of tears*
I hid from Him, and under running laughter.
*   Up vistaed hopes I sped; And shot, precipitated,*
Adown Titanic glooms of chasmed fears,
*   From those strong Feet that followed, followed*
after.

Francis Thompson,
'The Hound of Heaven'

The rhythm of my life was beginning to change as I slowly embraced this invisible invitation. I would often sit in the grounds of my local church listening to worshippers joyfully singing songs of praise. This continued for several years during which I concentrated on my career. Work was the hub of my life, but outside of that, I was unsettled and anxious. Andrew was stalking me. I would find him lurking outside where I lived and worked, or I'd see him from a distance cycling around the area desperately looking for me. He would suddenly appear at my window staring at me, an uninvited ghostly silhouette. He was haunting me. When I confronted him excuses were made such as he happened to be passing. He happened to be passing on his bicycle over thirty-five miles from where he lived!

I felt mentally assaulted as his unwanted and disruptive appearances frightened me. I kept moving from place to place. Afraid of living alone, on one occasion I took a lodger, while later becoming a lodger myself. The cumulative effect was draining. The lack of privacy and solitude at a time I was desperate for healing generated dread and worry. Again I felt I was to blame. It was my fault for divorcing him. I was the guilty one. I constantly reproached myself and was full of self-condemnation and self-loathing. I was aware that my childhood experiences and hidden memories were influencing me. I was prepared to dig deep into the rubble of my own psyche so that I could identify unhelpful patterns of thinking and behaving. An inner voice was telling me that new insights would emerge which would enable me to recover from the harm I had experienced as a child and more recently as an adult, but it was going to be painful and exhausting.

Experience has taught us that we have only one enduring weapon in our struggle against mental illness: the emotional discovery and emotional acceptance of the truth in the individual and unique history of our childhood.

Alice Miller,
The Drama of the Gifted Child

I had normalised the abnormal. As a consequence, I didn't hear the warning bells about Andrew. I didn't spot the pothole in the road. I was an emotional mess. My interior landscape was like one of the abandoned industrial sites I had left behind in my hometown. Sharp, rusty inner edges were witness to pain, shame and feelings of worthlessness. I longed to feel alive with a vibrant energy, or to rest with a serene contentment. I felt I was decaying. I was unlovable and emotionally fragile, more tearful than happy. I rarely laughed. Echoes of childhood and adult abuse howled round my inner emptiness. My memories could not protect me from these old ghosts. I was weary with all the unattended suffering and unshed tears. My heart was wounded and desolate, as my thoughts and feelings surrendered to a dark anguish.

Burdened by an arid listlessness, a dim light glowed deep within my soul. A small grain of wisdom was encouraging me to persevere. Despite the absence of hope and the pervading uncertainty of my life, I sensed I must travel this vocational journey. At times it felt like the road to nowhere. It didn't matter now. I had very little to lose. I was desperately hoping I could heal and transform into a stronger, wiser human being, regardless of the ultimate destination. It was not about where I was going but who I was becoming that mattered. I had to do something. I had to abandon harmful and destructive habits. I couldn't continue as I was. I couldn't live with an identity defined by past and present abuse. I had to let go and transform the pain and suffering into wisdom and new life.

Afraid of repeating past mistakes, I decided to go into long-term psychodynamic therapy. I nestled myself away in a secluded cottage in a small village. I changed my appearance. I wore frumpy clothes and allowed my hair to grow long instead of my usual short, tidy bob. I adopted three cats. Hiding behind my dowdy image, I wanted my past to disappear as I lost myself in relentless work and study.

Mistakes are, after all, the foundations of truth, and if a man does not know what a thing is, it is at least an increase in knowledge if he knows what it is not.

Carl Jung,
The Zofingia Lectures

Not to seek the truth would probably have culminated in the need for psychiatric care. It was only a matter of time before I would have drowned in a sea of unresolved pain and suffering. My health and well-being were at risk. I was delicately balanced on the edge of a deep dark chasm. The loss of my career, financial hardship and homelessness awaited me if I didn't try to better understand who I really was.

I met my therapist once, sometimes twice a week, depending on how much energy I had. It was an exhausting process. She was called Martha and was widowed, having been married to a minister. She became my Jungian skilled helper. Well-read and an accomplished painter, she was a deeply committed Christian who radiated wisdom and love. She blended scholarly authority with a concern for humanity. Martha listened attentively in a way I had not been listened to before. She had a serious disposition and shared very little of her own life. Her genuineness affirmed and validated me. Long, compassionate silences were allowed, giving me time to gain clarity in my thinking and to find the courage to choose to abandon my past.

I had a compulsive desire to discover who I really was, this stranger living in me. Conversely, the therapy was about who I was not. It was a melancholy process as together we crawled through my life map unpicking and unpacking the debris. Sometimes we would stop at a particular place and spend hours working through a story of my choosing. Martha engendered an atmosphere of empathy and warmth. I was held in a safe, loving embrace, like a child snuggling into a treasured soft, sumptuous blanket. I trusted her wise companionship. I was never probed but gently encouraged to stop and examine those aspects of my past which seemed relevant to me. I was not judged nor made to feel ashamed. I uncovered many unresolved issues buried deep within my wounded soul which had distorted my authentic self. It was as if my life had been a journey along a dimly lit corridor of sticky cobwebs and damaged mirrors, trapping me with false images. Until then I had believed the lies of those reflections. For the first time in my life, I was able to externalise repressed emotions such as anger, shame, guilt and sadness.

We become free by transforming ourselves from unaware victims of the past into responsible individuals in the present, who are aware of our past and are thus able to live with it.

Alice Miller,
The Drama of the Gifted Child

I found solace and deeper meaning by making sense of past hurts and neglect. When things seemed senseless, as much suffering is, I was helped to move to a place of grace, accepting that bad things happen to the good and life is neither tidy nor perfect. Beauty can co-exist with pain and suffering. At times I travelled through dark tunnels of depression, echoes of abuse ricocheting off the walls. It was a lonely time. Fear of being wrongly judged and the stigma of needing psychotherapy prevented me from telling anyone. Since

I didn't want to share what I was undertaking, I isolated myself socially. I was afraid that my need for therapy would jeopardise my employment and weaken my future prospects.

As I trudged through the slurry, I began to realise how my interior had become defaced by abuse and suffering. My grim inner experiences resembled images of obscene graffiti. And, like graffiti, they had been unlawfully inscribed, drawn and scratched onto my soul. Offensive slogans and vulgar drawings of crimes of hate and neglect were crudely scribbled or painted, leaving unique scars in my heart.

Undoubtedly, Martha was my mat carrier. Without her loving wisdom and care, I would not have been able to cope with reliving past traumas. This was not a journey for tourists in search of attractive sights and exciting adventures. I became a wandering pilgrim travelling through a bleak and threatening landscape. Week by week for almost three years we met in Martha's study surrounded by learned books and fine pieces of artwork. As we sat opposite one another, we slowly deconstructed the fragile pieces of my life. Without the warmth of sunlight and the sweetness of birdsong, we groped around my grubby inner ruins delicately excavating clues which told my life story. Many of these sessions took place on a Friday evening after which I would have to spend time over the weekend resting and recovering. The process was exhausting.

As our trust deepened so did our journey. False images of loving parents were abolished. This was agonising because I had to confront the truth: poor parenting by two hurting people. Between our sessions, I read prolifically. I had an insatiable desire to learn and grow, and I eagerly devoured the Christian books I borrowed from Martha. The Old Testament and the New, works of fiction and works of non-fiction, all infused me with images and language which influenced my healing and restoration. This was the beginning of my transformation.

On 3 April 1994, Easter Sunday, I walked into a beautiful medieval church in the nearby town and made my commitment to God. The church was dedicated to a local female saint, which mattered to me. I felt my place was alongside strong women in the communion of saints. I was drawn to the femininity of God, a God who is tender, gracious, steadfast and faithful. I identified with idealistic, spirited, brave and high-minded women, such as Eowyn in Tolkien's *Lord of the Rings*. I wanted to be associated with women who were accomplished because they were uniquely female, not in spite of being a woman. I needed to celebrate and exalt my womanhood, which became an essential component to my healing.

I became a disciple of Christ. I knelt at the altar, bowed my head and made my vow. The desire to make this decision was so compelling, its fragrance was irresistible. God was attractive to me, and She was attracting me to Her. I privately affirmed the faith into which I had been baptised and I promised to live a life of committed discipleship. So as not to practise my faith contrary to orthodox religious doctrine, this affirmation was later confirmed through prayer and the laying on of hands by my local bishop. This was a formality I was willing to undertake, not because I was afraid of heresy, but because I needed the institutionalised care and support of the church. I needed loving.

The church's doctrine and rituals gave me an inner scaffold of support. Exhausted by work and psychotherapy, the weekly Sunday service enabled me to relax and rest emotionally. I was aware of how my whole life had been governed by my struggle to cope with fear, guilt, shame and low self-esteem. It had been a constant battle for survival and self-preservation. With a strong work ethic and great self-discipline, I had managed to escape all forms of social difficulty until now. While my ambitions had enabled me to rise to considerable prestige at work, I was emotionally and spiritually bankrupt.

In the grip of this winter within my soul, I continued to journey. Just as the new fall of snow covers the countryside in waves and shades of beautiful, delicate white, so too did my bleak inner landscape feel frozen. I so wanted to trust the ceaseless calling of God's loving mercy to transform my barren heart, body and soul into unimaginable beauty and grace. Within days I began to change. The changes were ineffably subtle and yet irrefutable. The first thing to note was that I developed a comfortable mind as my inner disorder and chaos began to settle. I naturally adopted an imperturbable manner and calmer temperament. Instead of transmitting bitterness, anger, jealousy, fear and dread, I sensed an inner transformation of sweet gratitude and meekness. Like a child, without question, I trusted the grace of God could set me free from all my past hurts.

One day at a time, with its failures and fears,
With its hurts and mistakes, with its weakness and
tears,
With its portion of pain and its burden of care;
One day at a time we must meet and must bear.

One day at a time to be patient and strong,
To be calm under trial and sweet under wrong;
Then its toiling shall pass, and its sorrow shall cease;

It shall darken and die, and the night shall bring peace.

One day at a time – but the day is so long,
And the heart is not brave, and the soul is not strong,
O Thou pitiful Christ, be Thou near all the way;
Give courage and patience and strength for the day.

Annie Johnson Flint,
'One Day at a Time'

Gerard Hughes in his book *God of Surprises* describes how we avoid looking at our own inner chaos and destructiveness by projecting it onto other people. This habit of projecting blame onto others is insidious and damaging. It is usually so subtle that we are unaware that we are doing it.

The change in me became evident during a workshop I was delivering. I was teaching a group of highly specialised nurses about the concept of quality assurance and clinical governance. I had spent many hours researching and preparing for this. Previously I would have approached the session with trepidation, worried that a complicated question would embarrass me; I wouldn't have the answer, and my credibility would be undermined. This didn't happen. I vividly recall sitting among the students feeling humbled to be surrounded by such expertise. I was grateful and appreciative of them. When questions were asked that I knew little about I was not afraid. I felt inspired and motivated by their curiosity and thirst for knowledge. There was an atmosphere of mutual support and reciprocity. I was able to embrace the value of the question and explore its answer in a collaborative search with the group. I was no longer threatened by my own thoughts.

I began to feel safe in my own body and mind, liberated from my unreal fears. Truthfulness was the primary imperative. It felt like a homecoming. I was slowly admitting my deepest desire: to receive and offer genuine love.

It was an enlightenment that would change me forever.

Chapter 13

Paradox and Paranoia
1994 – 1996

*It takes great inner freedom to be a
follower of Jesus. His life is a choice, a
call, a vocation and we are totally free to
say yes or no or maybe. You do not have
to do this to make God love you. That is
already taken care of.*

Richard Rohr, *Eager to Love*

As my faith grew, the rest of my family became closer to one another
without me. Increasingly I felt marginalised and forgotten. I was
ambivalent about their coolness towards me. On the one hand,
I felt the pain of rejection, and on the other I deliberately avoided
them. I'd always known I belonged on the edge of this family, but
my perception of being the outsider seemed to be growing. It suited
me, and it suited them. My remoteness formed an invisible harmony
between us all.

Lee and his wife were convinced I had become an eccentric
religious nut and had joined a cult. Dad refused to discuss anything
to do with faith and the church; he was uncertain about the existence
of God. I was not a covert evangelist, but I longed for him to become
aware of God's love for him. I prayed that God's loving light and
peace would shine in his heart. Dad could still choose to believe and
therefore encounter the divine.

*The response of faith operates on a number of different
levels in human experience, but debate about it tends
to operate only on the rational and intellectual level.*

We are more than our rationality. We have depths to our nature – emotional, aesthetic and spiritual and if we lose touch with them we diminish and distort our humanity.

Richard Holloway,
Dancing on the Edge

It was plain to see a radiant springtime was blossoming in my heart. Gloomy clouds of sadness and doubt were being chased away by this hound of heaven. I was discovering a new clarity, peace and happiness.

Mum hid her faith. She was a closet believer, tormented by her Catholic guilt. She was torn between her belief in the indoctrination of the Catholic church of her childhood and my father's rejection of God. She would sometimes accompany me to church, on the few occasions I went home. Lee and Karen were adamant there was no God. Their lives were godless and angry. If there was a God then there was hell: Lee had been there. The legacy of his experiences of war bleached any sense of spirituality from their conscious being. He held these views with concrete certainty. He was scarred by the viciousness of humanity.

My friendships started to change as I changed. I struggled to connect with friends from my childhood and early nursing days. The longer they had lasted, the less we had in common. They became friends of habit and history rather than company I wanted to be with. I was attracted to others who were spiritually aware, who adopted a more ascetic lifestyle with a natural soulful shyness, women whose natures were compassionate and unassuming. There was a sense of unaffected authenticity about them as they made their lives sacred. In those times of ego-driven greed, consumerism and individualism, these women fostered an appealing collective solidarity. Their quiet lives didn't need brash boasting and feelings of superiority to those around them. Unlike other friends, these women were not driven by their egos but by an impulse for creative service with peaceful and loving hearts. Their company induced a calmness in me. My focus was shifting from the heroic to the transformative, from acquisition to giving, and from achieving to serving. It was an irresistible sweet perfume, which evoked loving graceful memories of lost days with my grandparents. I was living faithful to the sacred.

I was realising through the Book of Job that good people are vulnerable to suffering. Life is filled with pain, disillusionment and absurdity. God is no stranger to suffering, as seen in the crucified Jesus. But there is hope of new life in God.

The suffering of pain and abandonment is overcome by the suffering of love, which is not afraid of what is sick and ugly but accepts it and takes it into itself to heal it.

Ilia Delio,
The Humility of God

Was this the same love I had witnessed in the nurses caring for Mum during her rehabilitation or in the care shown by Alan and Brenda towards Gareth?

My newfound faith was meaningless to my old friends, and my spirituality became a taboo subject. I so wanted to share how my life had a new purpose. It was full of light, grace and love, God's humble love, and my response to that love was leading and guiding me in sacred and enlightened ways. Self-knowledge, patience, simplicity of life and listening to others with a compassionate heart were more important than the material world around me. My life was now orientated around my faith. I knew divine transforming love was essential for me to thrive. Yet I also appreciated how those who are true to their own conscience and profess no association with religion may also be close to God. I was turning away from a chaotic and egotistical life of vanity. It was my very own Lent whereby I was growing by dying. All the false faces I had worn, deceptions, collusion with conformity, loveless thoughts and unkind acts were being sacrificed for the pursuit of my truest being.

We arrive at truth, not by reason only, but also by the heart.

Blaise Pascal,
Pensées

I made choices based on gratitude, abundance and appreciation as I learned to decentre myself. I yearned for spiritual intimacy where there was no division by sex or age, colour or creed, wealth or status. My identity was no longer defined by the postmodern culture of outer accomplishments and popular competitive capitalism; it became socially focused, respectful of natural beauty, graceful and unconditionally loving. I was aware of an inner voice guiding me as it had done since I was a small child. I had been empowered to respond to tender, subtle senses of direction.

Nurturing my soul through the mess, mystery and magic of life mattered more than corporate positional power, materialism and financial wealth. I would not be defined by what I was but by the woman I was becoming.

To love each person, each creature, each element of creation as sister and brother not selfishly but for the sake of the other, to live in peace and reconciliation with all things, is to see God's goodness shining through the fragile, human nature of our lives.

Ilia Delio,
The Humility of God

I began to realise how the whole of creation was a manifestation of God. Beauty, grace and light surrounded me in all things. I was living in harmony with the life around me in ways I had not been able to experience before.

I knew my life was not about happily ever after and that pain is unavoidable if we are truly alive. But I was now able to celebrate the good fortune of not being in control and was learning to live in and trust the moment – there was a higher power in charge. While there was no certainty of living in the grace of God, my blighted ability to trust was healing. I was learning to believe that in every circumstance and detail of my life God was present. My response was not intellectual. I wasn't thinking my way to God. This was something much deeper. My soul was being beckoned from the prison of my self-limiting beliefs to the freedom of God's wonder, marvel and awe. An unnameable ache deep in my soul had been forgotten. I had rejected its call for a life of compromise and false promises of safety and security. Like a window being flung open to fresh morning sunlight, a holy and life-giving spirit had entered in. The voice of the sacred could be heard and I was responding. There was a sense of welcoming and deep bonding, which was growing stronger and stronger. My soul was flourishing with a joyful energy as I traded elusive, fickle feelings of happiness for an enduring story of loyalty, commitment and devotion. I patiently developed the courage to delay gratification and resist distractive and destructive impulses. I began to spend time in places with people who were my kindred spirits.

Rumbling in the background was my brother's diminishing mental health, camouflaged by his hedonistic lifestyle. Now discharged from the armed forces, his drinking was excessive, habitual and constant. He had no awareness of his antagonistic, inflammatory behaviour. He would unleash rage, abusing strangers, friends and neighbours for no reason. With no authority to answer to, such as his former employer, he bullied those around him. He was blind to the impact he was having on others; his conscience was dormant. Despite this, Mum and Dad continued to perch him on a pedestal of adulation, their denial making them complicit in his destructive behaviour.

After his initial breakdown, I would visit Lee's home on two further occasions. The second was to be my last. It was a pleasant summer's evening, and he was steadily drinking himself into a stupor. I started to feel anxious and uneasy. Buried memories were resurfacing of Mum's violent alcoholic episodes. Then, unprovoked, Lee betrayed me. If there had been any bonding between us, it was now destroyed. He exploded with an unflinching hatred I had not witnessed before. Sitting opposite me at the dining table he spewed out a series of horrid accusations. As I heard him call me a 'lefty feminist bitch' I froze in merciful deafness. I could see him, but my senses protected me by silencing him. It was like watching a frenzied Alfred Hitchcock film on the television with the sound turned off. Penned in by fear, I felt as if I were being pecked by a flock of angry carnivorous birds. Inadvertently I had stumbled and disturbed them. I was not a threat, I was not there to harm or steal from them, but now aroused they were attacking. There was no wizard Gandalf, fairy godmother or angel to rescue me. Suspended in time, I was terrified Lee would lunge across the table and act out his anger by physically attacking me. Visions of Mum lashing out drunk and out of control filled my mind. Paralysed by fear, tears trickled down my face. I felt broken and abandoned. I had no voice to retort. I was motionless, like a cold piece of stone. I became the repository of his reasonless, repugnant belligerence.

This was a man I had only ever protected, cared for and loved to the best of my ability. Despite our clear differences, I harboured no resentment towards him. His violent onslaught was senseless. Our relationship was dead, killed by his unmerited personal attack. My brother was no gallant gentleman but an emotionally derelict shell of a man. The abusive typhoon tore through me leaving a trail of emotional devastation. I drove away the next morning still dazed from the night before, as though I had just witnessed a fatal car crash.

He phoned a few months later high-spirited and drunk asking why I hadn't called. With wry amusement, he applauded his intentional wounding. It was deliberate, and he wasn't about to apologise nor could he assure me he wouldn't do it again. His voice was sinister and tormenting. He remained hostile towards me, and I would never trust him again.

The following couple of years adopted a settled rhythm as I distanced myself from my family. I had been appointed as deputy to Mary, the chief nurse and one of the finest leaders I have known. Her sharp intelligence, integrity, compassion and dedication to patients was an inspiration. She was an exemplary role model and influenced me far beyond the confines of my imagination. I was able to take on responsibilities outside my comfort zone, exceeding my expectations of what I was capable of. She constantly challenged me intellectually, enabling me to grow professionally and personally. At times I felt frustrated and uncomfortable. I became aware that I didn't always know that I didn't know. I moved from being surprised when I was wrong to being surprised when I was right. My self-perception was healing as I began to reach towards my true potential. Disabling images, which had previously limited my performance, were transformed. Their faces were being erased with new insights and a creative energy from deep within my psyche. I was becoming the woman I was intended to be, free from the chains of dark negativity. Crippling thoughts of poor self-worth and low self-esteem were fading. I was grateful to God and grateful to Mary.

To thine own self be true, and it must follow, as the
night the day, thou canst not then be false to any man.
William Shakespeare,
Hamlet

Mary's encouragement and loyal support enabled me to excel locally and nationally. She was my mat carrier. With her trust and respect, my self-confidence came alive. Deep unlived parts of my personality and capability thrived. I was in rhythm with my own unique nature as my life flowed and balanced naturally. I worked full-time, lived in an enchanting cottage with my three cats, and was studying part-time towards a Master of Arts in Leadership and Management. I had a loving circle of friends and was a member of my local church.

She who dwells in friendship dwells in God, and God
in her ... The fountain and source of friendship is love,
there can be love without friendship, but friendship
without love is impossible.
Aelred of Rievaulx,
Spiritual Friendship

I had ended my counselling with Martha feeling satisfied we had travelled far enough together, but my journey was not over yet, and my search for patterns of meaning and wisdom would continue.

Many words had been spoken over the past few years bringing profound insights and healing. Our inevitable separation brought sadness blended with a calm expectancy of new beginnings.

Occasionally I would see Andrew from a distance. He continued to search and patrol the places where he thought he could find me. I was confident he had no inkling of where I was living, a small village over thirty miles from where I worked. Exasperated and desperate, he resorted to his only other option.

It was late one Friday afternoon when I received a call from the hospital reception. It was Andrew asking to see me. A still small voice of calm accompanied me as I set off to meet him. My only thought was to make sure I stayed in a public place for protection. Despite my cool tranquillity, I was still wary of Andrew's unpredictable mental state. My anxiety was not unfounded. I hardly recognised him. I was shocked. His skeletal body was undernourished, his oversized eyes protruded from his thin, shrunken face and his clothing hung loosely from his emaciated body. He looked pitiful.

He asked me for help. He described how he had become romantically involved with a woman at work and now others were watching and talking about him behind his back. He felt persecuted and demonstrated an exaggerated suspicion of his colleagues. Then, like a pheasant scurrying away from a near collision at the roadside, his conversation swerved into erratic zigzags as he boasted about his physical fitness – he'd cycled over fifty miles to see me.

As I looked into his vulnerable, naked face, I spoke with considered truth and concern. I held up an invisible mirror and described what I could see and hear. He was paranoid and mentally very sick. Yes, he might be physically fit, but he was underweight, probably due to obsessive training, which was detrimental to his health. He needed professional help. He did not discount nor deny my observations. As he looked into this mirror, he saw who was betraying him the most – himself. He seemed relieved. Naming the root cause of what was troubling him, his diminished mental health, as opposed to coping with its psychosocial manifestations, such as broken or hurtful relationships, was reassuring. He could accept his paranoid imperfections rather than the idea he was being talked about and isolated by others. He needed hope, and by owning this suggestion, he had some degree of personal control.

He asked where he might get the support he needed. I gave him information about the British Association of Counsellors and suggested he discuss it with his GP. We parted amicably, and I never saw him again.

Chapter 14

Forgiving Dreams
1996 – 1997

We dare to set out on this perilous path,
endure moments of turmoil and even
crisis, because we trust that God is there,
in all the mess, to bless us.

Timothy Radcliffe, *What is the Point of Being a Christian?*

How did I know it was time to uproot myself and move two hundred miles away? Alone, with no significant other to test my thoughts, I was invited to choose uncertainty. It was February 1996. I felt a compelling mysterious call to travel back north to the land of my ancestors, nudged by a deep-seated, non-rational wisdom. I began to feel restlessly aware of an inner lonesomeness and a sense of separation from a place, people and purpose as yet unknown. Where I was living and working felt temporary and stagnant. I felt trapped by my success. I was doubting my capabilities and wanted to test and challenge myself; inner voices of longing were calling me to a place beyond the familiar.

As I ruminated on whether to move to a new place and space, something strange happened. In the early hours of one Sunday morning, a restless spirit woke me telling me to get in touch with Andrew. I tried to ignore it and return to the safety of sleep. It was impossible. I began to pray and listen. A voice within was guiding me to write to him. I surrendered and began to write. I asked him to forgive me, as I forgave him. I was sorry for all the pain and hurt that had passed between us. I was sorry I hadn't been able to help him deal with his mental health problems. I felt at times I had not responded with the grace and patience he deserved.

I posted the letter the next day. Two weeks later I received a reply. As I read the handwritten letter I sensed a slow but steady response had been constructed. It was considered and open. Andrew began by saying how grateful he was for the timing of the letter. He had just been discharged from a long-term psychiatric unit where he had been admitted under section. He was suffering from a paranoid personality disorder. He had probably developed it at an early age, and it was doubtful he would ever make a full recovery. He had lost his job and experienced financial difficulties, which thankfully his parents were able to alleviate. His only friends were his elderly parents and sister. All other friendships – of which I can only recall two – had disintegrated, leaving him further isolated and lonely.

It was shocking, but I was not surprised. It made sense and explained his extreme mistrust and suspicion. It also explained why he'd been packed off to boarding school, as his parents couldn't cope. Had this condition been discovered earlier, how different his life – and the life of his family – would have been. At last this enduring pattern of tortured inner experiences, which denied him the ability to live fully and intimately with those around him, had been diagnosed. Unwarranted fear and significant distress could be minimised. I was relieved he was now receiving appropriate care.

Andrew didn't make any reference to his or my forgiveness. The word 'sorry' didn't appear in his letter. But I had not written to him in the hope or expectation of reciprocal acquittal. What mattered was my acknowledgement that I had made a mistake by marrying him. It had been an honest, incapacitated failure based on lack of information and underdeveloped judgement. Despite this higher level of understanding, I felt sad and helpless. His needs had been beyond my ability to cope with. I had been arrogant, struggling to accept my own incompleteness and human frailty. I still felt guilty that my decision to leave him was to protect myself. I was sorry that neither of us had been aware of the divine presence living among us.

A couple of months later, as Easter was approaching, I wrote to Andrew again and described my newfound faith, how I had become a Christian and the transformative changes I was experiencing. I shared the joy and peace I felt, despite the inevitable unhappiness of life. I wanted to convey hope beyond the everyday to him. I was also seeking consolation from the remorse I was feeling. It was an innocent attempt to award myself the prize of freedom, freedom from regret and the thorn of self-contempt.

I enclosed a card with the following exquisite poem:

*One night I dreamed I was walking along the beach with
the Lord. Many scenes from my life flashed across the sky.
In each scene, I noticed footprints in the sand.
Sometimes there were two sets of footprints, other times
there was one only.
This bothered me because I noticed that during the low
periods of my life, when I was suffering from anguish,
sorrow or defeat, I could see only one set of footprints,
so I said to the Lord,
'You promised me, Lord, that if I followed you, you
would walk with me always. But I have noticed that
during the most trying periods of my life there has only
been one set of footprints in the sand. Why, when I
needed you most, have you not been there for me?'
The Lord replied, 'The years when you have seen only
one set of footprints, my child, is when I carried you.'*

Mary Stevenson,
'Footprints in the Sand'

Andrew wrote back to thank me. He was encouraged by my faith. *I
am going to find and welcome Jesus into my life* were the last words
he wrote.

*I behold myself standing in the presence of God our Lord
and of his angels and saints, who intercede for me.*

St Ignatius of Loyola,
The Spiritual Exercises

I was approached about a job in a large northern city. I applied and
was offered the post. Flattered by my success, I accepted. As soon as I
moved to the area, I joined a church in a pretty village where I found
lodgings with an elderly lady from the congregation.

It wasn't the most inspiring of jobs, as I soon realised. In contrast
to my previous manager, this manager was exasperating, her weak
leadership creating confusion and conflict within the team. This left
me feeling insecure and bewildered. Neither did the job content suit
me. Large projects collecting meaningless data were mind-numbing.
I had left behind a job which was inspiring and transformational for
one which seemed to have no point. Furthermore, the organisation
was in constant political conflict, with power struggles for promotion
and status outweighing patient care.

Once I'd moved into my new home, my landlady changed the house rules and insisted the room was only available from Monday to Friday to minimise the amount of time I spent in the house. She would sneak into my room, turn off the heating and acquaint herself with my possessions. I was bombarded with petty complaints. She rapidly became the landlady from hell. Known to the church as the kindly widow of a local VIP, she was admired for her charity work, but behind this facade was a mean and nasty woman.

At weekends I visited friends or went to stay with my parents. My difficult circumstances meant that I found myself spending time with my mum and dad which otherwise would not have happened. Was this a gift? I felt I was being prepared for future events. So I waited. Over Christmas 1996 I spent my two weeks' leave staying with my parents. I couldn't remember having spent this amount of time with them since I was a teenager, least of all over Christmas. It was peculiar. I didn't resist nor question, I just surrendered to the occasion. It felt mysteriously preordained and deliberate. It was no random coincidence.

Dad and I went hiking across the countryside together. Each morning we would eagerly assess the weather and the number of daylight hours before setting off. We would trek side by side with long stretches of silence for as long as the light permitted. An unspoken language drifted between us, its message clear: reconciliation. This man had changed. His company felt tender-hearted and humble. The raging baboon from many years ago had metamorphosed into a gentle, quiet man. Other than the natural signs of ageing, his outward appearance was little different, but his inner transformation was profound. I felt a deep peace across my heartland. An inner beauty washed away and healed the wounds from the past.

Free from morbid imagination, a voice whispered, *Appreciate this time with Dad, as it may be your last*. Was this to be my last Christmas with him? An unsteady apprehension started to creep in and disturb my thoughts. The future seemed brooding and threatening. Dark clouds were forming.

Only those who are aware of the tragedy that overhangs all human relationships and separates the light from the darkness can learn that everything, no matter how remote it now seems, will have its day of reckoning, leaving an indelible stain of suffering as a memento of its advent.

Martin Israel,
Doubt: The Way of Growth

Dad seemed content with his quiet, simple life marked by a daily routine involving reading the newspaper, doing the crossword and walking his pet Pekinese dog. Mum continued to torment him, her behaviour spikey, resentful and deliberately hurtful. She would try to provoke him into an argument, her nastiness irrational and her presence distracted and confused. Sparks would appear, which would multiply exponentially. In an attempt to stop her, Dad's anger would break out in shouting and thrashing against doors and furniture. Once again she deliberately became the victim, seeking sympathy as the target of his anger. Dad's loss of temper alleviated his exasperation, but he was also diminished by his disruptive anger. Old pathological patterns persisted like a chronic, painful disease.

The family crisis began after the New Year celebrations. I returned to my lodgings and an uneasy atmosphere at work. Financial pressures and ruthless ambition preoccupied the managers. It was tense and fragile. Closeted, secretive conversations by those in power engendered an environment of suspicion and suspense. I felt insecure and anxious.

Out of the blue, Mum phoned me at work. Her voice was quivering with desperation and fright. Dad was sick. He was acutely depressed, and she was worried about him. His mind had become imprisoned and tortured by dark, secret thoughts. My first reaction was to wonder whether she was attention-seeking again. Was her concern genuine? How could I discern what was real? Who was she afraid for – herself or Dad? Like an abandoned, terrified child in a haunted house, she was tangled up in her own anxiety. Confused and fraught she pleaded with me to help. Dad was not at home, having left her that morning to walk off his darkness. She believed Dad was at risk of self-harm. I knew she was only telling part of the story. Something had happened, and words had been said which had led to this situation. She hinted at bad, horrid things that had happened to Dad as a child, things too awful to describe, things which were unsayable. Hiding my scepticism, I reassured her and drove home, which was an hour away.

Dad returned unharmed but emotionally remote. It was as though he had entered a lonely, dark tunnel only wide enough for one person, a soulless, eerie place. We could all stand and shout at the entrance – words of love, concern and care – but ultimately Dad had to take steps to return or keep travelling further and further away. We could see he was becoming unreachable and the slow climb back into the light would be impossible for him unaided.

He agreed to receive medical attention and was admitted to an acute psychiatric ward for his own safety. I visited every weekend.

The ward was in the grounds of the hospital where I had trained as a nurse; its layout and decor resembled the wing of a decaying asylum. It smelled of cigarettes and stale urine. Even if patients weren't depressed before arrival, a stay of any length would certainly have rendered anyone, well or otherwise, mentally unfit. Many of them were elderly men admitted following the death of their spouses – lives shattered and broken from the anguish of lost love, wandering bereft souls unable to cope with life beyond the restraints of the psychiatric ward. Mumbling and dribbling, they would shuffle up and down the grim corridors in their fraying slippers and food-stained clothes, sedated on a cocktail of drugs.

My mind flashed back to my hands-on nursing as I imagined myself washing, bathing and tenderly caring for these fragile, vulnerable men. I would comb their neglected hair, shave their grey, crusted whiskers and trim their brittle nails, praying they could recover their dignity and self-respect. At times I felt I had walked into a scene from the film *One Flew Over The Cuckoo's Nest*, but this was no Oscar-winning film set with savvy acting performances. There would be no accolades, tributes and artistic honours to applaud these people. Nor was this a sumptuous, palatial setting. This was my dad, an inpatient suffering on a real-life psychiatric ward.

The staff were all male and dressed in casual clothes – jeans and T-shirts. They would sit and slouch in groups smoking and chatting or playing pool, ignoring the sick and hurting. I have no memory of them interacting with the patients. It was as though the patients had become invisible, like ghostly spirits. I do recall sitting with Dad and watching the staff as though we were an audience watching a group of actors in an amateur play. 'Look,' he said, 'they don't seem to know we're here. They don't care about us. They're only here to earn money.'

The following day I rang the consultant. I asked him what the plan was for my father's care, but he didn't even recognise his name. I felt impotent and deflated. It was a hopeless situation. My thoughts were scrambled by fear and dread. I had slipped into a fast-flowing river, and I was powerless against the force of the water as it repeatedly dragged me beneath the surface. I was not coping.

The weekend visits were spent watching Dad devour home-made ham sandwiches washed down with a flask of tea, while Mum described how tired and weary she was. Self-obsessed and jealous of the attention Dad was getting, she moaned incessantly. Dad seemed devoid of emotion. Numbed by his medication, he was oblivious to her smothering narcissism. Like a folklore zombie, he showed no reaction. I wanted to tenderly wrap him in a warm quilted blanket and reassure him all would be well. I wished for a miracle cure. It seemed too complicated, confusing and messy, but there were no simple remedies and no magic wands. The toxic, destructive dynamics between Mum and Dad, their own individual mental health problems, and poor psychiatric care were a recipe for an explosive disaster.

Dad was slowly slipping away down his tunnel of dark pain. Consumed by a desperate fear I wrote him a love letter, a letter which conveyed a heartfelt love for him and joy at our reconciliation. I had come to love my father in ways I thought I never could. Silently and unbidden, I had been blessed with the grace of a true, pure forgiveness. I had to share this loving forgiveness with him in the hope it would help to save him from this casket of pain. I pleaded with him to let go of any unresolved guilt and anguish which may be darkening his thoughts. Over and again I told him how much I loved him. I believed this would save him. I hoped his love for me would bring him back.

Each Sunday evening, miserable and tired, I would return to my lodgings and go to Mass at my local village church. Within the dark building, its shadows fragranced by incense, I would fall to my knees in solitary prayer and weep, my body shaking with abject anticipatory grief: 'God, oh God. Where are you? Please, please help me. Help my dad. Protect him from harm and surround him with loving, caring people.'

It was April 1997, and God arrived in a book. Unable to concentrate, I went to a Christian bookshop during my lunch break feeling agitated and desperate. There in the window was a recent publication, *God, Where Are You?* written by one of my favourite authors, Gerard Hughes. Once again I would be reminded that we read to know we are not alone. This personal journey of exploration into the mystery of God and of human life brought comfort and reassurance. His book was absorbing; I realised that our salvation is not outside the world, for God is in, as well as beyond, all things. The author's account of his own traumatic past became a source of life-giving strength. I felt as if my God, my very own personal God, was closer to me than I was to myself. This gave me the resilience I needed to accept the chaos around and within me. I let go of trying to control these unfathomable circumstances. I let go of feeling responsible. I let the river carry me without struggling, trusting the water to take me to a place of unknown destiny. Despite the depth of my pain, I was willing to embrace uncertainty and anguish. This book became a lifeline and my mat carrier. I clung to each chapter, sentence and word as it carried me closer and deeper into God's loving presence. I was falling into God's arms. A deep touching was taking place as I was aware of my mind being comforted and my senses opened. I was given the grace to be willing to surrender, to surrender to the naked now of true prayer and full presence.

Dad had been granted weekend leave. He seemed to be able to cope with short stays at home, but he and Mum continued to fight, and I would spend the entire weekend mediating between them. Mum's hatred towards Dad was so pathological that she attempted to poison him. I discovered she was dissolving up to six paracetamol in his evening mug of tea. I wasn't surprised, as she was mad enough to do such a wicked thing. I would never trust her, least of all with someone vulnerable. I was furious with her, while also being fearful. Haunted by images of her frenzied attacks when I was younger, I carefully made sure she agreed to stop this. What I really wanted to do was lash out angrily at the evil horror. It was shocking and vile. We were all vulnerable to Mum's venomous bites. She was calculated and devious enough to silently creep up and attack anyone who disturbed her, innocently or otherwise.

It was Monday, 28 April 1997 and Dad should have returned to the hospital after his weekend at home. I tried to call Mum to check how his return to the psychiatric ward had gone, but she didn't answer. Instead, I heard Dad's voice telling me Mum was in hospital. She had been admitted to the female psychiatric ward adjacent to his. He recounted a crazy, shambolic day. He and Mum had returned to his ward as planned and a review meeting was held with a junior female doctor. Mum dominated the meeting with her relentless, self-serving complaints about the burden of looking after Dad. She was emotionally ravenous. Like a predatory wildcat, she scratched and clawed at the flesh of the meeting. Hissing and spitting, her craving for attention became a histrionic drama. She demonised Dad, attributing her exhaustion to his demands. She was the victim and Dad was persecuting her.

Mum's manipulative tricks began to work. Her deluded demands convinced the doctor her needs far exceeded Dad's. Mum's insatiable narcissism, which neither medicine nor history could deflect, caused the meeting to fall apart. Wounded and abandoned, Dad fled to the refuge of his home. Staff at the hospital took pity on Mum and offered her a bed for the night to rest.

Dad was upset and angry. He was tired of Mum's lies. He talked about the meeting at the hospital and how abandoned he felt by Mum and the doctor. They had paired up and accused him of being a misogynist. Raging and exasperated he was forced to leave the appointment alone. He then calmly described how he was going to leave my mother. He should have done it years ago.

This was the last time I would hear his voice.

Later that evening I was contacted by the ward sister where Mum was staying. She described how they were concerned for her. She was exhausted due to the heavy burdens of looking after Dad (I wasn't convinced), but what was more critical was the threat of physical harm. 'Is your father capable of physical violence towards your mother?' She ambushed me with her directness. The words were flung at me as though I had been slapped across the face. Like a confident, swashbuckling musketeer, she pointed a rifle at my head. I froze as chaotic thoughts terrorised me. What do I say to Mum's allegations? Is Dad on trial? Will my testimony be used to convict him of a serious crime, or release him from the grip of this terrible ordeal? Was his destiny resting in my hands? Is he a condemned man? What verdict would the jury arrive at?

Our family history of domestic violence and abuse was publicly exposed. None of us was immune from the painful impact of this situation. I prayed for strength and wisdom and then spoke in truth: 'While there has been no evidence of recent violence, he has a history of such. There is one unassailable fact, Dad has been capable of beating Mum in the past.'

The nursing sister reaffirmed her decision to keep Mum in hospital overnight. The plan was for Mum to phone Dad the following morning to invite him back for further conciliatory discussions. She was underestimating Mum's depth of vengefulness and how she thrived on skirmishes and battles. But none of us could have predicted what was prowling ahead. Like a role-reversed scene out of Tolstoy's *Anna Karenina*, Vronsky was about to become the victim. Mum never phoned Dad. She alleged she had no change for the public call box, but I believe she was intentionally punishing and humiliating him. It was an opportunistic, cruel mind game and she was going to win no matter what. Basking in the warm attention from the nursing staff, the wicked power of revenge was leading to a shocking tragedy. As spring journeyed out of the cold winter darkness, from the invisible to the visible, our family was about to be thrust into deeper darkness.

Darker than dark.

Chapter 15

Tormented to Death

1997

Such a death is not freely chosen but is a desperate attempt to end unendurable pain. And this side of heaven, sometimes all the outstretched hands and the professional help in the world cannot reach a heart paralysed by fear and illness. It is not a sin to die.

Daniel O'Leary, *Already Within*

It was Tuesday, 29 April 1997. After a draining day at work, I arrived back at my lodgings at around 6.30pm to a call from Lee.

'Don't panic, but you need to get over to the hospital as soon as possible. Dad has taken a massive overdose. The police had to break into the house to allow access for an ambulance crew. His heart stopped several times, but he is alive. He's being transferred from the accident and emergency unit to Intensive Care on a life support machine. We are on our way and will see you there.'

Lee had phoned home by chance that afternoon. Dad told him what had happened and that he was quitting. Unsure of the meaning of his coded message Lee rang the ward where Mum was staying and explained the story to the nursing staff. They worked out what Dad meant, realising their plans to review him had been sabotaged by Mum. They summoned the police and ambulance.

The world around me plummeted into a silent, surreal atmosphere as though I had plunged into murky, deep water. The journey to the hospital was over sixty miles on a busy motorway. I didn't trust myself to drive. In shock, I grabbed my bag and ran to get help from a neighbour. Speechless and locked in bleak imaginings, I sat in the back of the car as I was swiftly driven to the hospital. My elderly neighbour and his wife respected my need for silence and were still and calm. Rendered mute by dread, I had neither the inclination nor the ability to converse. I sat gazing emptily out of the rear window at the white road-markings flashing by. I was frozen by anxiety as I strained to see through the sudden wall of darkness which surrounded my soul. I could neither pray nor cry. But I didn't doubt God's existence; the thought was too much to bear. I needed to trust God's spirit was closer to me than I was to myself. I couldn't face the question: Where or what is God? I was too threatened by meaninglessness, especially given the futility of what had happened to Dad. I was terrified of falling into an emotional abyss, which would devour me forever. I sensed the mystery of God in my deepest self. God was far beyond my thinking and imagination. I imagined being surrounded by God's holy angels who were helping to carry me through this terrible suffering. They would keep me company and soothe my wounded soul.

I have very few thoughts to recall. I was in shock as I travelled nearer and nearer to a situation which could only end tragically. Since I was a young child, I had sensed this moment was inevitable. I knew my parents were intent on seriously harming one another. Dad's overdose was a consequence of mutually inflicted hatred and cruelty. Long-term physical and mental abuse had now converged and imploded. Dark, destructive forces seemed to be at work – or perhaps this was part of an eternal script whereby Dad's imminent self-inflicted death had been sent as a solution to problems we couldn't solve.

Enter into the beauty of eternal tranquillity, in that place where there is no more sorrow, or separation or mourning or tears.

John O'Donohue,
Benedictus

I ran through the familiar disinfected hospital corridors where I had grown from an 18-year-old novice student to a competent registered nurse. For three years among these wards and corridors, day and night, I had gained hard-earned knowledge and the skills of caring for the sick and dying – young and old, male and female. It was one of the most dramatic, life-enhancing and transformational changes I would ever experience. Reversed by these horrible circumstances, nurses and doctors would now be caring for my family and me.

I approached the intensive care unit and was met by a female consultant. I saw Mum sitting in an adjacent waiting room, her face betraying anguish and terror, like the painting *The Scream* by Edvard Munch. The intensity of her wretchedness has been permanently and painfully carved in my memory. It's as though a hot, blunt knife has been dragged through my mind leaving the texture of my memory cauterised and jagged so that each time I revisit it, I feel a sharp, burning pain, which is instantly transmitted to my gut. My body never lies. This will be stored in my body forever. A permanent account of human suffering.

The consultant was aware of my nursing background and connections to the hospital; her account of what had happened to Dad was clear and concise. She made no attempt to converse with Mum, who was hysterical and incapable of any rational thought. The precipitating events and Dad's prognosis weren't embellished with soothing niceties. No time was wasted with social frills as I calmly asked for the truth.

Three attempts had been made to resuscitate Dad, who was now on a life support machine and would not survive the night. If his body should defy her clinical opinion, then he would unquestionably be dependent on the life support machine indefinitely. Any further attempt to resuscitate him would be futile.

There is something about the news of a suicide that cuts across everything we are doing or thinking. It has a chilling ring to it. We are stopped in our tracks. Everything else becomes unimportant. With deep gut reaction, we know that there is something ultimate here. There is no pretence in the minds of those who take their own lives. Somewhere in all of us, a silver shiver of fear begins ... With all its profound complexities, the propensity for suicide is, in most cases, an illness. We are made up of body and soul; either can snap.

Daniel O'Leary,
Already Within

It was not about *if* but *when*. It was certain Dad would die during the passage of this very night. Exiled and forsaken in some dark, hidden place, he had turned his anger and distress on himself. He had beckoned his escape from this torn and harsh world by consuming a large quantity of anti-depressants and sedatives and guzzling a bottle of Pernod. This bitter chalice would help to carry him into the beautiful, welcoming arms of his silent angels.

*We can die of cancer, high blood pressure, heart attacks,
aneurysms. These are physical sicknesses. But we can
suffer those, too, in the soul. There are malignancies
and aneurysms also of the heart – mortal wounds from
which the soul cannot recover.*

Ronald Rolheiser,
'Misconceptions about suicide' from the author's website

Mum, Lee and I huddled around Dad's bedside. He was surrounded
by machines, with coloured lights recording his transition from this
life to the next: moving lines, numbers and squiggles, which to the
untrained eye were baffling, but I knew described Dad's heart rate,
rhythm, blood pressure and temperature.

The providence of time allowed us, believers and non-believers,
to call upon the hospital chaplain. The Lord's Prayer and Psalm 51,
the Miserere, were quietly spoken over Dad in preparation for the
parting of his soul and the shedding of his body.

Each of us took it, in turn, to be alone with him. This interim
time was all we had to say all that was unsaid and unfinished, time
to snatch one last intimate moment before Dad's final farewell. It
was no time for brittle words or false belongings. In this crucible of
death, each of us graciously and passionately paid tribute to a man
whose life was closing. As Dad's inner light diminished and silence
deepened around us, I thanked him for being my dad. I reminded
him I loved him.

Then I read the 23rd psalm to him.

The Lord is my shepherd; I shall not want.
He maketh me to lie down in green pastures: he leadeth me
beside the still waters.
He restoreth my soul: he leadeth me in the paths of righteousness
for his name's sake.
Yea, though I walk through the valley of the shadow of death, I
will fear no evil: for thou art with me; thy rod and thy staff they
comfort me.
Thou preparest a table before me in the presence of mine
enemies: thou anointest my head with oil; my cup runneth over.
Surely goodness and mercy shall follow me all the days of my
life: and I will dwell in the house of the Lord for ever.

As the words were slowly spoken, there were subtle and
undisputable changes to the monitors reading Dad's vital signs.

His blood pressure strengthened and his heart rate improved. Somewhere in the depths of his being, Dad was responding. Was he peacefully embracing and welcoming God as his shepherd? Was he slowly passing to a place of rest and peace?

The anonymous Christian men and women who are true to their own consciences, who may profess no religion, attend no services, receive no sacraments, may be closer to God than any observant Christian.

Gerard Hughes,
God, Where Are You?

Lee and I waited pensively in a small room close by, while Mum was the last to sit with him. It was about 4 am when we heard shrieking and wailing. We hurried back to find Mum stretched across Dad's body sobbing and denying what had taken place. Dad had waited to be alone with Mum for their last intimate moment together. Just as he said he would when he spoke to me the last time, he finally separated from Mum. He crossed the threshold from this world to the next; he disentangled himself and slipped away.

May you be embraced by God in whom dawn and twilight are one and may your longing inhabit its deepest dreams within the shelter of the Great Belonging.

John O'Donohue,
Eternal Echoes

Cold and shocked, we drove home. The light of dawn brought no chorus of birdsong. A chilling silence deafened each of us.

In an agitated state, with knotted guts and a dry mouth, I dreaded returning to my parents' house. No one had been inside since Dad had been scooped up by the ambulance crew. What would we find? Would the house tell a story of his distress and abandonment? What were his movements leading up to losing consciousness? Was he dressed or undressed? I cringed at the thought of him being found naked, perhaps incontinent, with his face smeared in vomit. Or was his face covered in froth, like my friend who died in the nurses' residence? My fretful imagination created deathly dark images and foul smells, as though I were about to enter a disused house in a Tudor shambles. Dad had been found upstairs in bed. What would we find there? Empty medicine bottles ... Pernod ... soiled bed linen?

What were Dad's final thoughts as he approached the doors which would close his existence on earth? Did he leave a letter explaining why he had put his life in mortal danger? Was this brutal self-inflicted act a cry for help, or was he determined to end his life like this? Would he include angry, accusatory words? Would he blame others for his suffering, such as Mum or the hospital doctor at his last appointment? Or would he be able to write words of love and farewell wishes?

As we timidly entered the house, there was a surprisingly peaceful atmosphere, like the morning after a raging storm. I immediately went upstairs to look at Dad's bedroom. It resembled a silent, empty tomb. Unlike Mary Magdalene, I was not expecting to see a body, and I wasn't carrying spices and perfume. Feeling weak, my arms hanging heavily by my sides, I stood and gazed at the place where Dad began his final journey back to Mother Earth. The untidy bedclothes were like robes strewn across the bed. I was relieved to see the bed wasn't dirty. It mattered to me that there was no evidence of vomit, urine or faeces. Dad's death was ugly enough without it being soiled with undigested food and poo.

Unlike famous historical figures, Dad left no scripted words. There was no note, nothing. Dad had died without telling us why this was his only escape. No confession, no explanation, he owed us nothing.

There is nothing to compare with the pain of death.
You were here, and now you are not.
That's all.

I search for you in old photographs, things you touched,
things that remind me of you,
but they cannot fill the space you occupied.

The space is in me too,
bleeding round the edges where you were torn away.
In the night, strange shapes haunt the space...
regret, fear, fury,
all the things we might have done,
all the shattered dreams.

How Can I Go on with This Hole Inside Me?
Partial Person!
Don't let me fill the space with the wrong things.
Don't let me cover it up,

to eat me from within.
Give me courage to bear my emptiness,
to hold it gently
till the edges stop bleeding;
till the darkness becomes friendly;
till I see the star at its heart;
till it becomes a fertile space,
growing new life within it.

If I had not loved, I would not have wept.
This love you have given me;
this love I have carried;
this love has carried me.

And I know that though I cannot see you, touch you,
the love does not go away.
Carried by this love,
we are not divided.
And there will be no more weeping.

Kathy Galloway,
'You were here, and now you are not'

Lee immediately began searching through Mum and Dad's private documents. As drawers and cupboards were explored, he held out various bank and savings details exclaiming: 'Look how much Mum's worth!' I was disgusted with him and refused to be involved in his vulgar, disrespectful hunt for money. All I knew was that Mum was now a wealthy woman. She would profit from Dad's astute financial planning. But although rich financially, she was poor in spirit. Emotional and psychological poverty would not escape her, and no amount of money would reverse these horrid circumstances. She was blighted by this tragic suicide.

As Lee looted through the account books, he resembled a ruthless seventeenth-century pirate, a heartless criminal scavenging through valuable cargo from a shipwreck, his ill-gotten booty destined to enrich him.

Broken and wretched, Mum tried to block out her agonising pain with sedatives. Inconsolable, with pinpoint pupils, she lay on the settee like a collapsed wooden puppet whose strings had snapped. When she dared to drift into consciousness, she would chain-smoke, anxiously waiting for the next pill to carry her back to her numbing refuge. She couldn't take it in.

Lee started to drink can after can of beer. Drunk and delirious, he swung in and out of an angry stupor. He was going to lynch those responsible for Dad's death. They'd be blindfolded, bound and made to walk the plank over the side of his ship. I felt anxious and wary of his threats for fear he would once again project them onto me. The atmosphere around him was threatening and unpredictable.

Unaware of time, I sat on the back doorstep bewildered and devastated, clutching my knees into my chest like a vulnerable, orphaned child. I felt hollow and afraid I too would succumb to a life-threatening mental illness. The combination of my parents' genes was a destructive cocktail of uncertainty. Tears rolled in tramlines down my face as I longed and ached for a tender, comforting hug. I needed to be held in the arms of loving consolation where I could safely mourn and grieve. It was a cry from my soul, which would echo for many, many years.

One of us had to take responsibility for Dad's funeral. In an attempt to avoid my inner anguish and convince myself I wasn't mad or bad, I picked up the Yellow Pages and began looking for an undertaker. There seemed to be hundreds to choose from. How do you choose a funeral director when suffering from the trauma of a sudden tragic death? How do you avoid making reckless decisions, which you will later regret, as you struggle with the emotions generated by a suicide: denial, anger, grief and, above all, guilt? There would only be one opportunity to get it right. The deceased's widow was barely conscious and incoherent, and his son was making drunken threats towards the world, its uncle and aunty. It was emotional chaos.

I rang a number at random, and an appointment was made for that evening. I briefly explained the circumstances of Dad's death to avoid any awkward questions later on. With precise timing, the undertaker arrived at 7 pm. A tall man with grey hair carrying several cases, he was immaculately dressed wearing a heavy black woollen coat resembling a cassock and shiny black shoes. Without delay, as though he were auditioning for a part in a Gothic melodrama, he opened each of the cases and began to recite his script to his drunk and drugged audience. There were samples of wood for the coffin – mahogany, pine and oak; a choice of white, crimson or sky-blue silk to line the casket, and various handles in plastic, wood or metal. When he'd finished talking I was so angry I wanted to shake him. I felt he had come to exploit our pain and sorrow. It was a profit-making exercise; he was a salesman selling fancy goods to the bereaved. He was implying that if we really loved Dad, then we'd be willing to have the best quality – and most expensive

– wood, silk and accessories. The bereaved can ease their guilt by spending money; the more they spend, the greater their love and innocence.

Something inside me switched from vulnerable child to feisty adult. As he arrived at the point of stating the cost of Dad's elaborate funeral, I picked up the Yellow Pages I had used earlier and shoved them into his huge hands. He looked at me, confused. I glared at him.

'Look at that. There are dozens of funeral directors. Why should we choose you? Not only are we dealing with a sudden death, but this was a tragic suicide. Have you no respect?'

This seemed to snap him out of his detached commercial role. He became closer, more sensitive and present to our grief. No longer blinded by his regimented sales pitch, he seemed engaged and less preoccupied as he compassionately looked at each of us. I could see he was now aware of our pain and distress. I too changed my attitude as I traded my anger for an understanding of his initial selling approach. Could this have been his defence against the stress of dealing with the bereaved? How else could he cope with a job, the essence of which constantly touches the face of death – the young and the old, natural and tragic?

The next hurdle would be the funeral service. Since Dad was not a believer and Mum was insisting on a Catholic cremation with a requiem mass, we anticipated further rejection and shame. The Catholic Church opposes suicide. It claims that life ultimately belongs to God and so is not for us to end. Consequently, the preservation of our life is not something discretionary but obligatory.

Everyone is responsible for his life before God who has given it to him. It is God who remains the sovereign Master of life. We are obliged to accept life gratefully and preserve it for his honour and the salvation of our souls. We are stewards, not owners, of the life God has entrusted to us. It is not ours to dispose of.

The 1997 Catechism of the Catholic Church

According to the teachings of the church, Dad's suicide had violated God's sovereignty over life, attacked human dignity, and was an offence against the proper love of himself, his family, friends and neighbours. It was contrary to love for the living God.

Although suicide has traditionally been considered a mortal sin, there is an assumption of informed consent. The church also teaches that grave psychological disturbances, anguish and suffering diminish the individual's responsibility for committing suicide.

Given Dad's poor mental health, his thinking would have been distorted; Father O'Sullivan, the priest from our local church, must have taken this into consideration when he agreed to a full Catholic funeral without questioning Dad's entitlement to such a service. He unconditionally reached out and supported us with a silent love. This was a significant act towards alleviating the shame we all felt. Father O'Sullivan was a mat carrier for me and for Dad, and I am eternally grateful for his benevolent compassion.

In the lonely days preparing for the funeral, I escaped to *God, Where are you?* for solace and safe company. Gerard Hughes describes the deaths by suicide of his two sisters Marie and Margot and how, as happened with us, they were both granted a requiem mass before burial. I was stunned. Firstly, because of the remote possibility that I would be reading this book with similar stories just when my own father had committed suicide. Secondly, it shattered my false belief that bad things happen to bad people, that we are the authors of our own misery. I was reading about how bad things also happen to good, holy people from loving families. No one is immune from suffering and tragedy.

At night I was haunted by images of Dad lying in the mortuary, his body mutilated by the tools of the pathologist. Flesh and bones, which had so recently functioned with sophisticated collaboration, were now permanently terminated. Prescribed medicines, intended to alleviate suffering, by virtue of excess had caused a preventable death.

On the eve of Dad's funeral, I went to see Father O'Sullivan to discuss the eulogy. Neither Mum nor Lee made much contribution other than identifying a few dates such as Dad's retirement and Mum and Dad's wedding. Our hollowness and pain seemed to rob us of nostalgic memories. I felt everything had been taken from me, except the certainty and silence of Dad's death.

I walked into his study heavy-hearted, lonely and anxious. I could smell frankincense and candle wax, which soothed my nerves like an invisible holy balm. In a partially lit corner, shrouded in shadow, Father O'Sullivan's vestments hung in quiet sympathy: a white cotton hooded alb with tapered sleeves, a symbol of innocence and purity, and next to it the outer garment, the chasuble, its exquisite embroidery of red, gold and blue depicting the four gospels.

As I wearily glanced round this holy room, I spotted a copy of *God, Where are you?* on Father O'Sullivan's desk. We were reading the same book! I immediately became animated; this connection enabled us to converse on a more meaningful level. I felt respected and understood in ways which mattered to me as we explored God's presence in the face of suffering. I found strength and affirmation as the freedom of our sacred conversation unlocked my inner repository of unmet spiritual needs. This would equip me to face the days and weeks ahead.

But nothing could have prepared me to deal with the stigma which was awaiting me. Like Gerard Hughes' experience of his sisters' suicides, we each became afraid of judgement and condemnation – of being blamed for Dad's decision to take his own life. Because of this, we felt extreme isolation. This manifested itself in our relationships with neighbours, friends and colleagues.

My most painful experience during this raw time came from my school friend Julie. She was the friend who took delight in skitting me when I was a school girl. She was well aware of my family history. I went to see her a few days before Dad's funeral, and we sat upstairs in her bedroom, as we had done so many times as teenagers. As we sat among the clutter of her clothes, make-up and accessories, I sobbed; my grief and anguish pushed to the surface, insisting on expression from the innermost recesses of my heart.

Was this the sound of darkness calling out? My soul cried out in agonised disbelief at Dad's horrible death. Why? Oh why? I felt abandoned and angry that Dad didn't love me enough to want to stay alive. I didn't matter after all. My love had meant nothing. I was so angry with myself as I confronted my own fallibility. I couldn't save Dad with my love. I couldn't release him from his pain and suffering. Instead he asked for death to set his soul free from his body. I was mortal, not immortal. I was not God, nor the sun nor moon. I was just one of the many stars, insignificant and ordinary. But how else do we see the stars without darkness?

My eyes were hot and swollen. Tears ran down my face colliding with mucus from my nose. My body was shaking like a fragile branch, its dry autumn leaves defenceless against the tantrums of the wind battling to strip it bare. Julie sat watching me silently. I took her friendship for granted; I believed she could withstand watching and listening to my heart breaking. I was wrong.

I never saw Julie again. She wouldn't answer my phone calls, failed to arrive for a lunch date and didn't attend Dad's funeral. When I called at her parents' house, she was never home. As I was held in the stocks of grief, Julie had cut me out of her life. I fretted for a long time after that believing I was at fault. To share inconsolable grief with a childhood school friend was a crime worthy of punishment. Shame and guilt hovered over my worried mind.

I can't recall much about the funeral other than being invited to sprinkle Dad's coffin with holy water and bless it with incense before it disappeared through a purple velvet curtain with gold knotted tassels for cremation. I felt honoured by the privilege of this final act as we said our farewells and prayers of committal.

We need not worry unduly about the eternal salvation of those who die in this way. God's understanding and compassion infinitely surpass our own. Our lost loved ones are in safer hands than ours. If we, limited as we are, can already reach through this tragedy with some understanding and love, we can rest secure in the fact that, given the width and depth of God's love, the one who dies through suicide meets, on the other side, a compassion that's deeper than our own and a judgement that intuits the deepest motives of their heart.

Ronald Rolheiser,
from the author's website

We left the crematorium to the sound of Whitney Houston belting out 'I will always love you', not a song of my choice but one which Mum and Lee believed suitably expressed human indomitability. For me, it was the soundtrack to a turgid romantic thriller that should have been left to languish in development purgatory. I'm sure Dad would have preferred a Frank Sinatra song, perhaps 'Now is the hour when we must say goodbye'. But then, we were all so consumed by the blinding, deafening effects of Dad's needless extreme death that we were incapable of knowing our own minds, let alone what Dad would have wanted.

Dad left nothing behind other than dust and ash to scatter among the spring flowers and beauty of the earth.

Every death cuts off a story that has infinite possibilities. It can be seen as both a terrible story of our destructive end or our homecoming as we are liberated at the end of our story and entry into the longer story of eternity.

It is the deepest darkness and the dawn of light.

Timothy Radcliffe,
What is the Point of Being a Christian?

Chapter 16

Bare Dreams

1997 – 1998

The past was but the cemetery of our illusions: one simply stubbed one's toes on the gravestones.

Emile Zola, *The Masterpiece*

I returned to my lodgings leaving Mum to cope on her own. It was as though she were immersed in a fast-flowing river searching for water. Wasting away, she seemed to be dying before she had died; she was utterly lost within her inner dereliction. I worried about her ability to survive alone. I stayed with her every weekend, ensuring she ate at least one decent meal each day. On Saturday evening I would accompany her to Mass. We sat together inside the stillness of the whitewashed church surrounded by scented bouquets of delicate garden flowers. I preferred the evening service, as it was quieter, more reverent and contemplative. It was usually attended by people on their own, unlike Sunday mornings, which focused on young families. While the vibrant noise and colours of small children was a joy to see, it was also a painful reminder that our monochromic family had lost one of its cornerstones.

I never once questioned my loyalty to Mum and Lee, despite how they had behaved towards me. I chose to ignore their betrayals. I could not abandon them. To be anything other than loving, kind and patient would deny the existence of God. Was this an echo of Jesus's words from the Cross: 'Father, forgive them, for they do not know what they do', or was it just my own egocentric piousness? Was I misguided and weak, or was it a conditional hope, which would be rewarded with a long-awaited love?

I felt constantly anxious and frightened, even though I was not at risk of any harm. The trauma of Dad's suicide gripped my mind and body; I was filled with memories which both blessed and disturbed my soul. At times I felt paralysed, locked inside the arms of an invisible vice, which was squeezing and extracting any remaining sense of inner equanimity. Bad dreams, frightening thoughts and flashbacks tormented me day and night. My mood and ability to think clearly were damaged. I was terrified that I was somehow responsible for Dad's death. I was guilty, and it was my fault. If only I hadn't told the nurses the night before he died that he was capable of violence. If only I'd gone to see him on the same evening, after we had spoken on the phone, to comfort and console him. I should have taken time off work to be with him. If I had acted differently, he wouldn't have been left lonely and desperate. I could have rescued him.

Yet, in spite of this inner turmoil, just as in the days following Debbie's death in the nurses' residence, I was touched by the vivid beauty of life: strangers offering a quiet 'good morning', a faint smile from an innocent, shy child, and the bright yellow glow from endless fields of flowering rapeseed. The very act of living felt more precious, intense and glorious.

If only Mum and Dad could have loved one another, he would still have been alive.

There was no follow-up from the caring professionals, no clinical governance investigation in search of how and why Dad's suicide had occurred. He was just another statistic buried in a hospital tomb of meaningless figures. Was it preventable? No one seemed to care about the precipitating events which contributed to Dad's death. No one was asking any questions. No one wanted to know our story. All the coroner wanted to know was the cause of death; it was indisputable – drugs and alcohol.

Although the hospital involvement instantly disappeared like an ethereal vapour, I did go to see the junior doctor who had seen Dad in the clinic with Mum. I wanted her to know we didn't blame her, despite Mum and Lee attributing his death to her mishandling of his last appointment. I didn't want her to go through life carrying this burden of guilt. Maybe this is what I really wanted someone to say to me. Maybe she was a mirror I was holding up to myself. My soul was crying out for someone to tell me I wasn't to blame and it wasn't my fault. I wanted my dad back. I wanted to turn back time and speak to him on the phone, persuading him of hope and optimism. I wanted to buy him birthday and Father's Day cards. I wanted him to find peace.

It was a defining, life-changing time. There was life before Dad died and then life after Dad died. It was as if a deep muddy trench had been dug dividing these two periods. Life is never the same once you have been touched by the cold hand of death. Dad's death redefined my entire world and began to teach me who I really was.

My damaged, fragile self-esteem convinced me I had to work harder and harder. I had to keep proving myself. Full of dread and a sense of my worthlessness, I began to worry about what others thought of me. My colleagues seemed to avoid me; there was little eye contact when walking down a corridor or a casual 'How are you?' Office doors were kept shut to avoid any informal conversation. There were no invitations to share coffee or lunch breaks.

One colleague chose to be different. Her name was Anna. She was a single mum working full-time as a senior manager, a job which carried a huge responsibility in the prevailing adversarial culture. I admired her resilience and values-driven leadership. When hard times came, and others fell away, Anna was there for me, despite the many demands on her as a professional and a mother. She offered me more than tea and sympathy, it was friendship without judgement. Despite only knowing me for a short time, she'd invite me to stay at her home and share supper. We chatted about everyday things, such as music, fashion and even the latest lipstick. She invited me to spend Christmas Day with her extended family on my first Christmas after Dad had died – Mum was staying with Lee, and I hadn't been invited. I felt wanted and involved. There was no awkwardness, and I never felt I was being labelled 'This is the one whose dad committed suicide'. Family is not always about blood – this I had known for many years. It's about the people who want you in their life. They respect and accept you for who, not what, you are. They care about your happiness and well-being and love you no matter what. This sense of inclusion carried me through the anguish of facing these family celebrations alone and desolate.

I remember struggling to find something to wear. I had lost so much weight that nothing I chose seemed to fit me. I was waif-like and skeletal. My self-consciousness was exaggerated by my poor self-image. None of this mattered to Anna. She had a compassionate awareness that was generous and brave. No stranger to pain, she and her young daughter knew about betrayal; she had been abandoned by her husband. Anna could have transmitted her pain onto me, especially because I was so vulnerable, but she chose to transform it into acts of kindness and unconditional love. Anna was my mat carrier.

This friendship generated a transformative power. I was surrounded by a beautiful circle of light, protecting, healing and strengthening me during these terrible days. It was a power which didn't take sides but offered a compassionate indifference to the events threatening my annihilation.

I was having fewer meetings with my manager, and the atmosphere around me felt heavy and tense. A sombre mood seemed to filter along the corridors, as though we were captured in an old sepia photograph.

A new, fiercely ambitious director from a privileged background was appointed. Our respected and trusted common-sense director was pushed aside and encouraged to seek alternative employment. Young and overconfident, our new director's miscalculations resulted in a financial crisis. To keep the ship afloat, some of its cargo had to be shed. Long meetings took place behind closed doors. I sensed some kind of conspiracy was about to emerge. In an atmosphere of gloomy secrecy, I worried I was becoming paranoid as I struggled with the burden of grief and caring for Mum at weekends while trying to function effectively at work.

At lunchtime, I would go to a small rose garden close to where I worked. As I sat among the delicate beauty of the flowers with their stems of thorns, I would weep. I felt as though I had been pushed to the edge of society and I was losing my gravity. I was wobbly and emotionally unsteady. I could break out in sobs at any time in any place, public or private. Trivial, innocent reminders of Dad would trigger uncontrollable, indefinite episodes of weeping.

When nothing else subsists from the past, after the people are dead, after the things are broken and scattered ... the smell and taste of things remain poised a long time, like souls ... bearing resiliently, on tiny and almost impalpable drops of their essence, the immense edifice of memory.

Marcel Proust,
Swann's Way

Unexpected relief came in the form of a scrap of paper slipped underneath my office door. On it, my manager had scribbled: *Come and see me ASAP*. Like an anxious patient waiting for a cruel diagnosis, the ensuing lifting of uncertainty was more tolerable than constant unpredictability and chaos. Heart racing, with clammy palms, I went to see her immediately. Languishing in her own self-protective pity and guilt, she explained: 'This is the hardest thing I have ever had to do in my career.' Really? When you've nursed the sick, disabled and dying? Surely not!

She was about to change the course of my life and career. I was being sacked. I was told my post was redundant, but my perception was that I was the problem employee no one could face. I had to go so those around me could resume their cosy rituals and habits; my grief and the stigma of suicide made others feel uncomfortable. Did it knock on their inner door of mortality, reminding them that they too would die? It would be cleaner and tidier to let me go overboard than to cope with being alongside my emotional pain. This decision felt like discrimination based on human vulnerability.

Was I seen as psychologically disturbed and unlikable? I certainly didn't feel understood and supported during this time. Feelings of isolation howled around my inner landscape like a cold, bitter March wind. Its voiceless sound left me empty and abandoned. I felt doubly ashamed, afflicted by Dad's suicide and now my redundancy. I was an unwanted and unlovable wretch. I had neither the strength nor the inclination to contest the decision.

After seventeen years of uninterrupted full-time employment with the NHS, by Christmas 1997 I was unemployed. I returned to my lodgings and scurried up to my room pretending I was happy it was Friday, and I had a weekend ahead. I knew if I told my landlady her primary concern would be the threat to her income, as my redundancy would put at risk my ability to pay her rent.

I shut the door to my room and wept and wept. My body shook with a fierce inner distress. I stood naked in front of an old scratched wall mirror as I prayed and lamented at God – how could all this be part of God's divine intelligence in a land of grace and mercy? My nakedness was symbolic of how I was feeling: completely stripped, abandoned and powerless. I was a vulnerable failure. I felt too angry and desolate to hope for divine intervention. How can great holiness exist alongside such terrible darkness? There were no signs, wonders and miracles here in the desert of my soul. I couldn't hear a prophetic voice crying out words of reassurance, nor were there shepherds or wise men to comfort and console me.

I was afraid of the darkness that had descended upon me. My soul was overwhelmed. I imagined myself standing next to Mary at the foot of the Cross. I felt broken and dejected. There were no horizons of hope nor glimpses of light to strive for. Like Mary, I was in despair. I could not see how this pain and suffering could lead to anything but calamity. How could this be part of God's plan? A kind and loving God. I was lost in God's silence. My day resembled night, cold and darkly silent, as though I were lost in a deserted underground coal mine. Is this the colour of grace – black on black? I didn't care if I didn't wake the next morning. These unplanned forces of desolation were contorting my life into shapes I didn't recognise. I was afraid I would snap at any moment. I was at the mercy of God's grace as I struggled to see how this pain could sanctify me. As eventually, my secret tears faded, I fell into an exhausted sleep.

Grace is simply the last depth and radical meaning of
all the created person experiences, enacts and suffers
in the process of developing and realising herself as a
person. When someone experiences laughter or tears,
bears responsibility, stands by the truth, breaks through
the egoism of her life with other people; where someone
hopes against hope, faces the shallowness and stupidity
of the daily rush and bustle with humour and patience,
refusing to become embittered; where someone learns
to become silent and in this inner silence lets the evil
in her heart die rather than be spread outwards; in
a word, where someone lives as she would like to
live, combating her own egoism and the continual
temptation to inner despair – this is the event of grace.

Karl Rahner,
from 'A Copernican Revolution: Secular Life and the Sacraments'

By dawn the following morning there was inexplicable hope in my heart. My soul felt calm – consoled and renewed by sleep. It was as though an angel of light and compassion had watched over me throughout the night; during the bright darkness within my interior landscape of suffering, I discovered the friendship of serenity. The horizons of my imagination were slowly becoming tinged with subtle colours, like those from J.M.W. Turner's beautiful watercolour *Light and Colour (Goethe's Theory) – the Morning after the Deluge – Moses Writing the Book of Genesis.* I could glimpse the gifts of courage, wisdom and healing which in time would be born from the harshness of these losses. If you looked into my eyes that morning, there was no bleak abandonment but faint images of light and hope.

Throughout the days and weeks ahead, the burden of grief and loss entangled me in feelings of unworthiness. I had a heavy heart. The loss of my father ruptured our family, scattering us in strange directions. I felt increasingly drained of vitality and enthusiasm for the simple things of life. I was exhausted. I didn't have the energy to answer the telephone and chat to friends. Feeling unemployable compounded this. I was blighted by grief and rejection. It was as though a rapacious swarm of locusts had swept across my parched soul leaving me to cope with an endless famine. I felt stripped of everything: family, father, career success, income and status. My security, self-worth and self-image were all threatened. Again I would find comfort in music as The Verve released 'Bittersweet Symphony', the lyrics of which poetically described what was happening to me.

I used my redundancy money, which was the greatest sum I had ever acquired, to terminate the outstanding mortgage on my cottage in Cambridgeshire. While I had gained freedom from the slavery of debt, I was worried the stigma of suicide would deter any suitable employers. I felt as if I was balancing on a narrow rope. Like a novice acrobat, I could plunge and crash down towards homelessness.

I was continuing with my unsteady existence in my lodgings with the scolding landlady. She was neither sympathetic nor benevolent. Her main concern was to ensure she received her rent, which she would not reduce despite my extenuating circumstances. Not only did I have to vacate the room at weekends, but I was also expected to be out of the house during normal working hours, when she would visit my room to ensure I had turned the heating off. I was ensnared. She had the power to evict me if I did anything to offend her. To her Sunday church friends and vicar, she boasted of her charity, exploiting my misfortune to promote herself onto a social platform of grace and kindness. I was being used to conjure up images which would elevate her among the local gentry.

My fortnightly visits to the dingy dole office with its barred windows and gritty light were humiliating and degrading. Outside, slumped and stumbling, were the local winos weeping and chanting to themselves, lost in a vapour of alcohol; I wondered if they were praying to be rescued from their enslavement to drink or from the world around them. As I entered the shabby room, I was struck by smells which reminded me of the stale, sticky, urine-soaked carpets on the geriatric wards I worked on as a student nurse. The staff radiated an obsessive mistrust, and I was constantly quizzed about my domestic circumstances and entitlement for unemployment benefit. The threatening atmosphere was intensified as we were circumvallated by hefty barrel-chested security guards, who constantly seemed to be on the verge of resorting to artillery bombardment.

I was interviewed to establish my job options, but the staff only wanted my responses to tick the right boxes for their government statistic spreadsheets. We were viewed as lazy scroungers. They seemed too exhausted and disillusioned to undertake any serious challenge; it was all they could do to string a few monosyllabic sentences together, without even a glance at what I looked like.

We had to waste many hours queuing. There was a violent atmosphere: abuse and fighting were part of the daily routine among the unemployed. These most vulnerable people were anxious and afraid. For many, benefit sanctions threatened their ability to cope with serious hardship. It was fraught and grim; there was no light, no colour. I would stand motionless in this grubby chaos, avoiding any facial expression or eye contact for fear of a scabby tattooed punch or blood-red Doc Martin shin kick. Losing my teeth would be the final straw! Like a human mannequin, I fixed my gaze on the floor. I would then shuffle up the queue, just like patients I had nursed with Parkinson's disease many years before. I deliberately remained withdrawn, hoping not to be noticed.

I felt both sadness and fear towards my kindred unemployed. Sad because many reminded me of Mum during the terrible years she suffered from alcoholism, tortured souls feeling worthless and dejected, powerless victims of desperate circumstances spinning out of control. Each day took them further away from a threshold of hope and prosperity, with drugs and alcohol their only solace.

Being unwanted, unloved, uncared for, forgotten by everybody, I think that is much greater hunger, a much greater poverty than the person who has nothing to eat.
Mother Teresa

But somehow, through the smog and grime of this dismal situation, I was glad of the experience. I knew which side I was on if there were any sides. If power corrupts, then these poor, powerless folk were my unadulterated friends. It was worth meeting these individuals and being reminded of the hypocrisies of our civilised society. My own prejudices were being nailed against the wall for public display by this grim spectacle. Each of us was made to feel like a ragged scavenger desperate for scraps from the state banquet table.

I took time to stand and chat with those selling copies of the Big Issue outside the local supermarket. I realised that becoming homeless can happen to anyone. None of us, from teenagers to the middle-aged, is invulnerable from tumbling into this situation. Redundancy, addiction, domestic abuse, bereavement, mental health problems, poverty ... all can lead to having to live on the streets. Whatever misfortunes befall us in life, we all share the same hopes and dreams.

Was I becoming the victim of my subjugation? Were my circumstances really the result of stigmatisation or was that a delusion? Perhaps they were a direct result of reckless financial management and misfortune. I faced the choice of either accepting and moving on or falling into emotional and psychological dereliction. I could wallow in denial, pretence or projection, transmitting my pain onto others. I could blame others and become quarrelsome and bitter.

I wanted and needed to work. I was determined not to allow this setback to stunt my career, which I had striven so hard to achieve. Something within was fortifying me yet again, giving me the strength to resist and to persevere. This was not a new resolve to overcome adversity, but one I had called on many times since a young child. As a teenager I had crawled out of the gutter; there was no going back. I would preserve and protect my career, and I would not become homeless.

Like a farmer's field, my 17-year-old career had harvested rich, healthy crops. But now it was time to plough this landscape and let it lie fallow, waiting for new life and opportunities to grow. I began to ask myself how I could salvage meaning and purpose from these clumps of clay. What would become of me? Was I destined to become one of the winos from the dole office? I certainly carried the necessary genes, which at any moment could shunt me into their world.

I surrendered my ego to grace, which transformed my pain into the energy of hope and optimism. I accepted the pain of being a human being, and I carried my grief with me as I searched for employment. This would enable me to leave my lodgings and rent a place of my own. I could start again. The obvious choice was to move back home to be with Mum. It would help to alleviate her loneliness and provide me with a place to live. I would be a source of human comfort for her during these desolate days. But I feared going back more than becoming homeless. It would erase all my efforts to create a beautiful melody for my life away from the place I had suffered as a child. All those years of striving would be wiped out if I returned somewhere I only associated with abuse. I had felt an inner certainty that I had been invited to move away from a home and family where I did not belong. I felt sure my purpose was not to go back to live with Mum. Lee was also against this idea. I was puzzled by his resistance. Mum needed someone to help her, and if it wasn't me, who happened to be conveniently available, then who was it?

Lee was cooking up a ruthless and devious scheme. He was plotting his final betrayal, which I never would have imagined nor could ever forget. He was my Judas.

Chapter 17

The Prophecy is Realised
1998 – 2000

When someone lives as he would like to live, combating his own egoism and the continual temptation to inner despair – there is the event of grace.

Daniel O'Leary, *Treasured and Transformed*

I felt infused with an unfamiliar gift of invisible grace, which was carrying me through this strange rocky landscape. Grace was my mat carrier.

I bought myself a new suit and began visiting the local hospitals to introduce myself to the chief nurse. I wanted a job at a similar level to the one I had recently left; I was determined not to be demoted by my redundancy. I decided to develop professional networks, which would put me on their employment radar. This was my attempt to express a genuine interest in each hospital and create a memorable impression.

My endeavours carried echoes of the 17-year-old who had knocked on seaside hotel doors asking for a job back in the summer of 1979. Almost twenty years later, I resembled a Romani gypsy of folklore trying to sell pretty trinkets, and peg dolls to strangers, except I wasn't wearing a colourful costume nor would I cast a curse on those who refused to acknowledge me. After five months of job applications and endless interviews, I was eventually appointed as the clinical lead for professional services with a private hospital in a neighbouring town.

Lee dissuaded me from moving back home to live with Mum, stating his belief that she needed to be independent. In principle, this made sense. We agreed to support her through her grief along with the local priest, a close friend and her neighbours. But this was part of an undeclared cunning plan. Lee and Karen wanted Mum to sell up and move in with them. Strange things started to happen. All of Dad's hard-earned possessions – tools and fishing tackle – were moved to Lee's house. Then Lee and Karen, who could barely command the minimum wage, bought a large detached bungalow in a secluded spot, with extensive mature gardens and panoramic views across the countryside. A friend who was a local builder set about extending the property to include an additional bedroom, sun lounge, bathroom and kitchen. New high-spec cars appeared, along with an oversized caravan and several on – and off-road motorbikes. Karen then gave up work to become a full-time shopaholic housewife. They resembled a couple who had either won the lottery or had inherited a considerable sum of money.

Lee was now 'the man of the house' and his relationship with Mum was becoming toxic. There was an Oedipus–Jocasta complex between them. Mum had always had a fixation on Lee, which deepened after Dad's death. Intense adoration and hero worship dominated her thinking towards him. This made Lee feel special, as he was elevated to his podium of greatness. Similarly, Lee was obsessed with Mum. No longer having to compete with Dad for her affections, he was becoming emotionally dependent on her.

The option of Mum moving in with Lee and Karen was a thorny subject. There was a dark side to this. Lee was still drinking heavily and exhibiting bouts of angry, aggressive behaviour. I tried to persuade her to look for sheltered retirement accommodation close to where I was living. She ignored my pleas and would eventually choose to invest her ruined romantic longings in life with my brother and his wife.

I felt both excited and anxious about my move into private healthcare management. I was excited because it was a means to an end. I immediately rented a flat and moved far away from my sour landlady. But I was anxious because I had switched from the public to the private sector. Would I feel lonely and exiled from the familiarity of the NHS? Or would I embrace this new culture with its emphasis on choice and reduced waiting times?

The values between public and private healthcare seemed perverse, and this troubled me. It was immediately apparent that this private hospital offered a more timely and hospitable service to patients, but there was little evidence that it was more efficient, accountable or medically effective than the public sector. This made me feel professionally insecure. I struggled to appreciate and respect the private sector culture; I only detected cosmetic advantages such as doyleys on meal trays and individual ensuite rooms.

My primary focus was caring for the patients, which at times was tested beyond a threshold I never knew existed until I took this job. The conflict between my clinical priorities and the overriding commercial organisational imperatives was intolerable. The power systems of coercion, punishment, money and status with their capacity for self-serving illusions made me feel vulnerable and suspicious. The veiled greed of the consultants repulsed me as they flattered their patients' egos with their slick and facile bedside charm. I became an immediate target for them to vent their frustrations and tantrums. Many resembled spoilt, ill-mannered children. I quickly had to get used to daily torrents of abusive language and threats to my credibility.

One Friday morning I was summoned to theatre by a female consultant with a reputation for bullying and intimidation. What I saw next brought tears to my eyes. There, in the centre of the room, was a naked elderly man lying unconscious on the theatre table. He was surrounded by the theatre staff of nurses and technicians who, rather than being attentive to the patient's needs, looked more like a troop of idle, hung-over foot soldiers. The consultant was red-faced and raging about a piece of faulty equipment. I was horrified that no one seemed concerned about the dignity of this naked man. It was as though he didn't exist. He was like an unidentified corpse on a mortuary slab. With tears in my eyes, I drowned out the abusive language so that I could offer him a silent prayer for forgiveness. And then, out of the corner of my eye, I saw a missile hurtling towards me. The consultant was so uncontrollably angry that I was ignoring her, that she had launched a piece of equipment at me. I ducked, it missed and clanged on the floor as steel collided with ceramic tiles. I left the room feeling heavy-hearted and ashamed of what this man had been subjected to. We had all failed him and betrayed his trust.

A few days later I took the consultant by surprise during one of her outpatient clinics. I entered her office, closed the door and crept up to her. No words were spoken until I was a few inches away from her face. I was so close she could almost feel my breath. With piercing eyes and a calm voice, I raised a pointed finger to her face, and minaciously told her: 'Never ... never ... never ... subject my patients to such a degrading incident again. I hope I have made myself clear.' With a haughty and valiant stature, like Diana the goddess of the wild and untamed, I glided out of the office knowing I had prevented any further such occurrences. I glanced back one more time to see her face frozen like an arctic Russian lake. We never spoke again. This I was grateful for.

Once more, my life was about to take a dramatic turn. It was June 1999, and I had a week's holiday. Too exhausted to go away, I stayed in my flat to recover, read and go swimming. It was Wednesday night and I had a restless sleep, dreaming that a friend from church was in trouble. The following morning I called her. She was not okay. Driving into work that morning her car had broken down. I arranged for it to be towed to a garage and picked her up from work.

That evening we went out for supper, and it was while we were in the restaurant bar that she introduced me to someone she had known since a young child. His name was David. His family lived next door, so they'd grown up together. Not having seen one another for many years, they had a lot to talk about. I felt excluded and invisible, so I was surprised when David rang me the following evening.

It began as simple friendship, which is all I wanted. I wasn't interested in romance. I lacked the energy, inclination and interest in David for anything other than a casual acquaintance. I was anxiously seeking a new job in the NHS. I also wanted to study again and had enrolled for a masters course in Leadership and Management in the Public Sector.

David was seven years younger. I was a baby boomer and he a Generation X. The age difference was obvious. We had very different outlooks on life and how we each wanted to live out our values. He was strongly conservative while I was a socialist. He was obsessed with image and very materialistic. He had no hobbies other than nights out with the lads followed by a day of nursing a hangover. By contrast, I was unconcerned about image and looking like the majority. I disliked shopping intensely, so much so that if I needed new clothes then I would shop at a local charity shop. I relied on second-hand furniture and saved my hard-earned money. Particularly after my divorce and redundancy, any form of debt was scary. I lived well within my means. I yearned for long solitary walks in nature or spending time alone in my flat reading and listening to music.

So when David began to smother me with expensive perfumes, cards and flowers, I squirmed. I felt he was manipulating me to establish an emotional connection. He was using his charm to try to erode my inhibitions. I started to blame myself, believing it was my fault. I had misled him in some way and given him the wrong impression. I tried to be honest with him by making it clear his affections were unrequited. He responded by hand-delivering a long emotional letter pleading with me to reconsider. He was like a greedy, entitled child who had an insatiable appetite. Would he ever be satisfied?

I began to feel pulled in opposite directions as David repeatedly tugged at my emotions. Looking ahead along my life roadmap, I envisaged living alone and enjoying my independence. I was financially secure again and looking forward to returning to working in the public sector. I enjoyed visiting my circle of friends dating back to my school days, and I was excited about taking up my place on my master's course. Studying at this level was important to me given my poor results at school. Something within remained unresolved. I had to prove myself intellectually.

My life had been spared in spite of many trials and disasters; I was not about to squander it. I had emerged with a stronger sense of freedom and a lust for a dynamic, beautiful life. I felt an urgency, an inner rush to experience life's rich possibilities. Like someone who is aware that death is approaching through illness or old age, I was intensely aware of the brevity of life. I was deeply grateful and appreciative. As the captain of my own ship, I was eager to ensure I remained on a seamless pilgrimage destined for horizons alive with beauty. Would becoming involved with David risk a shipwreck? My voyage could be ruined.

We had nothing in common. I couldn't see any mutually attractive harmonies – culturally, spiritually, financially or politically. He seemed to be desperate to dive into a deep oceanic relationship, and his clinginess was dragging me down behind him. I was choking and feared he was engulfing me emotionally. I was drowning as I gasped for air, clutching the embankment with my fingertips. I was being slowly pulled in, despite my resistance.

If men are from Mars and women are from Venus, then it would take an apocalyptic disaster for our planets to converge.

And they did.

It was a cold February Monday evening in the year 2000 when the past came to occupy the present. Alone in my flat, tired after work, I received some news, news which was always destined to arrive, an inevitable echo from the past. Andrew was dead. My vision that we would be killed in a car accident was, in part, now playing out. He was killed in a crash in the early hours of Sunday morning on a dual carriageway close to where he thought I lived and worked. This was over two hundred miles from where I was now living. He had recently been discharged from a secure psychiatric unit having undergone inpatient treatment for schizophrenia. After drinking heavily on Saturday night, he drove his car and collided head-on with a van. He died instantly. The van driver survived.

The foreboding I'd had way back had arrived. I was not surprised, but it didn't protect me from shock and tears of deep sorrow. As with my father's death, I was sad that Andrew's life had ended in tragedy. I wondered whether he ever found respite from his mental anguish. Had he been able to visit an inner place of serenity and hope? It might be that he had mixed alcohol and drugs to induce a psychedelic world of escape.

Andrew's sister invited me to his funeral. Fine threads of unresolved guilt at my inability to cope with his mental state meant I felt unworthy to attend. If I accepted, would it be to redeem my ego, or perhaps to appease his sister? It would make no difference to Andrew and the passing of his soul. I was struggling to manage my grief after Dad's death and coping with a job that was threatening my integrity. I had little reserve to process the complexity of this sad news. I felt forced into the weighing of consequences; I had to make a choice. Confused and burdened by the fear that I would be hypocritical if I attended, I declined.

On the day of the funeral, I took the day off work and went to sit in my local church. In the dimly lit sacred space, with a heart full of sorrow, I lit a candle for Andrew. In the quietness I offered a private requiem of prayers that his tormented soul was now at peace, free from suffering and brokenness.

There is a necessary light that is only available through darkness that comes in those liminal spaces of birth, death and suffering. You can't learn it in books alone. There are certain truths that can be known only if we are sufficiently emptied, sufficiently ready, sufficiently confused or sufficiently destabilised.

Richard Rohr,
Things Hidden

Chapter 18

A Secret Lie

2000 – 2001

Illusions are to the soul what atmosphere is to the earth. Roll up that tender air and the plant dies, the colour fades ... By the truth we are undone.

Virginia Woolf, *Orlando*

I lied. I lied to my heart. I betrayed my own soul. I feebly gifted my trust to David and abandoned trusting myself. It was a deliberate naivety, which clung to denial and rejected the truth. Silenced by shame I would regret this for many years to come.

Despite our glaring inequalities, I deluded myself so I could please and not disappoint him. His attentiveness and endless gifts – perfumes, jewellery, expensive meals and surprise weekends away – made me feel special at a time when I was wounded from Dad's tragic suicide and Andrew's sudden death. I allowed myself to believe his flattery, hoping it would drown out the guilt that haunted me. I was hooked into a fantasy that we could be happy in a romantic relationship. I shut out my inner voice of wisdom. I hoped this would bring me my heart's desire: a contented, unconditional love. I denied my true feelings for a sphere of illusion and self-deception. It would be to my peril.

Further bad news would deepen my vulnerability and strengthen David's power and control. I was about to be hit by a wrecking ball, knocking me off balance and demolishing any sense of emotional well-being and self-confidence. It was rooted in my adolescent years when I first began my menstrual periods. These periods had always been heavy and painful, and I was now approaching forty. How time crawls when you can't control pain, especially at night. Nothing seemed to alleviate it. It was becoming unbearable.

I was plagued by suffering. It was as if an angry, bloodthirsty reptile was viciously ripping and chewing through the inside of my womb. On the outside, I looked fine, perhaps a little pale and with a bloated tummy, but on the inside, I was in agony. As the bleeding contractions increased, my adjacent bowel would be stimulated, resulting in an explosive evacuation of faeces. When I wasn't bleeding I became constipated, so much so I thought my bowel was obstructed and would burst, if not backflow. I also needed to pee frequently with little holding capacity. My poor bladder control meant my bladder would involuntarily release its contents of warm urine. It was unstable and unpredictable. I could be in the middle of a high street, driving my car, or on a simple countryside walk when, without warning, gush! Like an overflowing reservoir, down it would flow soaking my underwear and clothes.

At work, I was self-conscious as I fretted about staining my clothes with pee or blood or both. I had been appointed to a senior post back in the NHS with lead responsibility for organisational development. This included support for my master's programme. I felt thrilled and privileged. I wanted to prove myself to show I was worthy of this position, but I would sit in meetings distracted by a warm sensation oozing between my inner thighs, as dark red clots of blood were shed from my womb. Despite internal packing and wearing double-thickness long sanitary towels, I would flood whatever was in the way, as I was unable to dam the flow. I worried that when I stood up there would be a pool of blood for all to see on my chair and clothes. I wore dark colours to hide any stains until I could change into fresh clothing. I always sat close to the door for a swift exit should I need to go out. In the summer I was worried about generating a pong, as high temperatures intensify body odours.

At night I sweated, suffering intense abdominal and pelvic pain. Warm blood drenched the sheets as though an artery had been severed, allowing its cargo to be released beneath me. Exhausted and tearful, my only respite was to slump in a hot bath groaning in pain, my mind racing with the remnants of work from the day before blended with thoughts of the day ahead. How would I cope with the pain and loss of sleep?

Like looking out over the sea from the rear of a boat, the disturbed surface with its wave formations telling a story of travel as the vessel moves forward across the water, I realised how my heavy periods had not only stained my clothes, bed linen and furniture, they had also stained my life since I was twelve years old. Heavy bleeding saved me from the hands of a paedophile, but chronic pain, bloating, incontinence, hormone fluctuations and fatigue had also encumbered much of my life. Again I had normalised the abnormal. I was afraid any admission to anything other than wellness would hinder my employment opportunities. I had to work to pay my rent. There was no safety net to catch me.

As I stood in my local chemist's pleading for some new concoction of pain relief, the pharmacist advised me to go to see a doctor. Entrapped by shame and the stigma of my family medical history, I had avoided seeing my GP. In fact, I dreaded seeing a doctor more than the prospect of a painful dental appointment. Until now I'd had no reason as an adult to seek medical attention other than routine checks such as smears. This chronic selective attention and outright denial of illness and pain was about to be shattered. Horrid, uncontrollable pain was forcing me into an unconditional surrender.

It began when on my way to work one spring morning I took a detour to visit my doctor. After recounting my history of pain and heavy blood loss, she decisively prescribed stronger analgesics. Without warning, like a military chief sitting behind her large wooden desk of command and control, she launched a shocking missile. There was no place to hide and avoid this assault. It exploded, with lifelong implications.

'I'm referring you to a gynaecologist who specialises in endometriosis.'

There was no negotiation. This decision was strictly unilateral, with no opportunity for a veto. *Endo* what? Despite my nursing background, this term was unfamiliar. Why does my body need further inspection from another doctor? Why is the physiology of my concealed anatomy not functioning properly? Has it ever functioned correctly? The misery of pain and fear could only be abated by the truth. I had to admit I was suffering and I needed help. I wasn't coping.

A few weeks later I was seen by a professor who was renowned for his work with women with endometriosis. In a grey room surrounded by handwritten notices reminding staff to wash their hands and dispose of clinical waste correctly, he listened to my medical history. As I babbled on I hoped that somewhere within my story there would be something to negate the possibility I had endometriosis. It could just be heavy periods, which would eventually dry up as my body aged. I wanted him to tell me I was wasting his time. Instead he advised me I needed a pelvic laparoscopy. Under a general anaesthetic he would insert a small telescope with a light and a video camera into my abdomen so that he could view the area.

My only question was: 'What is the likelihood of endometriosis?'

'When I go looking for it I usually find it,' was the reply.

I would not see him again until a year later following major surgery.

Twelve weeks after this appointment I underwent my first laparoscopy. My memory is vague but I do recall lying in a hospital bed recovering from the anaesthetic. I was drowsy and bewildered when a young female doctor who had assisted the professor visited me. She seemed nervous, her expression grave, as she explained I had severe advanced endometriosis, which was affecting my ovaries, womb, bowel, bladder and pelvic cavity. She described the implications of this diagnosis in some detail, but I was in shock. I was looking at her but couldn't hear her. It was like watching a television screen with the volume turned off. I was listening inwardly to my own menacing sounds of panic. The only words I heard were something to do with needing major surgery and infertility. A tense chaos filled my veins and infused my body with fear. I felt hot and cold at the same time. My heart was thumping as I was being carelessly tossed around by towering waves of terror.

I desperately wanted to find a desert island of paradise to escape from the threat of this diagnosis, an uninhabited haven of tranquil beauty where I could warm my cold, shaking body in untainted sunshine, where exotic birdsong would soothe my soul and free me from wasteful worry. This was uncharted territory. Up to now I hadn't had to contemplate physical ill health. My world had been consumed by coping with work, Dad's death and Mum's poor mental health. I'd been blind to the signs and symptoms of this disease I'd had since puberty.

As soon as she finished, I hurriedly dressed and packed my small bag. David arrived to take me home.

I began to research what this disease was all about. I learned that endometriosis is a condition in which tissue that normally grows inside the womb grows outside it. The areas of endometriosis bleed each month, resulting in inflammation and scarring. A chronic and debilitating condition that causes painful or heavy periods, it may also lead to infertility, fatigue, and bowel and bladder problems. The more I discovered the more alarmed I became. It is an aggressive, benign neoplastic disease, not cancerous but nevertheless invasive. It deposits and implants endometrial tissue around various parts of the body, and these lesions are at risk of malignant transformation.

Dazed and numb I took a few days off work. I couldn't concentrate, my thoughts preoccupied with this monumental diagnosis. This assailing disease had been active in my body for nearly thirty years and I knew nothing about it. Or did I? Had I subliminally tuned out the truth? Was this quelling of pain, fatigue and stress a form of self-alienation masquerading as work and family pressures? The trauma of Dad's suicide blended with my redundancy had certainly contributed to my denial of my weakening health. At last the growing intensity of physical pain had forced me to confront this. My body was screaming: *You will attend to me. You will comfort and care for me. You can't avoid me any longer.* It was as though my body were a stage, its physical drama a response to my disregard for my health and well-being. My body was tired of self-neglect. I had not been listening to my true inner self, which was in need of nourishing care and rest.

A couple of months later, as I waited to hear about my ensuing surgery, David began to talk about our relationship becoming more committed. He was thinking of proposing to me. Gripped by the prognosis of endometriosis, I talked about the impact this could have on our future and on my ability to conceive. I felt blighted by this horrid invasive disease and how it could prevent me from any prospect of motherhood. My self-esteem once again was being undermined. It was as if an invisible infestation were slowly eating away at my anatomy and inner strength. I was riddled with self-criticism. I saw myself as a worthless, defective, unlovable failure. I couldn't keep Dad alive and fix his depression. Then I lost my job. I was the problematic poor performer.

David and I were on different wavelengths. We were travelling at different speeds in different directions. I was looking at the long-term implications of my diseased body, while David was more concerned about the possibility of a romantic wedding. I feared that his eagerness to get married was more about fulfilling his wish to marry a trophy bride to impress his friends and family. My income and professional status far exceeded his.

Did he fully understand the implications of my diagnosis? I wondered. How would he cope if we were unable to conceive? I wanted us to consider the potential consequences for our relationship. His response was simple. His love for me was far greater than his desire to have children. I felt flattered, believing he was willing to make this sacrifice so he could spend the rest of his life with me. My ego was being soothed and stroked. I allowed myself to venture into this mysterious land of illusion and fantasy. Like a defiant child in a cautionary tale, I disregarded my inner voice of wisdom whispering words of warning. Once again I succumbed to self-deception. I believed the lies I told myself. I was incapable of pulling back from the compulsion to prove my worth.

I can do this. I can have a successful marriage.

The residue from my marriage to Andrew started to bubble and blister beneath the surface of my conscious self. I was painfully reminded of failure – highlighted by his recent tragic death – the guilt of not coping with his mental illness and of giving up so quickly on our marriage. Deluding myself with self-affirmation, I believed I could weaken these painful feelings by proving I was capable of a successful relationship. If I chose not to become more involved with David, it would be giving power and control to the brokenness of my past. I told myself I wouldn't be debilitated by failure. I wouldn't be defined by my history of childhood and adult abuse. In fact, I believed my past had made me strong and resilient.

I rendered myself vulnerable by not being true to myself and not listening compassionately to my wounded heart. Scattered thoughts obscured my judgement. I was lost in a cloud of unknowing. I longed for clarity and certainty, but I was confused. I couldn't see myself married to David, and yet I couldn't see myself alone. I longed to find my soulmate, to be fully known and understood by my kindred spirit, to be accepted for who I was and the lovable, authentic human being I wanted to be. I did not want to be defined by career success, money or outer beauty. I was full of contradictions. I knew that greater achievements at work would not verify my true worth. Yet, at the same time, I was ambitious and determined to achieve academic success.

Should I resist David's desire to marry or should I accept? If I became the good, happy wife, would that mean he would stand by me? I wasn't fully in love with him. It was a partial feeling, as though something was missing. Would I learn to contentedly settle into married life with David? Would he become my heart's desire? Does true love evolve or is it instantaneous? I prayed and prayed for answers and insights. What I was really doing was asking God to take responsibility and rescue me, like a child at night afraid of the monster under the bed. In the darkness of my muddled thoughts, silence prevailed. Was this silence itself the answer? Was my own inner complexity making this decision unnecessarily difficult? Perhaps I should wait and allow time to wander and lead me to a place of empowerment, like a mountain stream which gathers volume and strength with distance. But in reality I felt more like a stream trapped beneath the earth searching for light and air. I was constrained by the heaviness of the damp earth and rocks blocking my way.

Which is the way forward? I felt as though time was running out as tomorrow became my today and today my yesterday. And still there were no clear answers. I had been altered by the pain of Dad and Andrew's deaths. Shame, blame and feelings of failure were blocking my senses.

Chapter 19

The Widowed Spinster
2001 – 2003

Truth is so obscure in these times and falsehood so established, that unless we love the truth we cannot know it.

Blaise Pascal, *Pensées*

David and I were engaged and planning our wedding. He agreed to attend wedding preparation classes with the vicar from my church. I naively believed these would enable us to ensure our decision to marry was embedded in strong Christian values. This investment, while it could not provide a guarantee, would certainly strengthen the possibility of us having a lasting marriage under God's protective wing. We discussed subjects such as commitment, finances, how we would deal with conflict, and our aspirations for the future. And still I ignored how we were made from different stuff. It was becoming more of a business transaction than a love story. At no point did either of us talk about being unsure. Like a train on its metal tracks, our path was fixed; its locomotion was rapidly gaining speed and distance, its destination a church wedding.

The private thoughts of friends were mostly of concern. Some had grave reservations, not only about our compatibility but also about David's character. They were sceptical and felt uncomfortable in his company. He seemed intense and indifferent towards them. But no one found the courage to tell me until many years later. Like me, my friends hoped things would work out happily ever after. Their dark worries lay in hibernation like dormice curled up asleep in their nest next to hazelnuts. The long winter of my soul was encased in a silent frozen climate.

David and I dutifully attended our weekly discussions with the vicar. Then a crater appeared when we were invited to hear our wedding banns, an ancient legal requirement whereby a couple's intention to marry has to be declared in church on three Sundays during the three months before their wedding. A fiery debate erupted when the vicar wanted to refer to me as a 'spinster of this parish' when reading out my name. Had Andrew not died, this particular church would not have permitted the wedding to take place as I would have been classed as a divorcee. Marriage is sacramental, permanent and indissoluble. According to the state, my previous marriage had been ended by divorce, but in God's eyes the bond had not been broken – that happened with Andrew's death. So, I argued, I should be described as a widow. I felt angry and upset. I was being labelled and categorised to solve the complexity of my past and make things tidy for the institution called The Church. I wanted to challenge this spoiling of my identity and the process of stigmatising me.

The institutions that claim to represent God ... have to earn their right to a hearing by the value of what they say, and not by virtue of who is saying it.

Richard Holloway,
Dancing on the Edge

Eventually, believing I would never be anything other than what society was telling me I was, and that to be accepted and loved I had to adjust to others, I agreed to be labelled a spinster.

At dawn on the morning of the wedding, as dew was dancing on the edge of spring petals and leaves, I went swimming. I needed the womb-like feeling of being immersed in warm, clear water. I had spent the evening before alone in my flat anxious about how I was going to adapt to David moving in. As I soaked away the final hours of my divorced spinsterhood in a long bubble bath I felt no excitement at the prospect of being together full-time. I knew I would grieve for the silent beauty of living alone. In the depths of peaceful solitude I had found the gracious presence of God. In this sacred space, inaccessible to the fantasies of my own making, was an invisible light which vanquished the darkness and cruelty of my life. I was trading this for a husband I was unsure about. I wasn't strong enough to disappoint others. I believed if others were happy this would protect and shield me from the anguish of mourning. I could escape enduring shame, grief and pain in a marriage which would bring love, support and loyalty. I could rid myself of the negative connotations attached to the label 'divorcee' so I would be socially acceptable. I was desperately seeking the good opinions of others.

Apart from friends, only Lee came to the wedding. Karen chose not to come and Mum was too ill. Her capricious mental health remained fragile; she was lost in grief and misery. I had hoped that just for one day she could be emotionally available for me. I had offered to take her shopping for an outfit and to find her somewhere comfortable to stay, but it was futile. She was too damaged.

Lee arrived at my flat at about 10am. He began to drink cans of lager and hung out of one of the large sash windows to smoke. I was worried I would reek of tobacco but was loath to challenge him for fear of an angry reaction. At last Jamie my hairdresser suggested he should slow down on the booze and go outside if he wanted a cigarette. Lee ignored him, muttering some obnoxious insult about the sexual identity of male hairdressers.

So, like Cinderella wearing a new pair of shoes and a ball gown, off I went to the wedding. Like Cinderella, I believed this wedding would change my life. It did, but it was never going to be a fairy-tale ending.

We arrived at the church knowing all the guests would be seated, a theatre audience anticipating a performance. As I reluctantly linked my arm through Lee's, I wished it were Dad beside me. My eyes filled with tears. Like the feet of ancient times, smiling through sorrow and carrying an invisible pain, we walked slowly down the aisle towards the white-robed vicar. The last time I had walked down an aisle like this was at Dad's funeral. To my right was a large pipe organ with scores of moving parts and a wind-breathing system integrated into a complex machine. It produced sounds which imitated the instruments in an orchestra, as it spoke a musical language of beauty, hope and love.

I was surrounded by an excited mosaic of expectant faces. Unlike a real theatre audience, each of these folk hid their true feelings. They hoped it would be happily ever after, but feared our marriage was doomed to fail and that it would only be a matter of time. I too felt like a member of an audience, helplessly watching myself living out a life destined for more unhappiness. My willingness to renounce the truth would be costly. I was robbing myself of my own essential integrity, which was a pearl of great price.

Witnessed by friends and family and in the presence of God, David and I made our wedding vows in this large Anglican church. These promises were sacred and binding and I took them seriously. I believed God would ensure we would make one another happy and fulfilled.

The wedding was then celebrated at a hotel with food and wine. The evening submitted to the blaring sounds of a disco.

Following a short cold spring English honeymoon I went into hospital for planned surgery. The operation would be major and lengthy. I was fortunate this pioneering surgeon was skilled at laparoscopic surgery, which meant I would not require an abdominal wound other than small keyhole incisions.

I was admitted on a Sunday and spent the evening sitting in the small, austere hospital chapel. In prayerful contemplation I began to unclutter my mind from its daily restless distractions, banishing petty worries created by my own self-absorption. An inner stillness began to fill my mind, freeing me from anxiety and doubt. A serene white presence embraced me as I sat alone, as steady as the stars in a winter's night. In this state of mysterious tranquillity I felt a perfect peace, the peace of God which passes all understanding, that keeps our hearts and minds in the knowledge and love of God.

I woke from four hours of surgery to the shrill sound of a machine calling out for assistance. I was alone in a dark room with clear plastic lines inserted into various parts of my body. Some were transporting fluids in, while others provided a route out for urine and blood. My oxygen supply was being supplemented through a green plastic facemask. It was night-time and an efficient but uncommunicative nurse visited me hourly to record my body's reaction to surgery.

My only visitor the following day was dapper David. He swaggered into my room looking immaculate and smelling of expensive cologne. He carried no flowers or card. A few days before my admission to hospital he had purchased his first sports car and he had spent the earlier part of the day speeding through country lanes with his kid brother. He was exuberant and preoccupied with his new toy; it was as if he had spent the afternoon at a theme park.

I lay in my haze of morphine, too sore to move, vulnerable and exposed, as when the tide goes out leaving behind a chewed shoreline. I felt like a forgotten starfish stranded in a rock pool waiting for the sea to return and carry me away. Wounded and anxious, I experienced a moment of sudden enlightenment. As I watched David from my bed, I realised the truth about our relationship. It was crystal clear. I wasn't being cherished by a loving, supportive husband – a grown-up. We were not in love with one another, but had been beguiled by the idea of love and marriage.

Desperate to honour God and my vows, and determined not to fail, I had chained myself to the theory of marriage instead of embracing the reality. Had I made a big mistake in marrying this man? My internal landscape was mangled both by surgery and by my unfulfilled emotional needs. Like Ingrid Bergman in the film *Gaslight* I'd fallen for a good-looking chap who displayed classic signs of narcissism. I'd rushed into marriage after a whirlwind romance, while I was still recovering from Dad and Andrew's deaths and the loss of my job. I hadn't had time to process the speed and savvy with which David had wooed me.

This disastrous misjudgement was rooted in my childhood where I had learned to be brave, congenial and helpful when in fact I felt frightened, sad and angry. No one ever taught me how to learn from and embrace these emotions. As a consequence I could not rely on my internal warning system to avoid a confident, well-groomed, expensively dressed man with a history of mistreating women. It was a pattern which would last for many years as he instinctively recognised my high tolerance for abuse and how he could use it for his own self-gratification.

My recovery was initially uneventful. I saw the surgeon once as he stood at the foot of my bed, muttered a few inaudible words and scurried off to his next patient. No one warned me about possible post-operative long – and short-term complications. A brief conversation with his surgical assistant told me of the difficulty they had in removing the deposits of endometriosis, but the operation had been a success.

About three months after my surgery I began to feel unwell, experiencing oscillating moods, insomnia, night sweats and fatigue, with unresolved urinary and bowel problems. I was referred back to see a gynaecologist who explained that I was experiencing a surgically induced menopause at the age of 39. No one had warned me this could happen after my operation despite my womb and ovaries being intact. I asked about the possibility of becoming pregnant and was told categorically that due to my age, and more specifically the endometriosis, I was unlikely to conceive, and if I did I had a high chance of miscarriage. The consultant was cold and dispassionate. I was devastated. I staggered away from the appointment carrying this hidden creeping disease like a drunk from a lunchtime drinking binge. I didn't know what to think or feel. My soul cried out to God in anguish.

I still believed that God is at the heart of everything, closer to me than I am to myself. So why all the inner chaos, confusion and pain? Every aspect of my being was challenged: my self-worth, my femininity, my profession, my marriage, my faith. It must be my fault, I concluded. I am not worthy of becoming a mum. My body is too old and diseased. My family medical history and diminished self-esteem were my witnesses. My self-contempt rose up triumphantly to solve the problem. Ruthlessly heaping blame onto myself I was able to justify the loss of the chance to try for a baby.

But just as the flick of a switch illuminates a dark room, so too did my whole being become instantly awakened to the intense desire to be a mother. Every cell in my body was aching for a child. I couldn't face commonplace occurrences involving mothers, babies and fathers. Everyone seemed to be blessed with parenthood. Even going to a supermarket could induce tears as I watched families shopping for groceries. Everyday life was an ordeal: colleagues taking their first, second or third episode of maternity leave, invitations to christenings, and then the agony of Christmas, which is all about the baby Jesus. At night I would dream of holding a baby in my arms and kissing her sweetly. My dream was my prayer, a prayer of concealed hope and an ingrained yearning like swirls and veins running through a piece of ancient marble.

I was clinging to hope, however false, however slight. I needed a fragile beam of light in so much darkness. I felt like two people: one who knew it was unlikely I would have a baby, and the other faithfully believing my prayer would be granted. As I indulged my dreams of motherhood, I tuned out one essential element: to conceive requires two people, male and female. I gave no thought to David being a suitable father for my child.

I can't quite recall when David's attitude to me started to change, but it was within a year of getting married. His charm had faded; the supply of excessive gifts and flowers had dwindled. He sulked and intimidated me with his brooding silences, ignoring me for hours on end, often into the next day. He had mood swings and emotional outbursts, constantly wanting to be the centre of attention. Obsessed with appearances, he had little self-awareness. At work he was repeatedly rejected for promotion and ignored by his colleagues. At home there was always tension. Like Michael Moran in John McGahern's *Amongst Women*, he began to display a bitter and jealous tyranny. Everything seemed to irritate him. His inner turmoil meant he was never at ease, especially with me. At times he seemed to despise me, mocking my natural disposition of playful eccentricity and my unwillingness to conform to social pressure imposed by fashion and materialism. He constantly reminded me of my shortcomings. These could be anything from the quality of my ironing, to my cooking, driving or style of dress. I often felt guilty and inadequate.

I wondered how he would feel if I threatened to leave him. Like Rose Brady, Moran's wife, I had married a man who is 'one sort of person when he's out in the open among people – he can be very sweet – but that he's a different sort of person altogether behind the walls of his own house.' In a climate of fear and doubt, he was becoming a psychological terrorist whereby everything was always my fault; I was always to blame for everyday domestic mishaps. Unprovoked hostility was manifested in eyes rolling, tutting, slamming doors and throwing objects at walls. I tried hard not to confront or contradict him for fear of reprisal. I became complicit with his behaviour believing my loyalty, patience and tolerance were honouring my marital vows and Christian values of love and devotion. As sure as an ancient tide beneath the guidance of a silvery moon returns to her shoreline, so too did I remain loyal to David, regardless of the topography of our marriage. I became blindly subservient as I pandered to his every whim. I wanted nothing more than to please him and to please God.

Then the big hook was cast in my direction and I bit. I received a call at work from David's supervisor. He had been sent home, as he wasn't coping emotionally. He was depressed. I tried to call him but he didn't answer the phone. Frantic, I tried again and again. I became more and more afraid and vulnerable as memories of Dad's last hours blew across my soul. Like a desert sandstorm, strong gusts of wind carrying painful rocks obscured my vision and ability to think straight. Eventually he answered. He sounded calm and relaxed. He was calm and relaxed because he had been relieved from the responsibilities of work. In the privacy and secrecy of our home he was indulging in an addiction which would seal our demise.

That evening, after a long conversation, we decided he needed professional help. He admitted he had been depressed for many years and had just been waiting for the right time to let it out. He'd been looking for something to empty his depression into. And he found me. I was his emotional dumping ground. The legacy of Dad and Andrew's deaths was a recurring pattern of behaviour which would endure for many years. David exploited my fear of suicide and mental illness and my eagerness to absorb guilt and accept responsibility. He took advantage of my earning ability, which far exceeded his. I was the goose that laid the golden eggs: the more I provided for him the more he wanted. He was never satisfied.

We spent a fortune on counselling, both individual and marriage, as well as buying cars, clothes, jewellery and other meaningless material possessions. We ate out at expensive restaurants, often to impress his friends, and went on many holidays. And yet he was still unhappy and dissatisfied. All the attention was on him and there seemed no room for me. I persevered, slowly being ground down on the lathe of time. The yuppie phenomenon, which seduced so many, upset the rhythm of our relationship. David was obsessed with money and prestige: having a beautiful body, being well-dressed, luxuriating in material comfort. His unashamed ambition was to set himself apart and above others. I was his means to accomplish this, as well as being a possession he could display like an expensive piece of bespoke furniture.

Alienated by life at home, I turned away from hopelessness and threw myself into my work and MA studies. My career success increased exponentially; the higher I rose up the echelons of the NHS the more confident and self-assured I became. I was able to cope with ever-increasing complexity and responsibility. I thrived on the day-to-day challenges of leading a senior team in one of Europe's largest organisations. This compensated for the converse conditions at home, where I remained insecure and uncertain. Within a year of my surgery I graduated with a distinction in my Master of Arts in Leadership and Management. The standard of my academic work generated articles and research which were published internationally. On the day of my graduation ceremony I wanted to return to my old school and boast of my achievements to those sadistic teachers. Like an excited cheerleader I wanted to jump, dance and parade around the building gleefully showing off my certificate. Instead, I was content with an inner sense of healing and reconciliation with my wayward youthful spirit. The teenager who was led to believe she was a failure had recovered her lost years of self-development and learning, as God's dream for her was steadily unfolding. I felt intellectually transformed, free from the ghosts of my absent childhood schooling. I had finally silenced the voices of cruel teachers.

As my MA studies ended I mourned their loss. Like the mother of an empty nest I felt increasingly lonely and lacking purpose. Throughout my studies I had flourished as I nurtured projects and assignments which were of particular interest to me. It was like losing a faithful friend and companion. This loneliness was exacerbated by David's growing dominance and control. I was made to feel like an idiot at home, undeserving of warmth and affection. Sadly, I began to believe him.

I had to get out and away. I was suffocating. I felt diminished and worthless. I was being slowly strangled by my own failings. So I was to make two significant changes, which would enhance the texture of my life. I was determined to find my inner peace. There was a small light and a gentle whisper within, beckoning across my river of suffering towards a horizon of still beauty and peace.

Despite all of this pain, I could not let go of wanting a baby. Like the homeless person who shoplifts to survive, I was desperate, and desperate people do desperate things.

Chapter 20

Sophia

2003 – 2004

The secret we keep forgetting, when the empty winds of despair blow across the winter wastes of our souls, is that it is always and only within these barren places that we can ever find the transforming comfort of a divine summer. Only then are we aware of God's astonishing bounty.

Daniel O'Leary, *Treasured and Transformed*

I needed another way of living. I was lonely and oppressed. David and I didn't confront our relational problems and misgivings and we avoided dealing with the roots of our mutual unhappiness. My senses felt dulled and segregated from the natural world; we seemed surrounded by consumerism, wealth and competitive social climbers. I needed to be free of the ego-serving trappings of greed and materialism. My soul needed to breathe and be stripped of illusions and pretence.

We moved to a small village in the countryside, leaving a busy urban lifestyle in search of a simpler existence closer to nature. I instantly fell in love with the house and the beauty of its surroundings. Panoramic views stretched undisturbed across wide, open fields, home to sheep, horses and cattle. Earthy country smells lifted my senses as they became the threshold to my soul. The calls of migrating geese carried my imagination to places of wild beauty.

I had arrived. I had been called to a place where I could breathe again. Exhausted by the demands of work and the strain of coping with David's controlling dependency, my soul had been gracefully guided to a secret, undiscovered sanctuary. It was as though I had been lost in a desert and had miraculously arrived at a lush oasis. There was an abundance of fresh, cool water to quench my parched interior, succulent fruits to provide vitality, sweet fragrance of blossom and colourful exotic birds praising the divine. The clear blue shimmer of heaven was smiling all around me. A vibrant energy was released as I discovered the simple joy of toiling to landscape our garden beneath the colours of rainbows above, in the company of dancing butterflies and chirping birds beneath floating fluffy clouds. As the dark soil softly slipped through my fingers and blackbirds waited patiently for worms, my soul danced to a tune called equanimity. Deep within there was a rhythm which was pre-tuned to the natural world, a longing to respond to nature. Layer upon layer of hurt began to heal as I knelt in the dirt to clear spaces for seedlings, bulbs, trees and shrubs.

These intense physical, emotional and spiritual experiences were a living encounter with God's grace and beauty. Never before had I felt so alive. The canticle of St Francis of Assisi became a living experience for me. I was in love with the beauty of Mother Earth, Brother Sun, Sister Moon, the stars, wind, air, the weather's mood, Sister Water and Brother Fire and nature's creatures.

But my social isolation bothered me. David made it so difficult for friends to visit I felt at times I was living in a dead end where the only life was the two of us. If I did encourage friends to come to our home he would either disappear for the day or stay upstairs sulking and brooding. Once the visitors had departed he would verbally attack and blame me for the misery I had caused, accusing me of unreasonable, selfish behaviour. His bullying tantrums and negative put-downs exerted an unwanted control. Eventually I stopped inviting friends as the repercussions left me feeling wretched.

Like a recurring nightmare, his emotional absence, manipulation and callousness echoed my father's behaviour. Why oh why had I married a man I didn't love and who didn't love me? Why hadn't I recognised the signs after years of living with Dad? I carried constant anxiety in my gut; like a rodent it gnawed away at my inner strength and self-esteem. Within me was a grave of guilt, shame and despair as I lowered my expectations to the point David could not disappoint me. This became a deliberate coping strategy. I believed I was unworthy of anything better. I did not deserve a tender-hearted, loving relationship.

My poor opinion of David was confirmed when I found shocking images on my computer, which revealed his clandestine pursuits. He was addicted to internet pornography. Sordid, unimaginable images of girl-on-girl sex gave him thrills and pleasures far beyond my world. I was devastated as I realised why he was so cold towards me and why I felt he was disgusted by me. He was programmed to respond to much higher levels of erotic stimulation. Or was I so undeserving of love and respect, he was unable to resist? He had hidden his addiction to powerful sexual imagery from me. He blamed his inability to show affection on his depression, telling lies about why he was so physically withdrawn. Once again, David was in control. His unwillingness to accept responsibility was destroying everything around him. Every particle in my body was outraged. I was livid. Tormented by memories of my father racing off to strip clubs, I felt raw with pain, degradation and betrayal. David's blatant lies and ugly lusting after other women's bodies made me feel sick. He was vulgar and warped.

This was his penultimate crime against me.

I wept and wept alone, too embarrassed to talk to anyone about this. Imprisoned by shame and shackled by the shock of his sleazy betrayal, my body and soul were infused with despair. Was this my fault? Was I really so unattractive and unloving that he had to resort to other women? A vicious jagged spear had torn through my flesh and pierced my heart. There was no sense of remorse or guilt from David. There was no concern about hurting me.

Like a moth flying into a flame, he was drawn to horrid adulterous images; nothing else could satisfy him, they owned his eyes and his heart. He was willing to risk our marriage so that he could dance once more to the haunted music with his fatal beloved pornography. For many years I would remain tormented and lonely from my discovery of his virtual infidelity. But there is no betrayal, loss or despair which is final. I resisted my primary feeling, which was to punish him, and I chose to help him. Believing my loyalty, compassion and devotion may reward me with reciprocal love, I imposed heavy conditions on our fragile marriage. It was an impossible dream.

David received more counselling, medication, time off work and marriage guidance. He even came with me to see our local priest. We sat with an uncomfortable separation between us in the austere surroundings of the vestry. I felt broken and sad. The priest emanated compassion and love with his gentle voice and non-judgemental words. His prayers stirred a sense of peace and acceptance deep within me. David made a full confession, asking God for forgiveness. It was as if we were taking part in a play, with David taking the leading role and the priest and myself the supporting actors. David acted out his story of shame and remorse like an innocent child wanting his parents to reassure him. His banal and predictable script didn't correlate with a man who was infinitely more devious and complicated. I was suspicious. He rarely presented the story for what it was. Instead he would describe a selective version of events bound in empty promises. So candles were lit and prayers said and off we went again on a merry-go-round of lies and deceit, as David pretended to abandon his addiction.

I was broken and desolate. Fractured parts within seemed to be withering. But without this brokenness I couldn't change and without change I couldn't thrive. I shared my misery with my faithful, constant garden, which became the essence of my strength and my mat carrier. Lost and lonely, I knelt in the damp soil and prayed for help. I endlessly dug, planted, fed, and watered, but emotionally I felt like a piece of arid wasteland, starved of care and attention. Destructive insects were eating away at my feelings, just like the plants in my garden. I longed for a warming sun and the nourishment of love.

But gradually the friendship with my garden and all her beauty enabled me to cope with this river of suffering. I could rest in the arms of her shade suffused by the scent of beautiful flowers, listening to exquisite birdsong. There was a divine sacred presence with an invisible embrace sheltering me from hurtful images. The wisdom of the land combined with a radiant light seemed to impart hope and transformation. My prayers were being listened to. It was a unique kind of inner brightness, a luminous darkness.

Disillusioned by organised religion, dogma and contemporary culture, I went on a two-day spiritual retreat in search of inspiration and direction. I was introduced to the notion of spiritual companionship, based on the writings of twelfth-century Cistercian abbot Aelred of Rievaulx. This course precipitated the second profound change I made to improve my life. Throughout this time away from home I began to realise how I needed to protect myself.

Make sure you have a 'soul-friend'. This is a person who will never deceive you, flatter you or wish anything for you but your true happiness. Your soul-friend will listen to you. Like a wise guardian angel, your soul-friend will always walk with you, defend you and love you. You are the most important person in your life.

Daniel O'Leary,
Prism of Love

I spoke to the chaplain at the hospital I was working in. We prayed together before he introduced me to Clare, a woman who would become my spiritual companion. For the following seven years, until she returned to her home in the United States, Clare helped to carry me across many rivers of further suffering. She taught and guided me with her intrinsic authority, becoming a model of selfless love and supportive understanding. She respected my doubts, fears and anger, as well as my desire for truth, justice and compassion.

Clare was my mat carrier. Through our loving friendship I developed a profound connection with God. My life filled with reverence, beauty, wonder and awe as Clare graciously helped me navigate through life's wayward storms. In the cellar of my lost dreams and memories we delicately searched for clues and glimpses of God's saving grace, love and mercy. Like prudent archaeologists sifting through layers of history, we recovered and analysed stories and images from my inner landscape. My awareness of life in God expanded, as wisdom and spiritual insights dawned within my consciousness. My spiritual musings enabled me to grow and develop; I felt I was on a cherished intimate journey with God.

> *God is closer to us than we are to ourselves.*
> *God is a mystery of silence and intimacy. God is*
> *incomprehensible and ineffable, far beyond our wildest*
> *imaginations, yet nearer to each of us than we are to*
> *ourselves.*
>
> **Ilia Delio,**
> The Humility of God

I wouldn't give up on becoming what I could be.

It was now November 2003. Since my surgery two years earlier my periods had been erratic so missing a period was not unusual, but it was significant when it coincided with other symptoms: sore, tender breasts, fatigue and nausea. My prayers had been answered! I was pregnant. I was going to be a mum. I would be able to put right all the wrongs that had happened to me during my blighted childhood. How could it be when we had only had sex once in the past twelve months, I was 41 years old, had endometriosis and was supposedly menopausal? It was a miracle.

While I wanted to shout out to the world how blissfully happy I was, David seemed shocked and bewildered. He had accepted the doctor's sentence of a childless future where I hadn't. I resisted being affected by his muted response as my emotions soared to the heavens.

Perhaps he was afraid that he would have to grow up and become a responsible adult. Might he be jealous of the affection the baby would attract, his inner narcissist whispering lies of rivalry and envy?

There was a small miracle being nursed inside my womb. I was elated. At last I felt worthy, worthy of this great privilege. There was nothing finer, nothing more beautiful and nothing else worth living for.

I told close friends and colleagues. They rejoiced in my good news. We could all share in my miracle. The eternal mystery of God had surprised me; like Mary, I felt as if I had been visited by an angel and granted my soul's desire. God is not remote or distant, dwelling only in tabernacles and temples of stone, but near to me. God is nearer to me than I am to myself. God is always present within me even when I am unable to be present for God; She is smiling and waiting to embrace me despite my confusion, bewilderment, anger and sadness.

I imagined my baby to be a daughter. I called her Sophia, which means wisdom.

Unlike all recent appointments with my GP, Dr Wong, I remember almost skipping to announce my good news. All the pessimistic predictions were wrong. 'I'm pregnant and it's a miracle!' I wanted to shout. She confirmed that I was pregnant and a further appointment was made for a scan. I would be able to see my baby and hear her heartbeat.

During those few weeks of sheer joy I never once thought the worst. This wonderful gift of becoming pregnant was such a strong and powerful life force, I was incapable of thinking about anything other than the day when I would hold my baby.

A few days before I was due to attend the hospital for the scan, I woke with the most horrific abdominal pain, pain which I didn't realise was humanly possible. I was bleeding. I was writhing in anguish and fear. My worst fear. An ambulance was called and I was swept away to the nearest hospital. I was losing my baby. This human being who might have lived would not. I clung to the sides of the bed almost too afraid to breathe as an ultrasound scan was used to search for life. Tears poured down my face as I prayed the scan would convey the heartbeat of life, but there was nothing.

I cried out to the hospital staff demanding to see their chaplain, only to be told he was in a meeting but would call in later. I was so angry. Attending a meeting was more important than a woman losing her unborn child. 'Later' never came.

Lifeless inside my dark red womb, Sophia clung onto me even in death; she was reluctant to leave me as my womb held onto her. This inner sanctuary was her home.

I would never kiss her. I would never hold her. But she would live on in my soul. I would never forget her short life within me; I would always remember her and celebrate her birthday, which would have been 1 July 2004.

As I lay wounded and inert with my legs apart, I granted permission for her warm remains to be removed from me. Using a cold metal instrument a doctor gently eased her from her dark sanctuary into the light of an unlived world. She was silently placed in a cold metal dish and taken away. I was never given the chance to see her. It was as if I wasn't there. I decided I might as well not exist. I felt too devastated to believe anything else.

I refused to leave until I saw the chaplain. Empty hours of waiting slipped by and no one came. Eventually I was told he wouldn't be coming as he'd had to go to administer the last rites to another patient. I raged and screamed. I felt abandoned by the church, God and myself.

A kiss never kissed
A dream never wished
An embrace never felt
A beauty never beheld
A tear never cried
A life never tried
A love never shown
A child never known

Anne M.R. Chiles,
'Lost Love'

Over the weeks and months that followed I felt as though I were living between the earth's atmosphere and outer space, an impervious place of nothing and nowhere. There was a dark void within and outside of me. Sadness, anger and guilt were constantly tormenting my broken heart. The pain of this unlived dream was disproportionate to the length of time I was pregnant.

It was all my fault. I was to blame. I wasn't worthy of becoming a mother. The genes any child of mine could inherit had to be halted. This genetic legacy had to stop, and it was stopping here with me. All the atrocities I had been subjected to within my family couldn't be allowed to afflict another generation. I couldn't bestow on my unborn child a future of alcoholism, suicide, depression and violence. It was as if I were in a furnace of affliction carrying an awful transferable disease for which there was no vaccination. I would be the author of my child's future misery.

No one seemed to understand. Other women would say, 'It's just a miscarriage.' Many friends refused to disclose their pregnancies until the end of the first trimester, after which a miscarriage is far less likely, so in the event of the loss of the baby they could pretend nothing had happened. Stories of friends depositing their unborn down the loo, mistaking a miscarriage for a heavy period, disgusted me. I was appalled to discover how miscarriage is trivialised and shrouded in silence and shame.

Never would I sing her a lullaby, never would I make her a birthday cake nor know her first day at school ... her first steps ... her first words ... Never would I forget her partial life, which would stay with me deep within my soul until the sun refused to shine.

In the midst of this I was concerned about Mum. Lee and Karen were moving her to live with them, three hundred miles away from her hometown, where she had lived for most of her life. I was anxious she would become increasingly dependent and socially isolated. I was unconvinced my brother and his wife had sufficient intellectual and emotional resources to cope with Mum's vulnerability. Their motives seemed to be driven by greed for money and not out of genuine care and compassion.

Mum and her daughter-in-law had quarrelled for many years. Mum believed Karen didn't love and appreciate Lee. She thought theirs was a marriage of convenience, a joyless relationship of false smiles and harboured resentments. Mum's embittered attitude towards Karen was malicious and vengeful. She seemed deliberately intent on engendering mistrust and conflict. This was a dark repetitive behaviour pattern from her own marriage. Mum was threatened by Karen's youth and jealous of her marriage to Lee. Lee was the husband Mum had never had. They were entangled in some kind of oedipal symbiosis. They could neither live with nor live without each other. It reminded me of Mrs Morel and her son Paul from *Sons and Lovers*, it was unhealthy and obsessive.

She's not like an ordinary woman, who can leave me my share in him. She wants to absorb him. She wants to draw him out and absorb him till there is nothing left of him, even for himself (or me).

D.H. Lawrence,
Sons and Lovers

Chapter 21

An Invisible Loss
2004 – 2008

Death is no enemy, but the foundation of gratitude, sympathy and art. Of all life's pleasures, only love owes no debt to death.

Linda Kohanov, *The Tao of Equus*

Christmas 2004 was empty. Surrounded by images of children, from baby Jesus to the quintessential family sharing Christmas together, I withdrew deep into my inner recluse sending no cards and giving no gifts. There was a darkness deep inside me which matched the dark outside. No tinsel, baubles and twinkling fairy lights were used to decorate our home. The house was devoid of any outward signs of joy. Christmas was all about babies, mums, dads, brothers and sisters. All around were nativity plays, small children carrying their Christingle oranges, and carols depicting wonderful scenes of the birth in the stable. I couldn't bear to visit a supermarket and be drowned by relentless crass Christmas songs, repugnant wasteful consumerism and human greed. I couldn't face it. I felt barren and hollow. I felt intense emotional pain and mental misery.

Christmas passed unnoticed, blurred and empty. I felt as though I didn't fit in. Once again I was on the edge, the edge of motherhood, my life-denying, oppressive marriage and my estranged family. At work I seemed surrounded by younger mums and pregnant colleagues. As their manager I had to authorise maternity leave. It was torture.

I felt as if I was on the road to nowhere as I mourned my invisible loss. There was no grave to visit and place flowers, no funeral to celebrate Sophia's short few weeks of life, where poems could be read and ancient hymns sung.

The pain and adversity did not bring David and me closer. Instead, we moved further apart. It somehow didn't matter. I didn't want him near me. He was ever more withdrawn. My suspicions of his retreat into the world of pornography tormented me, as he seemed to spend endless hours alone consoling himself with a computer. I was too tired and sad to confront him again. Given his persistent angry denial, it seemed futile to ask yet again for the truth.

I daydreamed about my lost pregnancy. As the months went by I imagined how my body would be changing. Visions of a small child in a cot, arms outstretched, wanting me, needing me, and giving my life purpose and meaning drifted into my consciousness. By night I could hear her calling out 'Mummy! Mummy!' Even God didn't understand. How could he? Jesus was a man not a woman.

As the date of her birthday arrived, I bought her a card: *To a very special daughter*, and planted a tree, an amelanchier, which in spring gave out snowy blossom as a sign of hope after the desolation of winter, and then radiant deep red colours in the autumn when it was the anniversary of losing her. I wondered what her favourite toy, nursery rhyme and bedtime story would have been. Who would have been her best friend?

Confronted with the truth of our failing marriage, I decided to resist the urge to try for another baby. I surrendered to my circumstances. I pieced together a broken picture. David was physically and emotionally cold towards me. I was the main breadwinner and we had a huge mortgage; he was regularly off work sick and we were spending beyond our means. If I were to conceive, it would be a path I probably couldn't cope with, given my ageing, diseased body and the state of our relationship. There was of course another scenario, which was to divorce David and search for another partner willing to father a child. At best this was untenable, at worse crazy.

I chose to remain childless. This was one of the toughest decisions I have ever made. I was struggling with a fear of abandonment and unbearable physical and emotional burdens, but I felt in control. I was making the decision; it was not being imposed on me. It was as though the yearning stranger in me was telling me: 'This is for your sake.' There was a secret path before me where hidden treasures were yet to be revealed. I felt as though I was being guided by a prophetic whisper and I had a deep knowing that I was being taken care of. My soul was taking care of me. My soul was my secret shelter, my inner mat carrier.

I slowly let go of the passion and addictive compulsion to have a child. There was no particular day or date to recall. I trusted that all would be well, but it would require patience and perseverance. I sensed a deeper and higher purpose to my life ahead. It was not without pain and grief, which seemed to own my days and nights. But God sends what we need – never in a hurry, but always in perfect time. I sensed the fulfilment of God's dream for my life was gently dawning, even though the reality seemed just the opposite.

I was asked to apply for an innovative new post at a northern university, a post which had recently been created in response to service needs. I would be responsible for developing leadership and management programmes for multi-disciplinary teams. It was an exciting opportunity and felt like a return to a vocation: the world of teaching.

To seek enlightenment, intellectual and or spiritual; to do good; to love and be loved; to create and to teach: these are the highest purposes of mankind. If there is meaning to life, it lies here.

George Monbiot,
How Did We Get Into This Mess?

I was thrilled. It was a welcome change. And so I switched my loyalties from the NHS to the world of academia, designing and delivering a range of courses from under – to post-graduate. I thrived on the students' enthusiasm and spirit of enquiry.

The job was flexible enough to consider having a new family member: a dog. I needed something other than students and garden plants to nurture. At times I was afraid I could easily slip into an unrecoverable mental illness if I didn't honour my need to care for another living being. The darkness of not loving frightened me. I feared that if I did not love then I wouldn't exist. I was plagued by recurring images of my placement on the geriatric ward when I was a student nurse. One of the patients was an elderly lady called May, who had dementia. She wore a hand-knitted woollen hat and at times was aggressive. A member of staff who was on maternity leave came to visit her colleagues with her newborn baby. May saw them and instantly became lucid. Her aggressive nature evaporated as she mellowed to a gentle spirit. Transfixed with the beauty of this baby, she suddenly said, 'Them that can 'av 'em don't want 'em, and them that can't do!' She walked away, grateful for her brief encounter, smiling and peaceful. I remember wondering why this scene was so vivid and profound. I asked myself, was I to become one of those that couldn't? It was like a prophecy, which had now come to pass.

As if by magic, help came bouncing along and I called her Bethany. She arrived in spring and we immediately bonded. It was love at first sight. She was more beautiful than beauty. I loved her instantly, with a love so pure and deep I never wanted to let her go. Bethany was a puppy retriever with fluffy fur and deep, dark sensitive eyes. She was playful, witty and loyal. Bethany saved me. I felt as though I was experiencing a resurrection. My feelings of worthlessness and emptiness were being transformed into a healing love. I was no longer emotionally bankrupt and craving affection, but was bursting with excitement and deep gratitude to the divine. I was trusting God more than ever.

Bethany was my mat carrier and I discovered a grace and companionship like never before. She knew just what I needed. Bethany was sensitive, patient, loving and kind. She embodied unconditional love and divine beauty. My innermost and outermost sense of God's divine presence was restored with unfaltering illumination. It was immediate and unrelenting. Bethany had no moods, was always pleased to see me, and above all else she was humbly forgiving. She had a wonderful sense of humour as we played together in and outdoors. And as I danced and sang songs to her, so too did she dance and sing with me. I gladly walked with her in any weather: wind, rain, snow, ice. Dark shadows of suffering disappeared in her radiant joyful light. I felt neither self-conscious nor inadequate, neither unlovable nor worthless. She was my soul's healer and restorer. I could trust Bethany without feeling vulnerable.

As we strode out across the countryside, surrounded by fields of farm animals, I began to notice the beauty and majesty of the horses we passed, standing patiently and watching us with clear, soft, intelligent eyes. I was falling into a blessed and charmed state each time I paused to watch these magnificent beasts. Their alluring graceful beauty was calling me; my deep-seeking, non-rational wisdom was inviting me to discover their mystery and magic.

I began to learn to ride at a local riding school. I became completely besotted with the spirit of the horse. This mutually respectful, trusting, empathetic rapport touched my soul in passionate and inspiring ways. Despite their size and strength, they were served by gentleness, patience and grace. Capable of such power and yet not violent. So beautiful without vanity. Alongside the love I had for Bethany, sharing the rarefied reality of the horse gave me the further unconditional intimacy that my soul had been longing for. I was hopelessly in love. Something shifted in me as I experienced a deep synchronicity with these amazing, graceful creatures. I discovered an emotional connection and rhythm with them and with the natural world around me. A mysterious spirit was ensuring

I was made aware of the life and love of horses. It was as though I had been asked what I knew of God, and I silently blossomed like a cherry tree.

How long had I existed without these wondrous creatures? Perhaps it explains why I have always felt only part person inside. When I am with horses I seem to have an expanded awareness. I feel connected to this stranger in me, who is more ancient and mysterious and more in tune with the rhythms of nature and her seasons. Some kind of ancestral echo had reached me as these sensitive beings taught me about collaboration and humility, never domination. I felt an even deeper sense of gratitude, affection and privilege as they awakened a more compassionate, patient and loving spirit within me. I was in harmony with myself and the natural world.

In parallel with my blessed state of equanimity, Mum's health was gradually declining. She would phone me crying and upset after another row – and on some occasions physical conflict – with Karen. I became increasingly concerned for her safety. I pleaded with her to consider moving into sheltered accommodation. It was a repeating pattern from my childhood. Familiar emotions of fear and dread returned. I wanted to speak out on her behalf, but she would never let me. She would not grant me permission to rescue her.

Then one evening I received a sudden call from her. Her voice was faint and laboured. She was asking me to visit her urgently; she was seriously ill and frightened. I took leave from work, packed a small bag and frantically hurried to see her. What I witnessed was repulsive. Her tortured emotions were having an adverse effect on her physical and mental health. As I looked through the shattered window of her soul, she resembled a small, malnourished child at Lowood School in *Jane Eyre*. She had become cachexic and needed much persuasion to tempt her to eat small morsels of food. She preferred to drink tea, hot or cold, and chain-smoke day and night. Her mood was lower than low, as she had sunk down into a pitiful place of despair. Devoid of any simple fantasy which would spark the tiniest fragments of healing, she had become severely depressed with little inclination even to wash her hands and face once a day. Mum was so vulnerable, I was afraid she would waste away through starvation and mental anguish.

The day I arrived, Lee and Karen were about to leave for a week's holiday in their caravan. Mum was in bed, emaciated and struggling to breathe. She was frightened and suffering from severe malnourishment and neglect. Her skeletal appearance was shocking. She had developed bedsores and was lying on sheets smeared with excrement.

Lee stormed into her bedroom demanding money, which he took from one of her cupboards. As he left, Mum said, 'He only comes in for money.'

He was controlling her and her finances.

I was shocked and angry. Why and how had this been allowed to develop? Why when Karen was Mum's registered carer did Mum have to pay for a private nurse to wash her? Why was she paying for Meals on Wheels?

I made an immediate appointment with her GP during which I struggled to describe the awful conditions Mum was living in. I sat shaking and weeping. The GP seemed nervous and alarmed. I told her that if she didn't take Mum into a nursing home that day I would put her in my car and take her to my own GP, who was three hundred miles away. Mum was admitted that same day. I spent the following few days visiting her and cleaning her accommodation. I found large sums of money stored in her linen cupboard.

Before I returned home I organised flowers to be delivered every week by a local florist. I told Mum that it was my expression of love for her. Each time the flowers arrived I wanted her to imagine that I was holding them.

When I arrived home, I wrote a letter to Mum's GP in which I detailed my concerns about the state I had found her in. I described her squalid living conditions and her social isolation and expressed my worries about Lee's behaviour. I asked her to evaluate Mum's needs and consider encouraging her to move to a residential care home nearer to me.

Mum was sent home a couple of weeks later only to be taken back to hospital by emergency ambulance. She had fallen out of bed during a domestic fight. I was told by the nurse that Mum was admitted for her own safety since the family dynamics had haemorrhaged. She never returned. Mum was later diagnosed with lung cancer. She died penniless in the nursing home in 2008, two days after her seventieth birthday. I later discovered large sums of money had been incrementally withdrawn from her bank account, the last of which was a month before she was admitted, resulting in an almost two-thousand-pound deficit.

Lee and Karen made no contribution towards Mum's funeral arrangements and neither of them offered a single word towards her final farewell. On the day of the funeral they looked as though they were on a Mediterranean beach holiday, wearing floral outfits. They not only dressed but also behaved inappropriately, telling vile jokes.

Once the funeral was over I wrote them one last letter. I reproached them for using Mum's money to fund their hedonistic lifestyle while ignoring her needs. I told them what I thought of their behaviour at the time of Mum's death; their disassociation with the funeral betrayed their lack of insight into her history, dreams, longings and spirituality. I finished by asking them never to contact me again.

But my saddest memory of Mum is that, despite my hope and longing, she never said she was sorry for all the hurt and pain she caused me. I never once heard her express regret for the poisonous regime she had subjected me to as I was growing up. But while she may have stunted my vitality as a child living in constant fear of punishment, she never succeeded in obliterating my authentic expression of my true self.

They all honoured their parents throughout their lives, even though their parents did them immeasurable harm. They sacrificed the desire for truth, self-loyalty, genuine communication, understanding and appreciation on the altar of parental respect, all in the hope of being loved and not rejected.

Alice Miller,
The Body Never Lies

Chapter 22

Herons and Horses

2008 – 2011

If you don't fit in; if you feel at odds with the world; if your identity is troubled and frayed; if you feel lost and ashamed, it could be because you have retained the human values you were supposed to have discarded. You are a deviant. Be proud.

George Monbiot, *How Did We Get Into This Mess?*

After Mum's death I was swept into a prolonged spiral of despair. It involved work, my marriage and ultimately my health. I was caught up in a cyclone of physical, psychological and emotional violence and I was deeply unhappy. I felt utterly lost. My exterior and interior lives were crumbling.

I made excuses for David's increasing hostility. This had become more marked since Mum's death. My denial of his resentment towards me was a form of self-protection. It was too horrid to imagine he was angry that I hadn't inherited any money. I couldn't – or wouldn't – see the truth because I was inside it. Not since my surgery shortly after we were married had I been able to stand back and see things as they really were. I was inside and brainwashed. He seemed to be solely focused on what was missing from his life: a better car, more holidays, expensive clothes and accessories. He was bitter about his inability to be promoted at work. He could think only of what his life should be, not what it was – what he wanted, not what he had. His existence was built on illusions. He was constantly dissatisfied with our beautiful home, garden, work and his family. He seemed to want more and more of everything. I dreaded him taking Bethany for a walk, knowing he would be fiercely intolerant of her juvenile behaviour. His way of reacting was harsh as he projected all his frustration and anger onto her.

I felt burdened by the impact of past memories: Andrew, Dad and now more recently the neglect Mum experienced towards the end of her life. There was always more I could have done: loved more, cared more, helped more, forgiven more. Guilt and shame paralysed me.

> *We have to assimilate the unpalatable details of our own complicity in the misfortunes that have dogged our lives and the potential harm we have done to others, not only directly but also at a distance by virtue of our lack of charity and our resentment based on jealousy and fear.*
>
> **Martin Israel,**
> Living Alone

I believed I was being faithful and courageous. My patient endurance of these hard times was my self-inflicted penance. I was punishing and blaming myself in an attempt to compensate for past relationships. I was also grieving for my lost childhood.

Deep down I knew that whatever – if anything – David and I had had between us was lost and we were irreparably broken. We could not be mended. I was acting the role of the loyal and loving wife, but it was all a pretence. The guilt of being otherwise was too frightening. Only with my dogs Bethany and Bonny was I true to myself. I lived an inward life inside my own heart companioned by my sheltering soul. It was an interior monastery where I was the only human inhabitant. I had built a sanctuary of resistance where no one else visited.

At work I had failed to notice the creeping cultural toxicity. Like a skin complaint that slowly spreads and worsens, you only notice when there is severe pain or your appearance starts to challenge your vain self-image. My need for security, identity and financial security had obscured my vision until the atmosphere was too uncomfortable and I began to feel threatened. The culture was suffocating as espoused values of student-centeredness, compassion and empathy conflicted with typical behaviours. Those at the top had got there not by leading, but by treading others underfoot. Cronyism and nepotism were prevalent; people were promoted beyond their level of competence. This led to poor decision-making, waste and inefficiency, and inevitably had a negative effect on staff morale. As a public service we faced unprecedented challenges, and yet there was a scarcity of competent management which was fit for purpose. There were deficiencies, particularly in ethics and values. Managers prioritised personal ambition and self-advancement over the needs of the service. Behind the rhetoric of the benefits of constant departmental change was the desire to wield power and control, which was generated through the dynamics of confusion and uncertainty. Existing structures were deliberately dismantled as staff roles and responsibilities were constantly reorganised. The justification for this often seemed irrational; it seemed more about managers proving they could rule us and wield power. The sequential dynamics of these detrimental changes created intolerable chaos and confusion for staff, which made them vulnerable and eager to accept their managers' agendas. Students were herded onto programmes designed for commercial benefit – to promote the profile of the department. This led to the neglect of its ethical integrity; there was insufficient management accountability for its virtuous capability and outcomes. The only guiding principle for behaviours was money. It was management by fear.

Teachers secretly berated the students. If they were conforming and performing well, then the atmosphere was jubilant. The students provided the boastful teachers with useful trophies for self-aggrandisement. However, those who were more challenging intellectually or behaviourally were ridiculed in the staffroom. Covert bullying of both students and staff was culturally acceptable. I would amuse myself with images of my colleagues as rugby players pushing and shoving one another around a rugby pitch. Like Rocky the Rhino they snorted and charged down the corridors muttering distasteful comments about students.

There is an inverse relationship between utility and reward. The most lucrative, prestigious jobs tend to cause the greatest harm. The most useful workers tend to be paid the least and treated the worst. If you possess one indispensable skill – battering and blustering (like a rugby player) your way to the top – incompetence in other areas is no impediment. The wrong traits were rewarded, as those who rose to the top were conformists and sycophants.

George Monbiot,
How Did We Get Into This Mess?

Monbiot describes an alarming study suggesting many bosses possess psychopathic traits. They are skilled in flattery and manipulation.

Their prospects are unlikely to be damaged by their egocentricity, strong sense of entitlement, readiness to exploit others and lack of empathy and conscience.

I had a mounting sense of incompatibility with this toxic, bullying culture. I began to feel drained and started to distance myself from the system to avoid becoming infected. My psychological contract had been breached and I needed to protect myself from further harm as the mismatch between my agreed and expected roles increased. Violations of trust and integrity caused me to withdraw. Each day I would carefully navigate through a hostile jungle; one slip and I could fall into a pit and impale myself on sharp thorns. The creeping imposition of autocratic power was eroding any sense of democracy. There was a pessimistic assumption that staff and students were to be mistrusted as they were fundamentally lazy. We were subjected to intolerable pressures and unsuitable role changes. It was as if we were being set up to fail. The atmosphere was fragile and insecure.

I often found myself in tears as I drove home. The relentless effort to conform combined with a heavy workload was exhausting. I wanted to use my voice to speak the truth, to tell the real story. A maelstrom of emotions and negative thoughts would whirl around my interior, desperate to be expressed. I kept doing what I knew I must do without throwing stones at the organisation. I quietly did my work without being antagonistic; I would suggest better alternatives to reframe and improve any issue. It did not seem wise to fight the organisation or cultural consensus, knowing full well I could be judged as negative, rebellious and arrogant. I was never remotely tempted to collude with this culture based on competing and comparing; I chose the ordinary everyday commitment of giving my best to the students. My primary focus was always about helping them to realise their true potential. Despite the chaos and confusion, I was blessed with a quiet conviction and an unequivocal intrinsic purpose.

I was unprepared for the lifeline I was given. It wasn't a win on the lottery, an unexpected promotion or a new job. It was far more precious and unique. There were no conditions, only kindness, the kindness of a stranger. He was tall, dark and gorgeous, strong but tender and deeply loyal. I immediately fell in love with him. He was an unmerited gift with a huge presence who became a wonderful friend. It was a perfect bonding. He had four legs, a white flash down his chiselled nose, a long luxuriant black mane and tail and a smooth reddish glossy coat; his eyes were deeply dark with a clear stillness. He was quiet by nature and smelled of sweetness. A 16-hand Irish Cob horse, he was about 15 years old and his name was Charlie. I was introduced to him through a friend. His owner was concentrating on other things and needed help with looking after him. I could spend as much time as I wanted with him, without any expense. He was a priceless gift from one brief encounter with a stranger.

Charlie became not only my mat carrier but a noble flying carpet. Throughout the changing seasons, together we would fly across fresh meadows carpeted with rich blue-green grass or casually crunch across dry yellow autumn stubble. As boggy black earth was illuminated white with snow and ice we would venture out into arctic mist before he was rugged up in a cosy stable of hay and straw. We would wade across clear dancing rivers and babbling streams and eat picnics by their side. The sound of the flowing water cleansed my soul, carrying away the dust and grit of worry. Beneath the shadow of the hunchback prehistoric blue-grey heron and dancing acrobatic swallows, shy deer accompanied us on our way home. His strength, agility, grace and beauty made him the perfect companion. We jumped logs and ditches as we reached for the sky. An ancient cobbled packhorse bridge led us to the different sides of the same place; covered in soft sumptuous iridescent moss it gently befriended its travellers. Never before had I felt so alive. In the shelter of his warm shadow I felt safe and deeply peaceful. Within these precious paradise moments, no thought, no act and no words could disturb the deep beauty of our friendship.

There was no end to our adventures as I thanked God for Charlie and the wonders of our landscape under the sky from dawn to dusk. Charlie was deeply willing and biddable. He didn't sulk and was never irritable. I was humbled by this creature's forgiving, trusting nature. There was no power, no judging, no infliction of pain or punishment, just silent devotion, mutual understanding and reciprocity. I felt wild and awake in his presence; he helped me recalibrate my inner misery. My soul could breathe as I was released from domesticity, oppressive control, fear and sadness. I felt more alive than my pain and loneliness were telling me. I was returning to my native wildness, to the natural and seamless fluency of my true authentic nature. It was an invitation to risk new ways of dwelling in the world. I was in balance and in tune with nature, instead of the marshlands of blurred emotions. I discovered my natural rhythm.

While my spirit was comfortably protected with an equanimity it longed for, physically I was struggling. I had secretly harboured recurring symptoms after my gynae surgery, which were now refusing to be silent. I was afraid if I told someone about these I would be deemed unfit to work and this would jeopardise my ability to earn money and provide a home for myself and my pets. Week by week their voices were getting louder.

My GP, Dr Wong, was perceptive and deeply caring in ways I have never experienced before or since from a doctor. She was to become a loyal, dependable mat carrier over the months and years ahead, before disaster struck like a near-fatal car crash. She began to ask probing questions, like a forensic scientist searching and examining trace materials. I trusted her. She was the first doctor who managed to convince me she genuinely wanted to help me. Eventually I disclosed the truth: I had bladder, bowel and womb problems.

I was referred to see an urologist, gynaecologist and a gastroenterologist. I was subjected to a range of procedures attempting to halt my heavy vaginal bleeding and stabilise my unpredictable bladder, which was capable of emptying itself regardless of time and place; this gushing of warm liquid was unannounced and unforgiving. I was also chronically constipated. Despite eating large quantities of fruit and vegetables, drinking gallons of water and leading an active lifestyle, my bowel was awkward and uncooperative. Its stubborn refusal to let go of its contents was frustrating and painful. Dry, hard pellets was the best I could manage.

And so I packed my dignity off to a future destination to be collected later. I was back on a treadmill of invasive procedures. Tubes, devices and complex chemical warm and cold fluids were inserted into almost every orifice as hospital staff paid more attention to each other than my naked, shivering body. Like lollygaggers standing around a market stall, they gossiped about holidays and kids, fashion and hair colouring, not caring that they were being observed. At times there was a complete absence of explanation, and consent was assumed by virtue of being present. I felt violated as devices were inserted to examine my interior anatomy and physiology. I was silenced by shame and disappointment – disappointment with my body and its failure to allow me a life without embarrassment, pain and humiliation. I felt utterly degraded and I blamed myself. Once again I was visited by the spectre of self-contempt. It was my fault that I was worthless and defective.

More gynae surgery was followed by the news that I needed colorectal surgery. I was unconvinced it was necessary. I needed more evidence concerning the risks and clinical outcomes. The physician recommending this referral seemed more excited about the hospital's newly appointed colorectal surgeon than concerned about my ambivalence. He was like a schoolboy showing off flashy new toys and boasting about his new friend. I didn't trust him.

I agreed to see the surgeon and discuss my case in more detail.

It was November 2010. On the day of the appointment I sat waiting alone in a windowless room. Fixed to the grey walls were tatty, grubby notices to staff reminding them of various hazards. The surgeon was running late. He eventually arrived not having read my notes. I was concerned he was not aware of my gynae and urinary malfunctions; given their close proximity to the bowel I knew this was significant. I asked him to explain the risks associated with the proposed procedure. His response was vague and could apply to any surgical procedure requiring a general anaesthetic. He was disengaged and distracted and made me feel as though I was wasting his time: he was too busy and too important for my trivial case. My quest for information was an irritation. I wanted him to realise that I was frightened and that I needed to understand the risks and benefits of the operation. I wanted him to assuage my fears. I knew it was serious and complicated.

Knowing when not to operate, is just as important as how to operate, and is a more difficult skill to acquire.

Henry Marsh,
Do No Harm

Despite knowing I was more certain about my questions than I was about the faint answers I was getting, after a few months of deliberation I decided to go ahead. I was living with ongoing suspense and anxiety. One thing was for sure: I wasn't going to alleviate my slow transit bowel problems with paracetamol. As my body aged, it would only compound the problem. Things slow down naturally as the body becomes older. Additionally, the risks of having a general anaesthetic would increase.

While I knew I needed some form of intervention, something to unblock my interior, no one told me of the catastrophic hazards associated with what was about to take place.

Chapter 23

A Sanctimonious Halo

2011 – 2013

When sorrows come they come not single spies but battalions.

William Shakespeare, *Hamlet*

On Monday, 4 April 2011 I submitted my body and soul to volatile gases and injectable anaesthetic agents. Like a pond swallowing a stone, I sank into oblivion. I lay unconscious on an operating table as the fresh young surgeon with his sophisticated technology and instruments attempted to insert plastic nylon mesh through keyholes into my lower abdomen.

I had resisted thoughts of mutilation parading as altruistic intervention being performed on my vulnerable body. The pioneering surgery was supposed to strengthen and support a torn wall between my bowel and vagina. This defect was allowing my bowel to herniate outwards and press against my vagina and bladder. How the wall had been torn was a question no one could answer. Large anterior rectoceles, or a bulging colon, commonly occur during full-term childbirth when this separating wall can be damaged.

It was a cold, uncomplicated recovery over four days in a noisy ward. It was cold because of a paucity of care. Human tenderness and compassion did not feature in the workings of this environment. Disorganised nurses rushed around shouting to one another, cleaners complained about their poor earnings and patterns of shift work, and doctors were abrupt. Medicines were missed or duplicated and no one had a clue about my true physical and psychological recovery.

I escaped home to the warm comfort of my two dogs and Chuckles, my chunky, cuddly black and white cat.

Fourteen months later, on 7 June 2012, I went to see Dr Wong. I was experiencing a range of distressing symptoms: profuse night sweats, bloated tummy, fatigue, explosive diarrhoea and heavy vaginal bleeding. I described how I felt my body was trying to spit out the mesh: 'It's like an alien monster and my body wants rid of it!' I explained. She looked aghast at this suggestion and immediately dismissed its plausibility. I sensed her mind was fixed into a medical model of systematic, evidence-based enquiry, a well-established traditional approach to searching for a recognised diagnosis. She didn't believe me. I felt stupid and embarrassed, like the child I once was asking for help to stop Trevor's abuse. I had shared with her detailed, intimate information only to be denied any sense of respect and serious consideration. I foolishly handed over my personal power and allowed her to take control of my well-being. This was my first mistake.

I was sent to see my gynaecologist, who immediately requested scans and blood tests. He diagnosed an absorption problem and wrote this in large capital letters in a letter to my GP.

I continued to record my symptoms:

Pain, pain and more pain
Tight and bloated tummy
Feeling full quickly after eating
Reduced appetite and nausea
Unable to swallow properly and sometimes regurgitating
Explosive foul-smelling diarrhoea
Excessive uncontrollable flatus
Excessive vaginal bleeding
Frequency of micturition
Fatigue and lethargy – feeling exhausted
Profuse night sweats, yet constantly cold

I was referred back to the gastroenterologist. I was reluctant to go to see him. I dreaded telling him about my symptoms as in previous encounters he'd been arrogant and aloof. His manner was like a bored headmaster facing yet another disagreeable child.

Another eight months went by and I finally had an appointment with him in January 2013. As I entered his palatial office he immediately seemed indifferent. It was the standard hospital doctor stance: *I'm too busy and important for this.* His nonchalance made me feel uptight. I composed myself and methodically began to list my worsening symptoms:

Explosive offensive greasy diarrhoea day and night (awake every couple of hours)
Stools pale, mucousy, watery, despite taking iron
Feel constipated with rectal discomfort

Mouth ulcers

Fatigue

Night sweats

Feeling very cold

Pain: rectal, abdominal and loin

Bloating

Occasional rectal bleeding

'Well,' he said. 'We can do a few mundane tests and see what happens.'

Mundane! Who said this was mundane? I wanted to scream at him to stop looking into his computer screen and take note of what I was telling him. Please take me seriously! Taking violent diarrhoea-inducing medication in preparation for a rigid pole inserted into a painful rectum in front of an audience of staff discussing skiing holidays is *not* mundane. How about we swap places and see if you consider this to be mundane; it is degrading and humiliating – not to mention frightening. My thoughts remained hidden as I clung to my self-respect and dignity. If I suddenly started acting out my true, authentic self, a frightened woman in pain, I would be seen as irrational and neurotic.

I was anxious and afraid. I found the indignities difficult to discuss and manage. I was ashamed, so ashamed I couldn't even tell close friends about my symptoms. I felt dejected and alone. All this just seemed to disgust David. His resentment towards me grew stronger day by day as his trophy wife was no longer available for display. His illusions were shattered and he was angry. My sitting on the loo every few hours squirting foul-smelling poo, especially throughout the night, was unbearable for him. The pungent smell and splattered poo created a scene I had rarely seen as a nurse, let alone one created by my own body. I felt as though I was rotting inside. None of this evoked any sympathy, tenderness or concern. He was too self-obsessed.

I continued to work when I should have taken sick leave months ago. My attachment to the students compelled me to keep going. I was also afraid if I took time off the department would adopt a draconian performance management approach with the implicit threat of constructive dismissal. Power and policy would be used to punish me and protect them. I was afraid no one would believe me. I would be labelled as stressed and not coping with work. It would have been easier if I had a broken leg or I'd had surgery. If there was something tangible and visible they could accept that, but not this unspecified condition.

My thinking became consumed in fear and anxiety as my health, ability to work and marriage were all rapidly disintegrating. I felt as though I were drowning in a septic tank. The tide of pain and anguish was unbearable.

I resorted to wearing big knickers filled with pads as my body leaked blood, urine and poo. I would only use single disabled toilets knowing there was no one else around to hear and smell my explosive bowel evacuation. It also meant I had a private washbasin and dryer where I could strip and wash. I was conscious of smelling so I took great care to scrub and deodorise myself after each visit. Only once did a woman in a wheelchair project her wrath onto me; to her I did not seem disabled, I had no legitimate right to use *her* facilities. I imagined myself whispering in her ear: 'When you have uncontrollable explosive diarrhoea, which smells worse than a sewer, there is urine flowing out of the sides of your pants and you are bleeding heavily, I'm sure you too would want access to disabled toilet facilities. Moreover, you would not want to have to explain and justify this to anyone. Like me, you would want to avoid further humiliation and degradation. Please do not assume the absence of a visible disability means that one doesn't exist.' That said, I would float away smiling and wearing my sanctimonious halo.

I felt utterly lost and displaced. I was losing my serenity. My sense of belonging was rapidly fading as I became sicker. I needed a loving shelter, a peaceful, undisturbed sanctuary. I wasn't sure who I was or what I was becoming. What would happen to me and to my animals?

David was acting strangely, more strangely than usual. The sicker I became, the happier he was. He continued to openly display his irritation and disgust towards me, but perhaps things were going well at work. He was helping out with Charlie, so I naively assumed it was Charlie's adorable magic rubbing off on him. Or maybe he felt powerful in the face of my weakness and vulnerability. I had neither the energy nor the inclination to discuss this with him. It would only lead to sulking and hostility.

On 5 February 2013 I went back to see Doctor Wong and complained of:

Acute and chronic pain becoming unbearable

Poor appetite and inability to eat due to pain

Worsening anti-social nature of bowel symptoms – explosive foul-smelling faeces

Poor sleep and excessive fatigue

Feeling very cold

Mouth ulcers

I was signed off sick and not one cell in my body was bothered. I was too weak and miserable. Tired and persistently cold, I took to my bed accompanied by my cat Chuckles. Never before had she wanted such close physical contact. Aloof and distant she had always preferred to live detached, as long as I fed her. Now she was providing comfort and company at a time of intense suffering. She was my mat carrier. As I lay in bed feeling totally unlovable, this small creature moved alongside me to tell me otherwise. Her presence felt divine as my craving for attachment was being met. Unlike the solitary child who plucked her pink blanket at night for comfort, here was a hurting woman in pain. I was being comforted across this river of suffering by a beautiful feline creature. Chuckles was fulfilling her destiny.

Time became blurred. Days and nights blended into one as I slipped in and out of a hypnotic sleep. I was marooned in the bedroom, my only exercise making trips to the bathroom. During short periods of lucidity, I started to piece things together. David's cheerfulness was peculiar. I had never known him to be singing in the shower at 6am on an icy winter's morning. This was out of character. His natural disposition was to be grumpy and irritable, especially around me. Other peculiarities included insisting on going to see Charlie alone, whereas until recently he had resented him, increased visits to the gym and boasting of his muscular physique, excessive texting, although he had only two pals, and encouraging my friends to stay, when he'd spent years isolating me.

It was Saturday, 11 February 2013. A close friend of mine came to visit and David went out for a curry and beers with his pals. He couldn't wait. He was excitable and agitated. He was also especially caring, making cups of tea and fussing both of us before skipping off down the road like a jubilant little boy. Why was he being so charming? I wondered. Exhausted after a couple of hours of chitchat, I went to bed. Disturbed by pain I lay awake staring holes into the darkness. David arrived home about 4am. Something about his behaviour was puzzling me. The long days immobilised in bed had given me time to notice both the subtle changes and the overt ones. Things were not making sense. I went downstairs and checked his phone. It was an automatic, unconscious act, as if I was being guided. It was almost like an out-of-body invitation to find the truth.

As I stared into the bright light of the message envelope I was shunted from a sickly, semi-conscious state to one of furious wide-awake horror. It was a defining moment. There was life before and life after this fateful illumination. I never knew I could react so suddenly, so sharply, especially when I was feeling so weak and poorly. I had been blinded by my denial of his infidelity, and the shock of this discovery rescued me from a dark wilderness. It was as if I had been buried underground and was slowly suffocating before suddenly being hauled onto the earth's surface where there was light and fresh air to breathe. I was alive at last. The sudden confrontation with his heinous, deceitful betrayal repulsed me. Text after text was from a friend of mine who kept her pony in the stable adjacent to Charlie. She was known to be a serial adulterer. Their clandestine affair described through the texts was vulgar and disgusting. When I look back now, it seems inevitable but at the time the obvious had become unrecognisable until pain and chaos stripped away my self-made denials.

I ran upstairs and found David sitting expectantly upright. It was as though he already knew what I was about to say. I forced the phone into his face. I screamed at him to get out, he was disgusting. He almost seemed relieved.

My life had been smashed into fragments like shards from a shattered lantern. But in my brokenness I felt a purification as my self-awareness finally emerged. I had spent years pretending I was happy with David. I had betrayed myself by ignoring my true feelings so I could accommodate his. I had abandoned my true self.

David packed a bag and left. He should have gone a long time ago. Chained to my vows I had tolerated abuse for years. His final betrayal granted me permission to protect myself and evict his creepy, sordid presence. Before he went, his last words to me were that he was fed up with my sickness and our loveless marriage. He knew he was behaving badly but believed that the wrongdoing was necessary to bring things to a head. He was giving himself permission to distance himself from the whole mess around him. There was no gentleness and no love between us. Any sense of affection had gone sour.

There was an immediate release of tension. I took long deep breaths of fresh air. The veil of deceit had been lifted, the smog had disappeared. I could see clearly. Like the return of a graceful migrating bird my serenity emerged. The oppression had evaporated as the truth within my soul was unleashed. I was true all the way through, in my words and all that I was. The virtue of integrity had blessed me.

If we are to hear the silent music beneath the noisy traffic of our thinking, we need to learn how to leave the mind and focus on the senses. The distractions of modern life prevent us picking up the rhythm of Grace.

Daniel O'Leary,
Treasured and Transformed

Even my animals seemed relieved and more relaxed.

David was braver than me. For years I had been paralysed by fear. I dreaded the change and inevitable losses associated with a broken marriage. I was haunted by the fear of being homeless and the threat of being unable to care for my animals. It was too painful. The idea of losing my security had terrified me. But now I didn't care. As I lay in bed day after day, lonely and frail, I slowly travelled through the longest season of suffering. I battled with my inner conflicts and moral failures: rejection, abandonment and humiliation, abuse, loss and my own imperfections. But I was still grateful for the present. I surrendered to God's loving grace and mercy. I was willing to accept what would happen next. Despite the pain and suffering, I was inwardly drawn to a secret place of mysterious love.

Only love and suffering are strong enough to break down our usual ego defences, crush our dual thinking, and open us up to Mystery. Love is what we long for and we're created for – in fact, love is what we are as an outpouring from God – but suffering often seems to be our opening to that need, that desire, and that identity. Love and suffering are the main portals that open up the mind space and heart space, breaking us into breadth and depth and communion.

Richard Rohr,
Radical Grace

This inner open window allowed me to embrace these impossible contradictions and untold miseries.

I rang only two friends: Anna and Beverly. Anna, the caring colleague who had befriended me after my father's death, was a strong, resilient and pragmatic woman. I knew she would drop everything to help. Bev was an old school friend I trusted for emotional, spiritual and physical support. Anna packed an overnight bag and raced up the motorway the next day. I was having a colonoscopy and needed someone with me. Bev arrived the day after to help me put my affairs in order. My priority was my finances. David was rapidly spending money from our joint account on his fairy-tale princess. Lavish meals, flowers and shopping for clothes were draining our meagre funds.

Within a week I had separated our finances and made an appointment with a solicitor to commence divorce proceedings. I arranged for Charlie to be looked after by friends at the stables. The stable owner agreed to put all livery bills on hold until further notice.

My health was deteriorating. I was seen again on 3 March by the headmaster gastroenterologist. I had the following symptoms:

Weight loss

Increased explosive greasy faeces, yellow with mucous and blood

Inflammatory pain

Bilateral loin pain

Flu-like symptoms with profuse night sweats and shivering

Exhaustion and malaise

Once again he seemed disengaged and unconcerned. Dr Wong had mentioned David had left me, which he seemed to think was aggravating my condition. Angry and frustrated at his presumptuous judgement I pleaded with him for help. I was afraid and becoming increasingly unwell.

He agreed to admit me to hospital. More tests were ordered and high doses of intravenous steroids were administered. But then I was abruptly discharged, due to bed management demands, despite no conclusive diagnosis. At the point of discharge I was advised a shadow had been seen on my CT scan and I should contact my gynaecologist urgently. I went home and collapsed that evening.

Desperate and frightened I later wrote to the chief executive to complain about my treatment. In my letter I set out the reason for my admission, which was my diminishing health and well-being. I told him I had been discharged with no diagnosis or treatment plan. At every stage of my illness there had been poor communication and lack of feedback. I explained the deleterious effects of this condition on the quality of my life. The hospital complaints department contacted me to reassure me they would investigatev. I didn't want an investigation, I needed medical attention. I was tired of the inertia and prolonged delay in diagnosis.

My gynaecologist reassured me the shadows on the scan were those of endometriosis. We agreed I should have a hysterectomy to alleviate the heavy bleeding.

On 23 May 2013 I was seen again by the gastroenterologist. The evening before this appointment Anna rang to check how I was. During our conversation she suggested the consultant probably thought I was a bunny boiler, a woman considered to be emotionally unstable and likely to be dangerously vengeful. While I was not about to boil any bunnies, guinea pigs, rats or mice, I was terrified and desperate. This may have appeared to others as instability. I may have made others feel uncomfortable, but I felt as though I was dying a slow painful death and no one was listening. In blunt opposition to this view, Bev believed I was too tolerant of the delays and inactions by both my GP and hospital consultant. She was furious with my composure and insisted I should be more dramatic and demanding. 'I get more upset when I've got a sore throat,' she would rant. But I had learned the art of tolerance and how to endure disappointment. I was also afraid of the power of the medical profession. I needed them to provide information for my employer to enable me to continue to receive an income while I was sick. Medical abandonment and alienation could threaten my security. Fear of harm and wrongful judgement silenced and trapped me into believing I was powerless.

During my appointment the next day I asked the consultant: 'Do you believe all this is psychosomatic – that my symptoms are exaggerated due to my husband's infidelity?' He anxiously noted this in my records and said 'No.' He looked pale and disturbed. I replied, 'So why do I feel you are not taking me seriously, especially as you seem to spend more time staring into your computer screen than listening to me? I hold all the clues to this, surely.' By now I was unafraid of causing offence. There were no egos to massage, only a desperate attempt to get some medical help. He ordered more investigations, but stated that he didn't expect to find anything.

On 5 July I was admitted for a hysterectomy. Before I went to theatre I had a long chat with my gynaecologist who seemed genuinely concerned and wanted to help. While I was signing the consent form, I reiterated how much pain I was in. I felt as if I was sitting on golf balls. I couldn't sit comfortably anymore, either in a chair or in bed.

As I woke from the anaesthetic I noticed the nurses seemed anxious and were avoiding eye contact. Within an hour I would receive both good and bad news. I was not expecting either.

Chapter 24

Surviving the Stitch-up and Smiling Through Pain

2013 – 2014

That survival instinct, that will to live, that need to get back to life again, is more powerful than any consideration of taste, decency, politeness, manners, civility. Anything. It's such a powerful force.

Danny Boyle, interview with *National Geographic* magazine

The good news came from my estate agent. He had sold the house to cash buyers. This was a rare occurrence in the prevailing financial climate. It was an answer to prayers, prayers of worrying desolation. The bad news was my hysterectomy had to be aborted due to clinical risks. On seeing inside my pelvic cavity the gynaecologist discovered my womb was firmly fixed to my rectum. Due to my distorted anatomy, the visibility was so poor he decided not to proceed. While I was under the general anaesthetic, he'd tried to contact Mr Fisher, the colorectal surgeon who'd inserted the mesh, to invite him to look and offer a diagnosis. He couldn't be located. So, instead, I was woken up and told the bad news. I felt stunned and confused. I was sent home with little support.

Friends reacted differently to the chaos in my life. Just like Job's three friends, Eliphaz, Bildad and Zophar, there were those whose unhelpful rhetoric made me feel ashamed of being ill. From their utopian world they acted as my judge and jury. All this mess was my fault. I was naive and gullible. Past failures dating back over many years were used to justify their poor opinion of me, thereby elevating their lives and false egos. Harboured resentments, jealousies and disappointments were dumped onto me. Despite the longevity of our friendship, I began to dislike these judgemental friends who weren't ashamed of being critical. They were like Green Shield Stamp collectors who had secretly saved up my past failures and were now cashing them in like elated lottery winners. Their betrayal deepened my sense of vulnerability as the foundations of our friendship began to disintegrate. The illusion of their loyalty was slowly fading as I realised their lovelessness had paraded as shallow compassion over the years. Some likened my life to a soap opera, others distanced themselves and became remote. I wasn't sure why. Perhaps it was their own sense of helplessness, or like David they were tired of my ill health and relational dramas. But others quietly helped me navigate an unforeseen river of unimaginable suffering by small acts of loving-kindness.

A few special women held me in loving compassion. I felt encircled by a string of precious iridescent pearls. They seemed to know exactly what I needed and made huge efforts to be present for me. They gave practical help, such as accompanying me to hospital appointments, lending money, walking my dogs Bethany and Bonny, feeding and exercising Charlie, and helping with all the legalese. They supported me with phone calls and text messages, providing compassionate, non-judgemental company and love. These were my mat carriers, giving of themselves and supplying practical, emotional and spiritual care. It was love and kindness for love and kindness' sake. Their inner beauty and emotional generosity became my mat, carrying me over this torrential river of suffering.

One of these friends was a stranger called Wendy, who had become aware of my plight through a mutual work acquaintance. Knowing I lived nearby she gathered some food and a bunch of home-grown gladioli, knocked on my door and offered to help. She was like the Good Samaritan caring for the traveller who'd been stripped, beaten and left half-dead at the side of the road. Her selfless willingness to reach out was like wrapping fine muslin bandages around my painful wounds. Over the following weeks and months she carried and cared for me in ways of undiscovered grace and beauty. Wendy became the older sister I never had. Her loving care was an angelic gift. She radiated patient humility, integrity and a gracious unconditional love. Our relationship challenged all my previous notions of friendship. Where I had previously assumed close friends would provide loving support by virtue of shared history, I now realised how untrue this was. Like a child discovering there is no such thing as Father Christmas, Wendy transformed my perception.

Once again I was liberated from the chains I revered. Like a river on its inevitable journey, I too was on an inner journey, a journey closer to God, for which I had both the desire and courage. I had been set free from a prison of gloomy oppression and stagnation, and now I was moving forward. Despite the threat of death, I felt truly alive and held by God's abiding love.

I grew sicker each day, so ill I began to leave my front door unlocked day and night for fear I would need an ambulance but be incapable of getting out of bed to open it. I felt as though I were swilling around inside the stinking putrefying belly of some unknown mammal. I was at the mercy of forces beyond my control. When and if I would eventually be spewed out was a mystery. Frightening images of my bowel bursting and spilling out horrid foul-smelling brown fluid terrified me as I lay in bed. I began to wonder if I was being prepared for something which was awaiting me in the future, something which was getting closer day by day.

Then one evening I knew I was probably dying. It was one of the longest nights of my life. Alone, in silence, in pain, feverish, weak and squirting foul-smelling fluid from a throbbing bulging rectum and bleeding from my decaying insides I lay on my bed with Chuckles, hoping for a miracle. I called my GP the following day but the call was not returned. So I asked a friend to take me to the hospital. I walked into the familiar gastroenterology outpatient department and begged for help. One of the nurses scurried out to see my consultant. Without an examination and assessment I was admitted.

Later that day the doctor who had inserted the mesh called in on his way home. He was looking forward to spending the weekend with his wife and newborn baby boy. I described my symptoms and my lengthy journey of ill health. His demeanour changed. He seemed agitated and hurriedly requested some urgent investigations.

At 8.30am on Saturday, 10 August 2013 I underwent a CT scan. At 9.30 the consultant reappeared. Surprised, I asked him why he was in the hospital on his weekend off. His reply was precise and dispassionate.

'I need to take you to theatre urgently,' he said quietly. He seemed nervous and awkward, as though he was afraid of my reaction.

'I know.'

'You need an emergency colostomy.'

'I know.'

'You have a perforated bowel and you're septic.'

'I know.'

It wasn't a shock to hear this news, but a relief. At last someone had taken me seriously.

I never once saw the gastroenterologist.

As I was being prepared for theatre I imagined what was going to happen to me. It was as though I was on a conveyor belt being carried towards a set of doors. On the other side was a room of masked, expressionless people, instruments, drugs and gases, which combined would permanently alter my body. Further scarring awaited me as I would learn to smile through pain. Indelible memories of this dystopian world were about to be created both physically and psychologically. My body is the guardian of stories of truth – it never lies; it will tell of the disregard and indignity I had been subjected to by the medical profession.

I went to theatre weak and empty, wondering if I would ever wake up. I had neither the energy nor motivation to care, just a few lingering thoughts that my animals would need to be looked after. I felt no emotion about the events I was facing. I was in complete surrender to my circumstances. My body was about to undergo intrusive, mutilating surgery. Lines drawn across my abdomen would be cut open to allow access to my sick, rotting interior. Others would see parts of me I never would.

Nothing seemed to matter now. I committed my soul to God and Her angels.

I woke in a six-bedded bay with five other women and their noisy visitors. I wanted to scream and run away, to hide in a remote place alone. My life was meaningless.

I had a hole in my swollen tummy, which was covered by a plastic bag. An opening had been made through my abdomen and my large bowel pulled through the incision. The bowel had been cut so that one end could be stitched to the outside to allow poo to escape. The remaining bowel no longer functioned. I had a colostomy. The surgeon had intended to remove the mesh, but I was too sick. It was too risky. A temporary stoma was fashioned so that I could recover and become stronger for further surgery.

I felt numb and indifferent as I realised how my body had been mutilated. Not only had my inner anatomy been ravaged by endometriosis and the nylon mesh, but my outer appearance was affected too, like a carefully crafted sculpture which had been defaced by ugly and angry graffiti. Before the operation I could conceal the inner malfunctions of my body, but not this, a swollen piece of bowel protruding from my abdomen expelling diarrhoea and gas.

I spent two weeks in hospital being pumped with antibiotics and painkillers. It took me four days to look at the stoma. As I looked down at this pink bulge smeared with poo, I felt dissociated from it. This wasn't happening to me. It was a horrible dream, a nightmare that I would wake from. I had become delirious with fever and infection. But then, why not me? Bad things happen in life and no one is immune from random tragedy. This I had learned from Dad's death.

Day and night I dreamed about the company of my animals, twiddling and stroking their ears, being lulled into a safe slumber by my cat. Is this how soldiers cope when facing the horrors of war, by transporting their minds to people and places of love and beauty? Reliving memories of roaming across fields and through rivers with Charlie and my two dogs helped me to escape my pain and wretchedness. Nostalgic images of these loyal loving souls soothed and comforted me. It was a displacement therapy as I filled my mind 'with everything that is true, everything that is noble, everything that is good, everything that we love and honour, everything that can be thought virtuous or worthy of praise.' I longed to be outdoors gently carried by Charlie through a sweet-scented wood beneath a clear blue sky and cotton-wool clouds, a place where the dew sparkles on undiscovered foliage in the company of barefoot elves and fairies, celestial beings, singing songs of love, light and hope. The embrace of strong trees would reassure me I was not alone.

I had one brief encounter with the stoma nurse. She escorted me to a cold, bleak bathroom, stood me by a sink and watched me change my stoma bag, like a prison warder checking I was fit to leave the compound. She then handed me some stoma care information and scurried off to her next appointment. Back at my bedside I began to read the glossy brochures produced by stoma companies. Supposedly educational, they were nonetheless promotional. I was shocked and angry. All the photographs were of retired white heterosexual couples, taken in exotic locations. It was like looking at a cruise liner brochure. Unlike these merry images, I was alone, penniless and at least twenty years younger. The only commonalities were our stomas, white skin and sexual orientation. I asked to see the stoma nurse again and, managing to contain my rage, with calm anger I pointed out the lack of diversity reflected in these images. My strong reaction was a manifestation of the grief I was feeling. Mounting disappointments, losses and fear were boiling inside me.

Bev took me home after a couple of weeks. Before I was discharged the consultant advised me I needed to have the lower part of my bowel removed and a permanent colostomy inserted in 6 to 8 weeks' time when I was stronger. Unthinkingly, I accepted this. I didn't doubt what he was telling me. I neither trusted nor mistrusted him. I was too weak and depressed to choose either position. It was as if I were lying motionless on the edge of a precipice staring into space. I had no energy to move out of danger. I was vulnerable and devoid of any sense of wisdom. Yet I was being kept safe and held by an invisible sense of grace and mercy. I could let go and allow these choices to evolve. My angels were watching, waiting, ensuring all would be well.

As I entered the house, I could feel the stoma bag moving across my tummy, a slippery warm foreign body sliding randomly across my skin. I went upstairs to the bathroom. The bag had become dislodged and I had poo all over my abdomen and clothes. I stood shaking as I wept like a helpless, abandoned child. I felt completely inadequate and unlovable. What should I do? I didn't know where to start with cleaning up my mess. The child within yearned for tender mothering care, loving warm kisses and reassurance. Bev offered help from the other side of the door, but I refused to let her in. I felt like an ugly foul-smelling useless monster. I was deformed and disgusting. Paralysed by shame and confusion, my self-esteem and femininity had been crushed.

As I tried to adapt to my disability, dark threats were advancing: unemployment, debt and homelessness. My employer was applying increasing pressure on me either to return to work or face disciplinary action. The house had been sold, the divorce sanctioned, and I was desperate for somewhere to live. Once again I was sailing close to becoming homeless and jobless. David remained remorseless throughout the entire demise of our marriage. Well-meaning friends suggested I rent somewhere to live until things calmed down. It seemed like a short-term solution and long-term problem. The thought of being controlled by an oppressive landlord horrified me. Rules and regulations, which would serve someone else's best interests, would irritate me and might tip my mental health into an abyss. I needed to live in a place of tranquillity where I was free to make decisions about my home and lifestyle. Furthermore, it was unlikely I would be able to take two dogs and a cat into rented accommodation. I was not about to give up my pets, not for anyone or anything. Like a mother fighting for the custody of her children, I would risk becoming homeless before I let go of them. It was a powerful, uncompromising energy coming from deep within my soul.

Bev and I set about house-hunting. We offered frantic prayers as we searched through estate agent advertisements. Everything was either too expensive or impractical; nothing was suitable. Bev stayed until I decided I could cope alone. The day she left I immediately missed her presence. My house felt like an echoing cavern. But in walked Wendy. I was never left to struggle alone.

I had a mission. My fierce teenage determination reappeared. I would not fail in my quest to find my own home. I trusted I would be guided and that a place was being prepared for me.

A few days after Bev left I received a letter from a distant friend. Shouting from the page was the word 'compromise'. She emphasised how life is full of compromises. Should I compromise, and if so how? Was I missing something? Blinded by grief and loss, was I being stubborn and unrealistic, afraid of more loss? Perhaps I should free myself of my own compulsiveness, resentments and obsessive patterns of thinking. Confusing images of Mum being deliberately irrational and difficult echoed in my mind. Fear of identifying with her was blessing me; I was somehow able to remain open to different options.

In the end, the only compromise I made would surprise and bless me in unimaginable and hidden guises. I moved to a small renovated cottage in a village close to where Charlie was stabled. I fell in love with my home, its location and the folk who lived around me. At last I could breathe and just be. Time seemed to deepen in an atmosphere of divine kindness. Nostalgic images of Nanna and Grandad's house stirred feelings of peace and security. It was a small village surrounded by beautiful countryside of rolling fields, streams, magical woods and wildlife. Indoors and out I was held in a place of peace and beauty, a place of refuge where I could shield myself from ongoing difficulties.

I barely slept and I struggled to care for my two dogs and Charlie. The cottage was too small and I felt too ill to look after myself, let alone them. I was frightened I would have to make some difficult decisions. I couldn't bear to see them suffer because of me. I was letting them down. Feelings of guilt and helplessness were absorbed into the swirling worries of lack of money and unemployment. Once again my psyche became tormented by fears of homelessness. This possibility was becoming more real every day.

I needed my animals as much as they needed me, if not more. They were my loving, loyal friends who enabled me to get out of bed in the morning and carry on along this road of hell. They too were my mat carriers; each time I stroked one of them a sense of grace and peace was transmitted giving me the courage and strength to keep going. They kept me in the here and now. l would often gaze into their eyes. It was like looking into a mirror whose light never goes out nor fades. This union with my animals was reassuringly blessed by grace, love and beauty.

Mr Fisher's opinion was clear and uncompromising. I would need part of my bowel resecting and a permanent stoma once I felt well and strong again. This would be done through a large incision down my abdomen. With the prospect of returning to work becoming increasingly remote, the threat of financial hardship and colostomy bags full of faeces and gas exploding day and night, I was feeling desperate. I would agree to almost anything that would enable me to avoid becoming homeless. I sold all I could to raise money to pay my bills. All the jewellery I had, including sentimental gifts given by friends, was sold. Furniture and clothes went onto eBay. The stable owner agreed to defer my bills for Charlie, and Wendy helped with feeding me.

Until now I assumed I would be entitled to employment and disability benefits, which would support me through this. It was a myth. Like the cynical images of lazy benefit scroungers depicted by the media, I too was made to feel like a deceitful beggar with no intention of reparation. As I sat sobbing in the Citizens Advice Bureau begging for help, I was advised the staff too believed the eligibility criteria for welfare benefits were harsh and failed to care for the vulnerable.

Every application for welfare assistance has its own debasing, money-guzzling protocol. It tramples on privacy and self-respect in a way inconceivable to anyone outside the benefit system ... it creates a noxious fog of suspicion.

Rutger Bregman,
Utopia for Realists

Despite paying my dues for over thirty years, I was tiptoeing along the threshold of homelessness and poverty. Once again, I was reminded this could happen to anyone at any time. This situation is not reserved for the undeserving, unlovable and marginalised. I was at the mercy of these destructive events, which I was gradually accepting rather than denying. It was no longer 'Why me?' but 'Why not me?' The centrality of my ego was once again being stripped of its power to delude me. My only way out of this debris and wave of hostile events was prayer. I was learning that it was the struggle itself and how I was responding which was leading me to a place of inner peace and sanctity.

An old friend from my student nurse days who was now a doctor gave me some unexpected advice. It was like snapping out of a hypnotic trance as I woke to the truth of these words: 'Before you submit to your bowel being dropped into a theatre bucket, you need a second opinion. You've been served badly and deserve better!' Consenting to this surgery, which would permanently disable and embarrass me, could be disastrous. I needed to obtain a second opinion. I was about to make both a good and bad decision. The better side to this spinning coin was travelling almost three hundred miles to see a world-class specialist. The dark side was he was known to Mr Fisher, the surgeon who had inserted the mesh.

This second surgeon, Mr Crow, by his own admission had a distasteful personality. His clear sociopathic traits meant patients and staff disliked him to the point some patients refused to be seen by him and staff avoided working alongside him. His licence to freely offend others was his surgical skill, which was superlative. He was an unchallenged rogue, trading emotional and psychological harm for surgical salvation.

Mr Crow disagreed with Mr Fisher and proposed to remove the mesh laparoscopically and repair any damage. Despite his affiliations with Mr Fisher, I agreed to have surgery with Mr Crow. During the five months I waited for surgery my employment was terminated. The relief was unimaginable. It was as if a lead weight had been lifted off my back. Although it felt strange not to have a job title to hide behind, I was now purely defined by being my true self. I was beginning to realise who this stranger was living in me. I was not someone who needed to belong to a group, organisation or establishment, but the naked me – a woman of God.

The decision to forfeit the income I earned from the world of academia was mitigated by the small pension I had accrued while working for the NHS. But it wasn't enough. I couldn't afford to pay the bills and care for one outdoor and three indoor pets. Like a mother who is no longer able to provide for her children, I had to admit to myself that we could not survive on my pension. I could not cope financially or physically. A force was developing within my heart that was making me feel uneasy. It was a moral dilemma between attachment and responsibility. I knew I didn't have the money or the physical health to cope with the daily demands of caring for all of us. Should I cling to these faithful, loving companions or let them go? Not meeting the needs of my pets was unthinkable. The fear of any one of us suffering because I had failed to confront the reality of this situation filled me with dread. I felt as though I was beneath a lowering, nihilistic cloud oscillating between the need for self-preservation and my bond with my animals.

I chose a moral mode of judgement. Concern and care for each of us was only viable if I let them go. The only option was to have them adopted. I prayed that the right folk would come along for Charlie and Bonny. Bethany and Chuckles would remain with me. Bethany was getting old and needed less exercise, which I would be able to cope with.

First it was beautiful Bonny to leave. She was taken by a wonderful family who were friends of a friend. The day she left was bitter sweet. Guilt and grief blended with the peace of knowing she would be loved and cherished. Her new family were immediately besotted with her whimsical personality. They needed her as she needed them. Bonny was about to fulfil her destiny. I thanked God for dear sweet Bonny as I mourned her loss. Bethany missed her terribly and became depressed. She wouldn't leave her bed and kept looking for her companion. I felt utterly helpless and guilty.

A few weeks later a home was found for Charlie and once again he would fulfil his destiny. He was adopted by someone who, like me, would value her relationship with him over horsemanship, kudos and image. Riding unsuitable horses had weakened her confidence, so we were both desperate and both needed this decision. I'd had many chats with Charlie leading up to his departure. I explained to him how I loved him and how he had saved me on many occasions from dropping into an emotional abyss. I'd had many dreams where I'd been on the edge of a cliff riding Charlie and afraid I was going to fall to my death, but he'd saved me every time. Through my relationship with him I had deepened my relationship with God. Charlie had not only been one of my mat carriers but a wonderful soul friend. Our adventures and happy times together throughout the seasons would live with me forever.

After I let him go I would often close my eyes to see his majestic presence and relive our happy intimate times together. I would touch his fine warm skin as I gently ran my fingers across his muscular body. I plaited his tail and combed his thick black mane as he quietly grazed on sweet-smelling hay. The senses truly are the threshold to the soul.

Two weeks after Charlie's adoption the date arrived for my operation. I revised my will and wrote a list of contacts in the event of anything awful happening. I was admitted for surgery.

I have several vivid memories. The first was on the day of admission. A student nurse handed me a jug of clear fluid with instructions of when to drink it. It was a potent laxative designed to clear and cleanse the large bowel in preparation for surgery. As I obediently drank, my tummy began to gurgle. Thank God there was a bathroom next door for what was about to happen. No sooner had I locked myself inside than I underwent one of the most undignified experiences of my life. Alone in this cold, sanitised, grey room, the explosive force of shit from my stoma was so powerful that it reached all four walls. Like an underground sewer which had been searching for the surface, it erupted with great velocity, spewing foul brown effluent all over the bathroom and me. It covered the walls, the wet shower area, the sink and the loo. I had warm shitty fluid and bits of undigested food in-between my toes, over my clothes and even in my handbag. It was a horrid scene of thoughtless neglect. I had more shit over me than when I was a 6-month-old baby in nappies. As I looked around I was more worried about who would have to clean the bathroom than I was about myself. The student who had deposited the jug of powerful laxative had gone off duty and no one was aware of who I was nor where I was. I didn't know whether to laugh or cry, so I did both.

The next scene was waking up after surgery to be told it was only a partial success due to the poor state of my abdominal/pelvic cavity. It was so inflamed and infected that the surgery was dangerous. Mr Crow told me he'd been close to killing me from perforation or haemorrhage and that the reason I was in this mess was because the initial surgery had been undertaken incorrectly. He looked traumatised and exhausted.

Mr Crow's comments raised more questions than answers. Was the mesh used appropriately in the first instance? Had it been secured in the wrong position? If I'd been made aware of the risks from mesh erosion, would I have given consent to this controlled violence against my body? The benefits did not outweigh the potential negative consequences. While I understood the need to balance risk, experience, skill and luck, I doubted that anyone had taken a measured rational decision in my case. Was Mr Fisher lacking in competence? It had been easier to trust him than to deal with the disturbing thought that he might lack the necessary skill and experience. Had my initial surgery been another statistic to boost his success ratings?

Surgeons find it difficult to admit to making mistakes, to themselves as well as to others, and there are all manner of ways in which they disguise their errors and try to put the blame elsewhere … it's quite easy to lie if things go wrong with an operation. It would be impossible for anybody to know after the operation in what way it had gone wrong. You can invent plausible excuses and dishonest operating notes.

Doctors need to be held accountable, since power corrupts. There must be easy access to complaints procedures and affordable litigation, commissions of enquiry, punishment and compensation. At the same time if you do not hide or deny any mistakes when things go wrong, and if your patients and their families know that you are distressed by whatever happened, you might, if you are lucky, receive the precious gift of forgiveness.

Henry Marsh,
Do No Harm

My final notable memory involved an exhausted staff nurse. During my recovery period I was receiving drugs through an intravenous line positioned in my left wrist. This had become inflamed and painful. Along came Nurse Burn-Out who began to insert some antibiotics into my arm. I protested, as the searing pain was like fire being injected into my veins. Her response was 'You'll have to grin and bear it!'. From thereon I knew her as Ms Grin-and-Bear-it. She was the archetype of many of the nurses I had come to know, not just in this hospital: disenchanted, disenfranchised, disillusioned professionals, weary and worn out.

After taking advice, I decided to commence legal proceedings. I wanted to know if it was a case of harm caused by delayed diagnosis, neglect, surgical error or product defect. It was futile. Mr Crow refused to provide a statement and the expert witness – a close colleague of his – trusted the medical records above my statement. These contemporaneous medical records, which stated what should have happened, did not necessarily reflect what actually happened. These supposed facts were not the same as the truth. Mr Crow's refusal to respond invalidated the proceedings and discredited me. There was no apology for my delayed diagnosis and the harm I suffered, nor any interest in the mesh as a harmful product. Despite Mr Crow stating twice in front of witnesses that the reason I was in this mess was because the surgery had been performed incorrectly, the legal system was unable support my case.

During my recovery from surgery, Mr Crow had strutted into my room like a puffed up peacock showing off his shimmering blue and green crescent sheen. He closed the door and nervously glanced over his shoulder to ensure no one could see or hear what he was about to say. He advised me to drop my legal case and get on with my life. He said that solicitors were out for profit and nothing more, and that there was no point in proceeding. This seemed like an abuse of power and a stitch-up. Mr Crow was protecting himself and his colleagues.

I've never seen him since, even though I need further surgery. I can't face him. The very thought of seeing him again leaves me cold and nauseous. His betrayal, combined with his cruel and offensive personality, is detrimental to my health and well-being.

I wrote to many folk who publicly proclaimed their concern about mesh erosion – politicians, surgeons, lawyers and senior health officials – and none replied. No one was held responsible and no one was made accountable.

Then came the bombshell. I was about to walk into another demolition ball. I received a surprise phone call from my GP's secretary summoning me to the surgery. I was anxious. Why did she need to see me so urgently? This had never happened before, even when I was seriously ill. It must be something dreadful to warrant such an urgent appointment. The request felt threateningly sinister. I fixed a time for the following day. It was a damp, cold November evening, one where you could imagine werewolves to be out prowling. I sat nervously in the reception area surrounded by sick people. Tatty magazines selling houses, holidays and fashion were scattered around the room. The patients were an eclectic mix, from grumpy, grizzly, rosy-cheeked toddlers with high temperatures to elderly people struggling to walk without pain and discomfort. Among the groaning, coughing and fidgeting I tried hard to appear relaxed and unconcerned.

My GP appeared looking pale and stern. Her face was filled with anger. I was under attack. I dutifully followed her into her office and sat in an armchair adjacent to her oak desk. I felt like a convicted criminal sitting chained to a torture chair. At any moment Dr Wong would pull a lever and I'd be ejected down a hatch into a rat-infested sewer, never to be seen again. As I sat looking at her in trepidation, she turned her computer screen round to face me. She began by asking how I was, but her interest was unconvincing. Her next question was about the clinical negligence case I was pursuing. I had been open with her about this to reassure her it was not about her. Like a terrified child who wanted to protect herself, this was my defence against retribution.

'What is this?' she exclaimed, a cocktail of emotions blended into her voice – hints of anxiety, fear and anger. But there were no sweet cherries nor the aroma of mint to soften and lighten the bitter intensity of our appointment. Before me I could see a webpage I had devised eight years previously; it was an assignment for a coaching course I had undertaken. I explained that the page was obsolete, a testimony to who I was, not what I was now. I was no longer registered as a practitioner. Dr Wong accused me of using the website to attract work, in addition to claiming my pension. She was so concerned she had discussed this with her mentor and legal representative. She believed I was soliciting private work, which could be seen as committing fraud. This was utter nonsense.

She had changed her views about me and was willing to uphold this revised perspective with other agencies if invited to do so. I was shocked. I struggled to breathe. I couldn't see straight. My mind raced in response to her half-baked, paranoid untruths. I felt threatened and bullied by her irrational views. My thoughts scattered in the winds of this shocking sudden confrontation. It was as though a hidden, faceless assassin had fired a gun inside my head.

I stated categorically I had never attempted to seek private work. I was not fit to work, and there was medical evidence to support this. I could not fake anaemia, inflammation, incontinence, fevers, bleeding, and so on. Furthermore, I was awaiting surgery. I could produce diaries and bank statements to prove I was genuine; the website host could provide activity data showing I had not used the website in years. All of this was completely disregarded. Something had transformed Dr Wong from a caring, compassionate human being into a threatening, irrational stranger. Had she been asked to provide a statement by the clinical negligence lawyers which had precipitated this paranoia? Her husband was a lawyer; had she panicked and asked him for help? Perhaps Mr Crow had contacted her and together they'd formulated this toxic plot to discredit me, believing it would deflect any prospect of being sued for malpractice. Was she so frightened she was willing to abandon her Hippocratic oath: 'the utmost respect for human life from its beginning, making the care of your patient your first concern'?

She stood as judge and jury as she advised me she could not and would not see me again. I felt abandoned and misunderstood. My eyes were brimming with hot tears desperate to be shed. Only a few managed to trickle down my face. I held them back with fierce determination. I felt like a powerless child facing a tyrannical headmistress, about to be punished for a crime I did not commit. I was no longer the wild, wayward 1970s teenager smugly proud of her truancy, or worse the 6-year-old terrified child facing her gorilla-like father at the school gates. I was now a defenceless, innocent middle-aged woman. Dr Wong would not believe me. I reminded her how difficult it had been for me to trust her, due to my background of abuse. I pleaded with her to see reason and respect our relationship. I agonised over every word, assuring her I would never exploit that trust in order to gain financially or in any other way, as it was not in my nature.

Our relationship had been a sacred gift which was now damaged beyond repair. I quietly left her office and never went back. I was silenced by fear, shame and blame. As I drove home through the foggy amber evening light, an inner strength seemed to stealthily infuse and warm my body as I returned to my own world of truth. It was like drinking a warm, soothing sweet liqueur. I only felt sadness for the doctor and the woman I once knew and trusted.

It is not I who am strong, it is reason, it is truth.

Emile Zola,
Truth

Chapter 25

The Song of the Nightingale
After winter must come spring

2014 – 2017

Even the Saints cannot mould events to their wishes, so our failure to do so must not dismay us. We are part of something bigger, and events take their course, driven by some other logic than our desires.

Sister Frances Teresa, *Living the Incarnation*

Winter within my soul was dying. I seemed to be living through the completion of several endings: marriage, career, health, and friendships both human and pets. It was a peculiar time, as I felt both relieved and bereft. The days seemed to crawl as I struggled to see beyond a dark and fallow emotional landscape. This was no field of dreams but a barren wilderness of broken promises littered with the bitter mystery of unanswered prayers.

Each day I strained against an ever-increasing awareness of life's brevity and an intense sense of urgency. I was no stranger to experiencing challenging emotions and the delicate fragility of our existence. The turbulent unfolding narrative of my life had forced me to face the inevitability of loss of relationships, health, financial security and prosperity. It seemed like a constant cycle of attachment and separation. The rubble of unfulfilled hopes and dreams surrounded me as I found myself once again kneeling at the foot of the crucified Christ. This was no icon of beauty but a mysterious place of sorrow, suffering and compassion.

A still small voice was whispering that this chapter was destined to unfold. I prayed for the emergence of a broader hope and kinder light.

I prayed that bitter, resentful shadows would avoid my soul. I was slowly realising the painful chaos associated with the interruptions and disruptions of loss were in fact a shedding of internal images of an egocentric ideal life embellished by addictive illusions. In the quiet solitude of my cottage, I nestled myself away as I almost became a recluse. I sensed this was a time of healing transformation and resurrection.

When my energy allowed, Bethany and I would wander through grassy fields, silent woods and purple-carpeted moorland. We watched clouds and streams with quiet eyes as my heart sang to the beautiful call of curlews in soft flight. Nature with her divine beauty was once again calling me into her healing, loving embrace. Her adorable remedies brought me peace.

My relationship with God became transformed as increasingly I was reminded God is both 'out there' and carried within. God herself was my counsellor: 'At night my innermost being instructs me,' says the Psalmist. The secret mystery of God was deepening day by day and night by night.

Strolling about the village with Bethany enabled us to make new friends, which helped to minimise social isolation. These were shy, authentic folk unaffected by greed and externality. They had a natural kindness, which did not attract attention to itself. Nor did they take advantage of my vulnerability. They lived quietly and observantly; they too had known hard times. Each offered support when things were difficult and were ready to celebrate happy, joyous occasions. They were considerate and gentle both in their words and actions.

Away from the toils of social gratification, popularity and public image, in the quiet spacious rhythm of this unassuming place, I surrendered to a slow, hesitant beauty and grace. With no conscious effort, there was a slow letting go of harmful memories as I began to hear an ancient, inescapable echo. A power was being invoked – a primal force was emerging within. This could not be faked nor invented. No one could bring me news of this inner world living within me. It was hidden behind a false image. Its anonymous presence had been silenced by years of pain, shame, blame, ambition and fear, which had presented in various forms: the pursuit of status and recognition, rejection, humiliation, abandonment, loss and abuse. The power of pain and the distracting facade of image were rapidly diminishing. I befriended the unknown and yielded to its call.

A clearing was being created, like the space that emerges in a harvested autumn cornfield. I began to be free and uncluttered from the grip of the past as I sensed a true vitality within, a hidden longing. It was as if the wreckage was being swept away after a long, exhausting battle. I was betwixt and between. It was as though I had left one room but not yet entered the next. It was a time of grace and expectant uncertainty. I knew I was not in control but that something genuinely new was about to happen. I was approaching a threshold of beginning.

Deep longings began to stir. Their fulfilment could not be forced as I patiently waited and listened to my profound desire for love, togetherness and intimacy. I needed to be loved. My soul was ready to meet its true other. I decided to go back. I could not give up. I had to find my soulmate and kindred spirit – two friends and one soul. An ancient cycle which had separated us had been broken. I had to find him. There was a journey ahead which I had to take. To resist or deny this would be an act of self-neglect.

Once I admitted to myself what I truly needed and yearned for, it seemed that a secret message, which had for ever been concealed, was at last to be unveiled. I had learned from my near-death experience how precious life is; its ordinariness was more beautiful than ever, and miracles were happening all around me. Nothing was going to stop me from finding him. It was only four weeks since my last surgery; I was grey, weak and frail, but something was calmly compelling me to set off. Like a scene from *The Adjustment Bureau*, a romantic film about a politician and a contemporary dancer who are being kept apart by mysterious forces, I wondered if the events of my life so far had conspired to prevent me from finding my one true love, my soulmate.

I was invited to join a close friend for a Christian retreat. We had attended many conferences in this secluded Georgian country house over the years. Standing in a commanding position facing out to sea, it was a familiar place of rest, inspiration and peace. I decided to make the three-hundred-mile pilgrimage and return to this wondrous sanctuary. Here I could let myself be carried away by beauty and mystery.

This journey heralded a dramatic change to my life. It was to become an epiphany of luminosity as a divine spring within my soul was about to burst into life. A stream which had been long underground was searching for light and air. I felt like Bilbo Baggins setting off from his front door on a warm, sunny spring morning. I had a sense of curious excitement as I drove towards familiarity blended with uncertainty and the unknown.

Throughout the weekend, like one of Anthony Gormley's life-sized sculptures, I spent many hours on the beach in contemplation before the timeless sound of the sea. In the shelter of this sacred space I silently prayed for healing.

It's Another Place
Where the Mersey meets the Irish Sea
And time and tide wait for no man
Yet two miles of men
One hundred strong
Cast from Iron, rooted deep
Stand apart – as lines in the sand
And wait for ever.

I am like them
Transfixed
And lost in the moment
I follow their gaze
To an infinite horizon
And fancy there is longing in their eyes.
Returning tides will lay them bare
And I wonder if – or is that when?
Their time will come
To call for me
Our vigil broken
To finally swim home.

Lesley Young,
'The Crosby Lads'

I knew I could not thrive if I lived in the past with all its pain and suffering. Like a funeral procession before me, residual images of past harm were carried out to sea and abandoned. All the horrid memories I'd preserved within the inner recesses of my mind, like specimens in jars of formaldehyde lined up on dusty shelves, were collected and offered up for disposal. I wanted them to be permanently cast out so that there was room for new life and new beginnings.

I experienced a sudden encounter with my innermost unspoken secret insights and desires. These flashed before me as I silently called out to God. Like the 17-year-old girl I once was, who had sat on a Welsh beach asking for a purpose in life, this time I was longing for love. Perhaps this is what I had always wanted and needed. It was a moment of epiphany as the dream of the winds and oceans was gently preparing to be born. And like the miracle of birth, once again my life was about to indelibly change.

That weekend I received two seemingly inconsequential messages. The first was from the address given by the guest speaker. He was a Baptist minister who described how a chance invitation changed the course of his life. He was invited to a local football match, which led to him meeting his wife. He concluded by saying we should never underestimate what can happen from one single encounter. I didn't give it much thought, probably because it was contextualised by football, a sport I am only remotely familiar with.

The second piece of information I received was while reading a random article in a magazine in the coffee lounge. A *Guardian* columnist described the heartache of her divorce and how she coped with it. She related three years of emotionally exhausting internet dating and its turbulent ups and downs. Eventually she met someone and became happily settled in a long-term loving relationship. She concluded by critiquing several internet dating sites.

Sheltering from reality, I returned home to the warm, loving companionship of Bethany and Chuckles. Like me, they were unaware of what was about to happen. Over the following few weeks, I meandered my way through various online dating sites. I was nervous and hesitant. Many of the profiles were banal and tedious, despite their portfolios of solvency and rapture. Boastful men, whose age was betrayed by the story sketched on their faces, described their pseudo-colourful lives as bursting with adventure. I doubt even Richard Branson's life with its leisurely trips to the moon could surpass these guys. Their brash existence was ego-driven and revolved around expensive cars, fine dining and shopping. Their perfect lives were depicted by glorious heroic success, achievement and acquisition. It was the Trinitarian ethos for the modern age: me, myself and I. Others were limping along barely disentangled from their persecution of previous partners. They had little insight into their self-perpetuating suffering. Their solution was to invite another unsuspecting relationship onto their doomed merry-go-round.

As I continued to search, there was not one profile with the slightest flicker of modest consciousness and alternative values – someone whose life and its worth were not measured by modern culture with its emphasis on power, prestige and possessions, but the primacy of love. I knew it was essential for me to meet someone who paid attention to different things. Living a simple life free from the trappings of modern living was important. He should have a sense of humility and care about social justice. Nature must be honoured and revered – animals, birds, plants and trees. He had to be able to see beauty manifested in each other and the natural life that surrounds us.

The search seemed futile, my hopes seemed impossible and unrealistic. To respond to these profiles might risk becoming embroiled in a bitter divorce or, even worse, the trophy bird would once more be kept in a gilded cage. I could not, and would not, risk blistering my life once again by this mistake. I was not going to repeat the toxic destructive pattern I had succumbed to in the past. Through abuse, brokenness and despair I had learned how to recognise the falsely charming flirtations of insincere men. Anyone disconnected with their inner world and lacking in self-knowledge would also be given a wide berth. My deep-seeking, non-rational inner wisdom was telling me not to squander my dreams on the manipulations of a self-adulating and emotionally immature male. I vowed I would be faithful to my true self. I knew I had the courage to resist that which was artificial, superficial and disingenuous. I was tired and weary of it all. I asked myself whether I should give up. But each morning, deep within the delicate sound of silence, I woke to the beating heart of my deep longing.

It was October 3, the 276th day of 2014 with 89 remaining. The day of the week was Friday. Bethany and I took our usual morning woodland stroll, arriving back at my cottage about 11am. It was a bright cheery autumn day and the sunshine was streaming into the kitchen as I filled the kettle to make a mug of tea. My laptop computer lay dormant on the kitchen table. As I waited for the water to boil, I switched it on and my longing closed its weary eyes as I saw for the first time the man I'd been searching for. There before me was a face I had not seen before but I recognised. The universe at last had conspired to bring us back together. He had a masculine beauty and radiance I knew and understood.

It was the sublime moment I stepped out of this world and into another, a world which had been waiting for this very moment to arrive. I imagined ethereal laughter from angels around me. Bethany and I danced around the kitchen in joyous celebration. I had found him!

Unknown to me, this man was simultaneously looking at my profile having the same inner experience and thoughts. Our encounter was a breathtaking synchronisation of our lives. I had found the person I truly loved by trusting an act of ancient recognition would bring us together; it was as though we'd been wandering in search of one another. Previously separated, we both carried a never fading memory of one another. Although silent at times, but always faithful and true, an invisible guide led us back together. Love opens the door of ancient recognition. You enter. You come home to each other at last. I had come out of the loneliness of exile and home to the house of belonging.

As I carefully read and reread his profile, I was mesmerised by his description.

His name was James.

James was unusually open and honest about who he was and what he was looking for. He had even included a short testimonial from his sister describing his playfulness and his culinary skills, especially chocolate desserts! It was clear he was from a close and loving family. There was no hidden agenda or mind game being played out. Here was a deep-thinking man from a creative, artistic background unafraid to be true to himself. There was no hiding behind a facade of pretence and embellishment. This man had profound insight into who he was. He knew what he needed and, more importantly, what he was not looking for.

James was a self-aware man of integrity with no entanglements. He had a spirit of fun, humour and love for the beauty of life. His determined search to find his one true love had never wavered, despite not knowing if and when this would be accomplished. James also knew that when this happened everything else would take care of itself. And it did.

The similarities shared between our profiles were astounding. This was what miracles were made of. It was as though we had written them side by side, like two excited schoolchildren copying one another's stories. Our profiles were almost a carbon copy. But why shouldn't they be? For at last our hearts of longing had found their true love. Our shared passion for nature, art and literature was immediately apparent; so too was our mutual dislike of consumerism and greed. We shared the same intrinsic values about love and social justice.

As we began to exchange emails I discovered how our life paths, despite involving hundreds of miles and several cities, had almost crossed several times. We were born forty miles from one another and could very possibly have visited the same parks as children. More recently we could have been sitting in the same pub in Scotland where I had celebrated a past birthday. It was as though we were being given the opportunity to meet, but the messiness of life had steered us away from one another. But all roads, with their twists and turns and gruelling topography, were brought through a forest of dreaming into the light of this unique connection. Despite the darkness of the journey, we both had an instinctive hope deep within our souls that our quest would eventually be granted.

Our first sumptuous telephone conversation lasted four hours and our first date twelve. James arrived carrying a chocolate torte, which he had made himself and decorated with a white sugar heart, along with a bunch of perfumed lilies.

I knew I loved James even before I met him face to face. We were one and we both felt the same about one another. It was as though I had met him before. I recognised his face, but because it was out of context I couldn't recall his name.

Loving James is so very natural and effortless, like breathing fresh pure alpine air or gently floating in an endless warm sea. The effect leaves me with a deep vitality and undiscovered energy. Being separated was unbearable. The trajectory of our lives had kept us apart for far too long. Despite our ability to live comfortably alone and independently, we minimised any time away from each other. The pace of our deepening relationship was fast and slow. It had a rhythm which rapidly compensated for the years apart while soothingly bathing us in a peaceful tranquillity.

The only challenge was Bethany. She was so used to being alone with me and the centre of my attention that she would howl and howl when she had to share me with James. She became quickly consoled and adjusted once James bonded with her, which was expedited by the endless ball games he taught her. Additionally she was getting lots of loving attention from James's family. Her new granny found great pleasure in buying her soft toy gifts and tasty biscuit treats.

Everything made sense. Music, literature and art celebrating romance, love and commitment suddenly had a significance neither of us had been able to appreciate before. Love songs and poems were no longer lifeless relics but expressions of our deep feelings for one another.

Come live with me and be my love,
And we will all the pleasures prove,
That Valleys, groves, hills, and fields,
Woods, or steepy mountain yields.

And we will sit upon the Rocks,
Seeing the Shepherds feed their flocks,
By shallow Rivers to whose falls
Melodious birds sing Madrigals.

And I will make thee beds of Roses
And a thousand fragrant posies,
A cap of flowers, and a kirtle
Embroidered all with leaves of Myrtle;

A gown made of the finest wool
Which from our pretty Lambs we pull;
Fair lined slippers for the cold,
With buckles of the purest gold;

A belt of straw and Ivy buds,
With Coral clasps and Amber studs:
And if these pleasures may thee move,
Come live with me, and be my love.

The Shepherds' Swains shall dance and sing
For thy delight each May-morning:
If these delights thy mind may move,
Then live with me, and be my love.

Christopher Marlowe,
'The Passionate Shepherd to his Love'

Encouraged and unafraid to be my true self, I have to learn to live as a woman who is loved and cherished for love's own sake: no agenda, conditions, demands and expectations. James loves me and our life together in ways I have never before experienced. His tender-hearted devotion and natural humanity enable me to dance with the beauty of the life we share. I feel like the girl from the Renoir painting *Dance at Bougival*. Each day is a creative encounter with the divine as we nourish one another with a rare and precious love. Unforeseen happiness and exciting possibilities have created new horizons wanting to be seen. Sometimes the only words I have to express my joy are in tears. Ordinary days are graced with endless laughter and spontaneous acts of kindness, romance and affection as I let go of fear, fear of rejection, abandonment, punishment and betrayal. I know I belong with this man and always have.

On 1 January 2015 James proposed to me and on 25 July 2015 we were married. It was a simple, graceful ceremony surrounded by close family and friends. There was a beauty which manifested itself throughout the entire day. Everything was beautiful about James: his eyes, his face, tender touches and sweet kisses, my wedding gown and our promises of commitment and love, the ceremonial blessing and applause, the many colourful outfits and hats worn by guests, sweet sensual perfumes and colognes, excited photographs beneath the summer sun, floating confetti, delicious food and wine, and proud speeches of celebration and deep gratitude.

This was our wedding blessing:

As spring unfolds the dream of the earth,
May you bring each other's hearts to birth.

As the ocean finds calm in the view of land
May you love the gaze of each other's mind.
As the wind arises free and wild,
May nothing negative control your lives.
As kindly as the moonlight might search the dark,
So gentle may you be when light grows scarce.
As surprised as the silence that music opens,
May your words for each other be touched with
reverence.
As warmly as the air draws in the light,
May you welcome each other's every gift.
As elegant as dreams absorbing the night,
May sleep find you clear of anger and hurt.
And as twilight harvests the day's colours,
May love bring you home to each other.

John O'Donohue,
'For Marriage'

We now live in a small rural village surrounded by forests and rivers. Our everyday lives like others still face challenges, disappointments and upsets. My health issues are ongoing and will be for many years as I journey towards old age. But we live in a climate of love and peaceful devotion towards one another. One another's well-being matters more than life itself.

During a hazy late summer's day James and I were exploring our local countryside when I realised I recognised the landscape. I suddenly stopped walking as I recalled a lost dream I had as a small child when I was nestled in a safe shelter of high sweet-smelling golden stalks: a dream of living in a remote place held by green hills, forests, silver flowing streams and colourful wildlife.

And now I know.

Fairy tales, dreams and prayers have come true, as my soul sang with grace, beauty and love. I gave thanks, knowing I will love him until the sun refuses to shine.

The Nightingale

The nightingale has totemic significance for me. Not only am I drawn to the symbolism of this bird of love and loss but it is also the name of the founder of modern nursing, Florence Nightingale.

In 1859 Florence Nightingale wrote *Notes on Nursing*, a book that is still considered a classic. In 1860 she opened the Nightingale School for Nurses whose mission was to train nurses to work in hospitals and to care for the poor. She was an advocate for women's rights and argued strongly for the removal of restrictions that prevented women from having careers. Considering the severe constraints on the kinds of activities deemed suitable for women by Victorian society and ferocious male opposition, her achievements were truly remarkable. Perhaps without Florence Nightingale, my own life path would have been very different, one which could have denied me a fulfilling and successful career.

The nightingale also carries literary symbolism; not only does its song presage love, but it is also a symbol of the connection between love and death. In *Romeo and Juliet*, it signifies the lovers' undying love for each other, but also that both are in mortal danger. It traditionally represents melancholy and joy, love and loss, and life and death.

The nightingale will sing for its mate all through the night and thus also symbolises the spiritual person practising love and visualisation. Its sweet song brings to light what is mysterious and hidden; it gives inspiration as the harbinger of personal dawn. It guides the listener into connecting with old beliefs and thoughts and encourages her to take charge of her mind. What is learned in the night is to be incorporated into the day. She shows us how to move through different levels of consciousness and use the inspiration of higher realms while keeping grounded. She teaches us to sing loudly – above the cacophony of the mind chatter and above what others think and say. Timid and shy at times, she can show us how to act with grace and elegance.

When it comes to parental love, the nightingale's timidity changes to a brave ferocity, she demonstrates the balance between the two, asking us whether we are sharing what we know and acting what we believe.

Those who have the power of the nightingale love poetry and music; they respond to its power to educate and inform without indoctrination. Songs are used as a way of healing our souls and hearts. Music brings motivation and life to the depressed; it heals the wounds in our lives and soothes our spirit.

Bibliography

Aelred of Rievaulx, *Spiritual friendship*, ed. Billy, Dennis, (Ave Maria Press, 2008)

Bregman, Rutger, *Utopia for Realists: And How We Can get There* (Bloomsbury Publishing, 2017)

Delio, Ilia, 2005, *The Humility of God: A Franciscan Perspective* (St Anthony Messenger Press, 2005)

De Mille, Agnes, *Martha: The Life and Works of Martha Graham* (Random House, 1991)

Frances Teresa, Sr, *Living the Incarnation: Praying with Francis and Clare of Assisi* (Darton, Longman & Todd Ltd, 1993)

Galloway, Kathy, *Talking To The Bones* (SPCK, 1996)

Holloway, Richard, *Dancing on the Edge: Making Sense of Faith in a Post-Christian Age* (Fount, 1997)

Hughes, Gerard W., *God of Surprises* (Darton, Longman & Todd Ltd, 1985)

Hughes, Gerard W., *God, Where Are You?* (Darton, Longman & Todd Ltd, 2010)

Israel, Martin, *Doubt: The Way of Growth* (Continuum Publishing, 1997 used by permission of Bloomsbury Publishing plc)

Israel, Martin, *Living Alone: The Inward Journey to Fellowship.* (SPCK, 1982)

Jung, Carl, *The Zofingia Lectures*, Volume 22 of The Jung Collected Works, (Princetown University Press, 1983)

Kohanov, Linda, *The Tao of Equus* (New World Library, 2001)

Marsh, Henry, *Do No Harm: Stories of Life, Death and Brain Surgery* (Weidenfeld & Nicolson, 2014)

Miller, Alice, *Breaking Down the Wall of Silence: The Liberating Experience of Facing Painful Truth* (Basic Books, 2008)

Miller, Alice, *The Body Never Lies: The Lingering Effects of Hurtful Parenting* (W.W. Norton & Company, 2006)

Miller, Alice, *The Drama of the Gifted Child: The Search for the True Self* (Virago, 2008)

Miller, Alice, *Thou Shalt Not Be Aware: Society's Betrayal of the Child*. Translated by Hildegarde and Hunter Hannum, © 1984 by Alice Miller (Reprinted by permission of Farrar, Straus & Giroux, 1998)

Monbiot, George, *How Did We Get Into This Mess?: Politics, Equality, Nature* (Verso, 2016)

O'Brien, Teryn, 'Wild-Hearted' from the author's website, www.terynobrien.com

O'Donohue, John, *Benedictus: A Book of Blessings* (Bantam Press, Reproduced by permission of The Random House Group Ltd UK and Inkwell Management New York USA © 2007)

O'Donohue, John, *Eternal Echoes* (Bantam Press. Reproduced by permission of The Random House Group Ltd. and Inkwell Management New York USA © 1998)

O'Leary, Daniel J., *Already Within: Divining the Hidden Spring* (Columba Press, 2000)

O'Leary, Daniel J., *Prism of Love: God's Colours in Everyday Life* (Columba Press, 2016)

O'Leary, Daniel J., *Treasured and Transformed: Vision for the Heart, Understanding for the Mind* (Columba Press, 2014)

Radcliffe, Timothy, *What is the Point of Being a Christian?* (Burns & Oates, 2005)

Rahner, Karl S.J., Extract from 'A Copernican Revolution: Secular Life and the Sacraments:1', lecture published in *The Tablet* (6 March 1971). Reproduced with permission of the publisher: *The Tablet: The International Catholic News Weekly*; www.thetablet.co.uk.

Rohr, Richard, *Eager to Love: The Alternative Way of Francis of Assisi* (Hodder & Stoughton, 2015)

Rohr, Richard, *Radical Grace: Daily Meditations* July-Sept 2009 vol. 22 no. 3. Copyright © 2018 by CAC. Used by permission of CAC. All rights reserved worldwide.

Rohr, Richard, *Things Hidden: Scripture as Spirituality* (St. Anthony Messenger Press, 2007)

Rolheiser, Ronald, 'Misconceptions about suicide' (27 July 2003) and the second quotation in Chapter 15 (28 July 2013) are taken from the author's website www.ronrolheiser.com. Used with permission of the author, Oblate Father Ron Rolheiser. Currently, Father Rolheiser is serving as President of the Oblate School of Theology in San Antonio Texas, www.ronrolheiser.com

Schaar, John H., *Legitimacy in the Modern State* (Taylor & Francis Group, 1981)

Stalls, Jonathon, 'What Really Frightens Us' in *Evolutionary Thinking*, Oneing, Vol.4, No.2 Copyright © 2018 by CAC. Used by permission of CAC. All rights reserved worldwide.

Young, Lesley, 2013, National Poets Day.

Acknowledgements

I am especially grateful to Helen Fazal, my gifted editor for her belief in my story and her constant empowering support throughout the writing of it. There were times I was weakened by vulnerability and exhaustion from writing these memoirs. Helen was able to respond with compassion and a willingness to share the load. Throughout the entire editing process, Helen remained cheerful, diligent and coped admirably with my creative messiness. It has been a blessed privilege to know and worked with her.

I wish to thank Lesley, Wendy and Chris who have carefully read the manuscript and asked questions and made suggestions which enabled me to consider the content more carefully.

I am in gratitude to Evleen with whom I have walked the inner journey. Her loving compassion and commitment have helped me recover and become the woman I was intended to be.

Without my 'mat carriers' with their unselfish kindness and love, especially my animals (to be loved by animals enables my soul to feel the divine) I would not have been able nor would have wanted to survive.

A special thank you to Anne for her faithful prayers and loving arms which held me in a place of grace and beauty.

I want to thank Sandra David and the Arrow Gate Publishing team. Thank you, Sandra, for taking the time to sensitively read the depths of my book and decide to share it with the world community. You are a joy to work with, and I will always be grateful for your encouragement and passion.

To Father Daniel, who in my darkest times brought transforming light, love and hope.

Finally, to all those who are willing to read this book. May there be something within these pages which brings you hope, love and healing. May you be blessed throughout your journey.

May I give thanks and praise to Mother Nature, her wild spirit, her wonderful creatures and her abiding beautiful landscape.

It is only in showing ourselves as we truly are that we may give ourselves to other people.

Martin Israel,
Doubt: The Way of Growth

CPSIA information can be obtained
at www.ICGtesting.com
Printed in the USA
BVHW021342220419
546169BV00011BA/18/P